29.95

THE TRIAL LAWYER'S ART

THE TRIAL LAWYER'S ART

Sam Schrager

TEMPLE UNIVERSITY PRESS

PHILADELPHIA

Temple University Press, Philadelphia 19122
Copyright © 1999 by Temple University.
All rights reserved
Published 1999
Printed in the United States of America

Text design by Gary Gore

Poem on page 36: From SHAKER, WHY DON'T YOU SING by Maya Angelou. Copyright © 1983 by Maya Angelou. Reprinted by permission of Random House, Inc.

Library of Congress Cataloging-in-Publication Data

Schrager, Samuel Alan.
    The trial lawyer's art / Sam Schrager.
        p.   cm.
    Includes bibliographical references and index.
    ISBN 1-56639-673-5 (cloth : alk. paper)
    1. Trial practice—United States.   2. Forensic oratory.
    3. Persuasion (Rhetoric).   I. Title.
    KF8915.S263   1999
    347.73'75—dc21   98-39076

In memory of Bill and Perle Schrager

We have heard talk of justice. Is there anybody
who knows what justice is? No one on earth can
measure out justice. Can you look at any man and
say what he deserves—whether he deserves hanging
by the neck until dead or life in prison or thirty
days in prison or a medal?

—*Clarence Darrow*

Our activity, then, is largely concerned with
moral matters, but as performers we do not have a
moral concern with them. As performers we are
merchants of morality.

—*Erving Goffman*

CONTENTS

ACKNOWLEDGMENTS

A great many people helped with this study. Lawyers gave their time graciously and pro bono. Often they seemed intrigued by the idea that, as peculiar as it sounds, folklore *does* have something to do with jury trials.

The Smithsonian Institution abetted this view by inviting trial attorneys to demonstrate their skills at the 1986 Festival of American Folklife, where they took their place on the National Mall along with practitioners of traditional crafts from Japan and Tennessee—the sorts of groups far more often associated with this annual summer rite celebrating American and world cultures. The Smithsonian's Office of Folklife Programs sponsored my field research on lawyers, the American Trial Lawyers program, and the initial phase of the writing. Peter Seitel, who inspired me to study lawyers, was responsible for this. I've benefited a great deal from his curiosity and counsel.

The Association of Trial Lawyers of America (ATLA) made the project possible with their generous financial support. Bruce Desfor pitched the idea to ATLA, Marrianna Smith endorsed it, and Judge Jim Carrigan took a personal interest.

Not being a lawyer, I depended on the indulgence of members of the profession throughout the research. I was especially fortunate to meet Germaine Ingram at the start. Lawyer and tap dancer, she seriously entertained my clunky notions about courtroom performance. She also tipped me off to the importance of Cecil B. Moore. Among Philadelphia attorneys, I am deeply indebted to Roger King and Robert Mozenter for the frank, intimate explanations they gave me of their courtroom tactics. Gerald Litvin went far beyond duty's call to tutor me about civil advocacy. Dennis Eisman and LeGrom Davis oriented me to the workings of the criminal courts. Suzanne Reilly humanized the law. Oscar Gaskins explained much about Cecil Moore. In San Francisco, Tony Serra kindly invited me to observe him in battle from the inside. Harold Rosenthal did the same, and counseled me over the long haul.

During the Festival phase, Edward Stein offered savvy guidance from his experience with trial training workshops. He, Germaine Ingram, Harold Rosenthal, and Barry Scheck were resourceful onstage presenters.

Herb Shore showed me how to design the program for dramatic effect. Joanne Mulcahy skillfully coordinated and transcribed the sessions. Her trenchant insights about lawyers' styles helped form my ideas about cultural identity. Lyle Rosbotham photographed the attorneys at the Festival and contributed his work to the book.

I extend my thanks to all the lawyers and judges who participated in the Festival. While many of them appear in these pages, I regret that others, for reasons of space, do not. My gratitude goes to Tom Alexander, Roy Barrera, Sr., Charles Becton, James Brosnahan, Penelope Cooper, Stephen Delinsky, William Dwyer, James Ferguson II, James Goetz, Jo Ann Harris, Boyce Holleman, James Jeans, Roger E. King, Albert Krieger, Ralph Lancaster, Jr., Arthur Mallory, Diana Marshall, Thomas McNamara, R. Eugene Pincham, Lorna Propes, Arthur Raynes, Keith Roberts, Sr., Kenneth Robinson, Frank Rothschild, Murray Sams, Jr., Lawrence Schwartz, J. Tony Serra, James Sharp, the late John Shepherd, Jacob Stein, John Tierney, Michael Tigar, Mark Tuohy, David Webster, Patrick Williams, and William Wilson, Jr., as well as to Jim Carrigan and Douglas Hillman, who presided over the demonstrations.

My folklore colleagues Debora Kodish, Peter Seitel, and Steve Zeitlin perused the entire manuscript and steered me into clarifying the presentation at many points. Don Finkel and Pete Sinclair, colleagues at The Evergreen State College, also offered valuable advice. For my view of the authority of experience in stories, I am indebted to Pete's highly original thinking. By a lucky choice, Temple University Press sent my manuscript to Milner Ball, whose incisive criticism showed me crucial ways to avoid embarrassment and strengthen my argument. Frank McClellan and Penny Cooper read the book sympathetically, even though they're trial lawyers.

Roger Abrahams, Keith Bucholtz, Stephanie Coontz, John Dorst, Margaret Gribskov, Peta Henderson, David Simon, Kirk Thompson, and Judge Robert Wollheim made helpful suggestions on various chapters. Bob Horan gave deft encouragement when I was midway through the writing. Patrick MacMahon planted the seed for the conclusion by asking me to consider the ends that writers serve. Howard Schwartz helped me think about ethical reform. Justino Balderrama, Susan Dwyer-Shick, and Kim Stafford passed along good references. Randy Stilson, Ernestine Kimbro, and Sara Rideout directed me to many sources in the Evergreen library. Paul Conway brought me up to speed on current indigent defense policies in Philadelphia. Hideo Yagi arranged to have the manuscript copied when I was teaching at Kobe University of Commerce. Doris Braendel and Sherry Babbitt handled the editing process gracefully.

None of these people, of course, are responsible for my mistakes and misunderstandings. *Mea culpa.*

I am grateful as well to the lawyers, judges, and others who spoke with me about trials in Philadelphia and elsewhere; to the folklorists with whom I shared conversations about the project; to the lawyers and judges who recommended lawyers for the Festival; to the Festival staff and "witnesses" who helped stage the program; to the National Institute for Trial Advocacy for permission to use their case files; to Temple University librarians for aid with research on Cecil Moore; and to my fellow faculty and students at Evergreen with whom I have studied culture over the years.

Finally, I thank Leah, Ben, and Jocelyn for their great good spirits while having to grow up with this book. Above all I thank Laura, whose judgment is unerringly true.

THE TRIAL LAWYER'S ART

A STORYTELLING CRAFT

> We tell stories to talk out the trouble in our
> lives, trouble otherwise so often unspeakable.
> —William Kittredge[1]

I t was Monday morning of the week before Christmas, and I was sitting in a small, packed courtroom in Philadelphia's cavernous City Hall, waiting with other spectators for a murder trial to begin.

I was there to watch the lawyers. The previous week, my first in the courthouse, I had walked in on scenes of misery and folly, of life gone wrong. I had seen a defense attorney press a rape victim about the precise details of her ordeal until she became speechless. I watched a teenage girl on trial for murdering her child's father: she had locked him in her closet when he refused to marry her, and, after two-and-a-half months inside, he'd died. I heard a public defender coax a robbery victim into identifying the defendant from a photograph, but it was a trick: the man in the picture was really the defendant's brother. I came upon a woman, her son just convicted of murder, sobbing in an anteroom while her family milled nearby.

As I went from one courtroom to another the roving jurors noticed me. "Roving," or "floating," jurors, as they call themselves in the criminal courts of Philadelphia, are regulars, connoisseurs of good trials. Retirees mostly, they choose to pass the time observing human nature in the raw, not packaged for consumption on TV. On a blackboard tucked inside a

City Hall entrance, they post the locations of trials they're following so members of the group know where to meet.[2]

Some of them spotted me jotting notes and asked if I was a reporter. I told them I was a folklorist doing a project for the Smithsonian, studying how lawyers go about their work. They had advice. I should see a *good* trial, they said. There was one about to start, which they were going to attend. The prosecutor, Roger E. King, was Philadelphia's best, they said, very impressive in front of a jury. It was a death penalty case, a triple homicide. King had shown one of the group, Lillian Torrance, police photographs of the victims. The faces, she told me, looked like shiny leather that had burnt and lifted up.

So now I was part of the crowd marking time—waiting for Judge Juanita Kidd Stout, who, true to her reputation with roving jurors, was late. Roger King, a forty-year-old African American with a trim, muscular look, was sitting at one counsel table. He was chatting with two men in the first row about the Eagles, Philadelphia's football team. It had been reported over the weekend that they wouldn't be leaving town after all, and King was expounding on the costly concessions Mayor Wilson Goode had made to keep them, their defeat on Sunday in the season finale, the problems with season tickets at Veterans Stadium, and the Eagles' lack of a credible wide receiver. His voice carried to the back of the room.

Across the aisle, facing forward inconspicuously, sat the defendant, a skinny African American man of about thirty wearing a dark pin-striped suit. Next to him was his court-appointed counsel, a white-haired, genial older white man who kept silent except when he turned to wave a cheery good morning in the general direction of the audience behind him. I wondered if his client had any supporters in the room. The front row was taken by detectives and patrolmen involved in the case; the next three, apparently, by the murdered people's family and friends. Behind them were a dozen roving jurors, most of whom assumed the man was guilty because Roger King was prosecuting him.

When the jurors filed in, King snapped forward in his seat. The judge entered and wordlessly turned the jury over to the crier. He administered the oath to them, then to the defendant, and then, with the defendant still standing, recited the charges. "LaRue Blaylock," he intoned, "this is bill of information number 166 charging you with possessing instruments of crime generally, the instrument of crime being a pipe, a knife, ice pick, and scissors. To this bill of information how do you plead, guilty or not guilty?"

"Not guilty," Blaylock said in a low voice.[3]

The other charges followed, phrased in the same way. The defendant pleaded not guilty to them all: to the burglary of the house, the robbery of the three victims, the rape of one of them, the murder of all three. "Pleading not guilty," the crier concluded, "how do you wish to be tried?"

Blaylock seemed confused, then said, "By jury."

"Ladies and gentlemen of the jury," the crier concluded, "the defendant, LaRue Blaylock, pleads not guilty to all charges and has requested a trial by jury. You may be seated."

The judge now spoke for the first time. "Mr. King," she began.

The prosecutor stood. His manner was almost leisurely, but the words were spare and precise.

> Good morning, ladies and gentlemen of the jury.
>
> This is my first opportunity to speak to you about the facts and circumstances in the case of the Commonwealth of Pennsylvania and LaRue Blaylock.
>
> We will take you back in time and space to Monday, December nineteenth.
>
> We will take you back to a household preparing for Christmas.
>
> We will take you back to that Monday when
>> one Marci Jones
>> one Audrey Jones
>> and one Donald Jones
>> were three
>>> alive
>>> people.[4]

I glanced around the room. Everyone's gaze was riveted on King. He was pacing in front of his counsel table, addressing the jurors but not looking straight at any one of them.

King introduced the defendant as Marci's and Audrey's stepuncle, noted his whereabouts at certain times that day, and then described the crimes. Marci Jones was stabbed repeatedly, raped, and hung by an extension cord from the rafters. Donald Jones, her father, was struck thirty-five times on the head. Audrey Jones, Marci's sister, was stabbed in the head and drowned in the bathtub.

I felt torn between revulsion at these ghastly acts and fascination about how they could have happened. The cadences and rich tonalities of King's voice were like those of an African American church sermon. Then it dawned on me that what Roger King was doing was very much *like* preaching. He was putting on a performance.

This was not what I had expected. I knew, as everyone knows, that trial lawyers engage in a certain amount of acting. But how much? And of what kind? I hadn't considered the part performance might actually play in their work. When I'd discussed my project with Peter Seitel, director of the Smithsonian Institution's Office of Folklife Programs, we had focused not on lawyers' stagecraft but on their rhetoric and logic. I'd thus gone into court on the lookout especially for rationally persuasive speech.

But here, instead, was performance—not performance as trickery, with the lawyer mounting a show he or she knows to be false, but rather full-fledged performance in the anthropological sense: performance as an artfully enacted event, a skilled display of communication that holds an audience, stimulates their senses, provokes their emotions. A performed event, like all forms of artistry, evokes and comments on aspects of reality yet remains at a distance from it, in a time and space of its own. Every society has many kinds of such occasions. Most are formally marked as performances; *some,* only tacitly so.[5]

Later I tried to reconstruct what had signaled to me that Roger King was performing. Right from the start of his opening statement he'd used devices that scholars have identified, in a wide range of societies, as signs that oral performance is taking place. He used stock phrases (*ladies and gentlemen of the jury*), parallelism (*we will take you back*), rhythmic language (*one Marci Jones/one Audrey Jones*), poetic diction (*three alive people*), and unusual body movements (his way of pacing and rolling his head). Also, the crier's archaic invocations and oath-takings just before King spoke were set formulas of the sort that, scholars have found, telegraph that a performance is about to start. They take the trial across a threshold into a consecrated space.[6]

My realization in Judge Stout's courtroom that day—a day to which I will return in detail later—is at the root of this book. For what was true of Roger King's actions is true, I soon recognized, of the actions of all practitioners of his trade. The jury trial, from beginning to end, is an artfully performed event. From the moment opposing counsels first appear before prospective jurors until the moment the verdict is in, they are performing.

They must. And it's not that certain flamboyant attorneys like King choose to perform, while others, who present evidence more factually, don't. The jury trial is inherently a performance situation, and trial lawyers are always manipulating its artful possibilities.

To see lawyers at trial as performers is not to say that their advocacy is faked. On the contrary, such a view helps to explain—and puts a different slant on—the widespread contempt felt toward trial lawyers in our media-saturated society, cynicism that has intensified in the wake of the national spectacles surrounding the O. J. Simpson trial and other high-profile cases.

This cynicism stems from the betrayal of certain cherished convictions about the conduct of jury trials. While everyone knows that the legal system is flawed—that justice misfires, that the innocent are punished, that the guilty go free—most of us grew up believing that trials are a rational search for truth, or would be if only the attorneys played fair. The lawyer's job, we thought, is to put evidence before the jury. The jurors' job is to listen to the evidence and then, reasoning together, to determine the facts. This is our society's official view of trials. And lawyers' refusal to limit themselves to this assigned role, as revealed in stratagems now routinely exposed on the news and Court TV and dramatized in movies and TV series, easily becomes, in the public mind, a failure of moral character.

Yet the belief that jury trials are rational proceedings has always been a legitimating tactic of the justice system, a grand oversimplification. It does not square with the trial's nature as combat. A trial is a last resort, undertaken in the small portion of legal disputes in which parties can't reach agreement, in which a binding judgment about the truth has to be made and no one is in a position to say, authoritatively, what that truth is. In these circumstances some societies consult oracles. Others rely on judges. American legal tradition has a democratic preference for nonprofessional juries. Consequently, we have an adversarial system that requires lawyers to show zealous allegiance to their side's version of truth. The need to be believable to jurors pushes lawyers well beyond giving a straightforward presentation of evidence. It forces them to try to create the *appearance* of truth.[7]

Performance, as we shall see, is the lawyers' means of crafting the appearance of truth.

When trial lawyers speak in their public role as agents of the court system, they espouse official rhetoric about truth and justice. But when they talk shop, they often talk craft. They act as if no matter what may *actually* have happened in the events under litigation, the evidence is by its very nature inconclusive. They talk as if the outcome of a case may be decided more by the skill they muster than by the evidence they have to work with, as if they can make do with the materials at hand.[8]

Most lawyers (I'll use this word, along with "attorneys" and "counsels," as shorthand for "trial lawyers," the small subset of criminal and civil attorneys who regularly argue cases before juries) speak as if their skill can compensate for weaknesses in a case. They believe that the more skillful you are, the more likely it is you will prevail. Their conviction is borne out by the knowledge that certain of their numbers, like Roger King, have uncanny success with juries. Such attorneys win (or do better than was expected) even when the evidence seems to dictate defeat. As a result they enjoy formidable reputations among their peers.

Gerry Spence, an attorney from Jackson, Wyoming, who is widely regarded as one of the best in the business, likes to admonish lawyers for betraying their craft tradition. He decries the profession as a whole for having "lost its light, its ability to speak to or hear ordinary people."[9] He takes as example one of his most famous trials, the Karen Silkwood case. What lawyers typically do wrong in such complex cases, he writes, is to "dump tons of garbage on the jury—the government rules and regulations, the company reports, thousands of hours of testimony that inspect every tedious nook and cranny of fact, scores of witnesses dragged up to the witness stand and whipped endlessly by the brilliant examination of the lawyers." That, to him, is failed craft. How can it be done right? "[I]t could also be a story," he says. "Let me tell you the story":

> Once upon a time there was a courageous young woman who discovered that her fellow workers were being contaminated with a terrible poison, an insidious substance called plutonium, that, when even the tiniest amounts were breathed into the lungs, could cause one of the most dreaded and deadly diseases of all—lung cancer. They were ordinary folks, trusting folks—red-faced farm boys and housewives, people who worked hard and tried to get ahead and who took their children to church, and who wanted to be good citizens and to live decent and honest lives.
>
> But some of this woman's fellow workers were already dying

and others soon would be stricken and, worse, they didn't know it. They went home at night and watched television and played with their children. But this young woman knew, and she decided to tell her fellow workers the truth. Then something happened to her.

The drift of Spence's story is clear, whether you saw the film *Silkwood* or know that Karen Silkwood died in suspect circumstances. A villain, the corporation Kerr-McGee, was killing residents of a community. A heroine fought to save them. We know the situation, and know that situations like this happen again and again. We hear in it an archetypal struggle of a brave, vulnerable human being against impersonal, grinding evil. The words *once upon a time* mark this as the realm of the folktale, a point Spence stresses when he advises aspiring lawyers to practice their case as a bedtime story for children. "[F]or if you can explain it to your children," he writes, "then you have finally acquired the skill to speak to a jury."

Why would juries be swayed by simple stories rather than by massive compilations of evidence? Because we think with stories. We depend on them more than on any other form of thought to make sense of lived experience. Stories give meaning to things that happen to people, things that in the absence of stories about them may be too complicated or confusing, too painful or mysterious, to figure out at all.

Good lawyers compose their stories with careful attention to the evidence and the law. But they reach beyond these givens to tie the circumstances, which are always unique, to plotlines already deeply embedded in listeners' minds, to mythic narratives whose familiar moves reveal how the world is and how people, faced with fateful choices, act for good or for ill. This larger meaning is crucial to the story's effectiveness as a means of persuasion, a rhetorical device.[10]

The lawyer's selection of plotline is shaped by his or her self-made identity. Gerry Spence's tale about Karen Silkwood, for instance, has affinities to his tale that more recently won acquittal for Randy Weaver in the slaying of a federal marshal at Ruby Ridge, Idaho—a verdict that led to congressional hearings on the excessive use of force by government agents. At the trial, while federal prosecutors painted Weaver as a Nazi-sympathizing white supremacist, Spence portrayed him as a separatist. The marshal was part of a team of agents who, Spence said, had been spying on Weaver for fifteen months on trumped-up charges. Weaver's son was shot in the back, and the next day his wife was gunned down while holding her baby. Spence claimed that the agents were the murderers, that Weaver's son and wife died because of their political beliefs, that the marshal was killed in self-defense.[11] Randy Weaver and Karen Silkwood had diametrically opposed politics, but the lawyer found common mythic ground in their fates. Isolated and independent, each held fast to convictions that aroused the wrath of their nation's mightiest dragons. Spence, who sees himself as a populist defender of individual freedom, is fascinated by this plotline and extremely adept at plumbing it with jurors.

In craft work of all kinds the outcome of one's efforts is at risk throughout the project, with the chances of success depending on the skill one applies from start to finish.[12] Like all professional storytellers, lawyers shrewdly orchestrate myriad elements to make a convincing story. Witnesses have to be controlled, the jury's makeup fathomed, the judge catered to, one's adversary outflanked, one's self-image sustained, the evidence molded to fit potent cultural understandings. This work is full of risk, because the story is constantly being contested.

I first realized how tricky it can be to tell a story convincingly when, after a month in the Philadelphia courts, I witnessed the frustration of a lawyer whose strategy had failed him, despite seemingly strong evidence to support his case.[13]

This trial too was for first-degree murder. Henry Rawlins, the defendant, and Sidney Loud, the victim, were young men, neighbors. The killing occurred when Rawlins approached Loud as the latter sat in his truck. The question before the jury was what happened next—who was carrying the gun, which had never been recovered, and how Loud was shot five times, twice in the back. Rawlins claimed self-defense, but the five bullets made roving jurors think he was guilty as charged. I agreed with them.

The prosecutor, Jonathan Dunn, was cross-examining Rawlins. During a break he confided his strategy to a couple of us. "I'm just setting the stage," Dunn said. "We're getting there. I'm building up his feelings toward me." By inducing the defendant to show anger, Dunn explained, he would show the jury that his calm demeanor was a facade. Rawlins, he said, "doesn't know yet how he feels. I'm getting him in touch with his feelings." Dunn asked the roving juror with me his opinion of how it was going. "I don't envy you your job," my companion replied. He was being polite. Minutes before he'd told me that Rawlins was holding up well on the stand and might succeed with the claim of self-defense.

But as it turned out, Dunn could not get Rawlins to express anger. "Did you dislike Sidney?" Dunn asked. "No, sir, I didn't like him. If that's dislike, okay." "Did your feeling of dislike increase over a period of time? "Not so much dislike as fear." They went in circles like that. When testimony ended for the afternoon, the mood among the roving jurors had swung toward anticipation of victory for the defense. One said of Rawlins, "He's very cool"—unflappable—and my companion said, "If I was on the jury I'd let him off."

In the hallway Dunn asked me pointedly, in the presence of several police detectives, "What do you think?" The question embarrassed me; I thought it had gone badly for him that day and didn't know how to say so tactfully. Dunn persisted, wanting to know how I'd reacted to what the defendant had and hadn't said. His basic question was whether I found Rawlins believable. Personally, I didn't. Then one of the detectives ventured the opinion that Rawlins had handled himself well by sticking to his claim that he couldn't remember the details of the shooting. Dunn was unhappy, irritated by our replies. I guessed he was worried that, despite all his ballistics evidence, the first-degree murder conviction might slip away.

Dunn's trouble was his opponent's plot. Russell Goldman, the defense counsel, was pitching *his* story of the murder as a vigilante action. In an earlier period Goldman may have taken a different tack. But this was at a time when the sensationalized case of Bernhard Goetz, a middle-aged white man who shot four African American youths on a New York City subway when they hassled him for money, was still in the air, and lawyers in Philadelphia, who took the popular sympathy for Goetz seriously, saw potential payoff in a vigilante defense. Race wasn't overtly at issue in this case—both defendant and victim were African American, as was the prosecutor—but class was. In Goldman's rendering, Henry Rawlins and his family were leading members of their community, whereas Sidney Loud and his family were the dregs, the kind of people who, Goldman said, we're "scared to death might come into our neighborhood." For ten years they had carried out "a reign of terror" against the Rawlins family. Rawlins's polite, confident manner and his middle-class way of speaking confirmed this story, and so, inadvertently, did the victim's family, who all seemed uncomfortable and inarticulate on the witness stand.

Suppose the prosecutor had succeeded in his plan and Rawlins had flashed at him in anger. Would that have demonstrated guilt? Not at all, but Dunn would have seized on it as a symbol of the anger that had provoked

Rawlins to commit murder. Even a momentary loss of control by the defendant could be made to stand, imaginatively, for the murder itself. To create this appearance of a propensity for violence, Dunn had to be able to manipulate Rawlins's emotions. His failure to do so could have been due to Rawlins's unanticipatable cool. But it could also have been part of an unfolding dynamic that, by this stage of the trial, had led Dunn into a perilous corner, where he felt compelled to "break the witness." I think Dunn felt the pressure to land a big blow, for he sensed Goldman was outmaneuvering him.

In the end it was Dunn who betrayed anger, lashing out at Goldman. In his summation, Goldman revealed that he had grown up in the very same neighborhood and had gone to the very same grade school that the Rawlins kids had attended. In response, Dunn in his closing told the jury that he resented Goldman presuming to speak for the neighborhood. There was a racial subtext here: the white folks of Goldman's Jewish childhood were gone, and Dunn was laying claim to speaking on behalf of the current black residents. But Dunn, as he had seemed for much of the trial, was in the position of responding to his adversary. Once on the defensive, he got stuck there. What ultimately determined the outcome of the case—a conviction on involuntary manslaughter, the lowest possible charge—was not, I think, whether the defendant had actually committed premeditated murder or acted in self-defense, but rather the lawyers' effectiveness in plying their craft.

Such outcomes violate our sense of justice. Justness of outcome is, after all, what the public cares about. Was the verdict the right one, we want to know. But from the craft viewpoint, this is not what mainly matters. The task, from a craft perspective, is, in a strict sense of the word, fictive: an elaborate fabrication of meaning for an audience. Thus lawyers' work is allied with that of novelists, actors, directors, salespeople, and politicians—all fabulists with whom attorneys often are compared and often compare themselves.

When Gerry Spence calls the jury trial "the experience of the tribe around the fire," he summons a primordial image of performance. Trials, beneath their fact-finding function, are collective rituals. They are moments for what the sociologist Emile Durkheim saw as the purpose of ritual: "moral remaking," when members of a society assemble in groups to "reaffirm in common their common sentiments."[14] The lawyer's part is to perform a story that gives jurors a convincing account of their shared circumstances, their unvoiced dreads, their evocable faith.

*   *   *

In every jury trial the attorneys construct rival stories from testimony and evidence whose meaning is unclear. A trial is a competition over the framing of this ambiguous material: *how* should the jury interpret the testimony and evidence? And it is also a competition over the authority of the lawyers: *whose* account of the meaning of this material deserves to be believed?[15]

Consider how these questions played out in the second trial for the bombing of the Oklahoma City federal building. Prosecution and defense did not dispute certain key facts in the case against Terry Nichols, such as Nichols's friendship with Timothy McVeigh, who'd already been sentenced to death for the bombing, or Nichols's fingerprints on a receipt for a ton of ammonium nitrate fertilizer purchased under a fictitious name, or Nichols's absence from Oklahoma City on the day of the explosion. But the stories they framed from the evidence were irreconcilable. Larry Mackey, the lead prosecutor, argued in his closing, "What has emerged is a complete and compelling picture that it was Terry Nichols and Tim McVeigh together, side by side, who are responsible for the bombing in Oklahoma City and the deaths of those innocent people." Michael Tigar, lead defense counsel, claimed that his client had cut his ties with McVeigh in the months before the bombing and was starting anew: "Terry Nichols was building a life, not a bomb."[16]

The Nichols verdict—guilty of involuntary manslaughter and conspiracy but not of first- or second-degree murder—was a major, if qualified, endorsement of the defense's framing of events. Despite incriminating circumstantial evidence, the jury bought Tigar's and his co-counsel's story that Nichols was not a true partner in McVeigh's evil design. The defense went on to prevail in the death penalty phase of the trial (conspiracy is a capital offense under a new federal law), when a minority of the jury refused to impose the death sentence, despite graphic, wrenching testimony for the prosecution from survivors, family members, and witnesses of the disaster.

Why did some jurors side with the defense? "Michael Tigar is one heck of an attorney," declared the forewoman, Niki Deutchman, a leader of the holdouts against the death sentence, at a press conference. In her eyes, Tigar possessed great authority. What led her to put such faith in him? Lawyers who observed the trial noted that Tigar had cultivated rapport with each prospective juror during jury selection and had sustained these connections through the trial, most prominently with Deutchman, who often smiled at him when the jury entered the courtroom. She is a nurse and natural childbirth instructor. In jury selection Tigar chatted with her about the Lamaze childbirth method and their mutual challenge of raising teenage daughters; in his summation he slipped in a defense of home birth and mentioned that his son had been born at home with the help of a midwife thirty-five years ago. Deutchman is also a convert to Judaism who had studied for six months in Israel. In his summation Tigar made Old Testament references and argued, "Even the Supreme Court of Israel freed from a death sentence a man found to have no direct participation in the deaths of people he had been accused of killing."

Michael Tigar's close attunement to selected jurors—a traditional craft technique—is just one arrow in the quiver of his polished performance style, with which I am familiar. He was one of the attorneys I invited, at the end of my field research, to the Smithsonian Institution's Festival of American Folklife, where, in a tent on the Mall in the enervating summer heat, they staged public demonstrations of their craft.[17] Tigar, in a mock death penalty plea, mounted a powerful defense of a man convicted of the brutal murder of two elderly women. His performance exuded the same impassioned questioning of moral beliefs, the same deep identification with his client, and the same fluid, literary diction and effortless self-confidence that would later lend so much authority to his defense of Terry Nichols.

As it happened, a federal judge who saw and was moved by this demonstration proposed, when Nichols was arrested, that Tigar be appointed to represent him.[18] In the interests of justice, judges thus made sure that the man accused of the deadliest terrorist act in American history would get a strong defense. Tigar was an inspired choice.

There is an enormous literature on persuasion in trials and in law. Its beginnings in the West can be found in the philosophy of Plato and Aristotle, in the rhetoric of Cicero and Quintilian, and in Jewish and Christian traditions of Bible interpretation. Its contemporary forms are both scholarly and popular, each with many intertwining branches.

Scholars have looked, for example, at numerous facets of the use of language in court by lawyers, witnesses, and judges. They've shown the necessity of using stories in litigation and law; described how disputing is woven into the daily affairs of society; and made law a tool for surveying wellsprings of meaning and power in human life. All these areas of inquiry are relevant to this book.[19]

So too is popular culture, where trials have proved an inexhaustible source of entertainment and instruction. Media portrayals range from journalistic accounts of real trials and real lawyers to the fantasized scenarios of novels and screen, often authored or overseen by trained lawyers. Whether true, like O. J., or fiction, like Grisham, trials presented for mass consumption are theatrical performances, with dramatic pulse and story line.

This book's concern with performing, then, reflects long-standing, widespread understandings about what a trial is. What is new about this study is that it investigates in a sustained way the meaning of performance in a trial. It explores how stories are actually staged as artful performances, as part of a living craft tradition. How, it asks, do lawyers—especially masters such as Michael Tigar and Roger King—go about framing their stories in front of a jury? And how do they summon the authority to get their stories across?[20]

These are American trials, American stories. To follow them as performances is to chart intensely fraught dynamics of symbolic communication with American audiences. The search leads far beyond the legal arena, since what lawyers try to achieve with juries is indebted to—and sheds light on—the ways in which Americans grapple with truth in daily life.

For every trial that crosses the radar screen of national consciousness, thousands proceed in obscurity. Even our country's most accomplished trial lawyers pass much of the time toiling in the trenches, on cases more often than not unknown outside local venues. This is the terrain of day-to-day advocacy covered in the first part of this book. The central figure will be an exceptionally skilled prosecutor, Roger King. I'll describe his exploits in two homicide trials that occurred in the course of my research, with glimpses of several others. The focus will be on how he frames his stories and on how his opponents frame theirs.

By staying with a single attorney to look at his use of craft in various situations and against more than one adversary, we can picture tests of performance all trial lawyers face. Thus, Chapter 1, which describes how Roger King employs drama to great effect in one trial, also demonstrates the potential of drama to move jurors toward judgment in any trial. Chapter 2, in which King and an opponent square off in a protracted battle shaped by their personal styles, depicts sources for performing that all lawyers (and arguably all storytellers) depend upon to give authority to their framing of events. Together these chapters are a scaffolding for viewing trial advocacy as a performance craft.

An interlude follows: a sketch of a lawyer whose bold, fractious style has had formative impact on criminal trial practice in Philadelphia, and whose commanding presence has made him a legend in the legal community and the city at large.

The second part of the book widens the inquiry into lawyers' exercise of authority. It features a cast of distinguished criminal and civil attorneys who, like Michael Tigar, participated in the Smithsonian program. They are men and women from places like Chicago, San Francisco, and New York; Charlotte, San Antonio, and St. Louis; Bozeman, Montana, Gulfport, Mississippi, and Portland, Maine. On the Mall, they engaged each other in intense impromptu matchups and relaxed exchanges of "war stories." With these interactions as evidence, I consider how leading lawyers perform and regard their work.

As I watched these lawyers in action, I was struck by how, subtly but persistently, they manipulated cultural identity—their own and others' racial, gender, class, and regional affiliations—to make themselves and their stories mythically persuasive, in the American grain. Chapter 3 studies this strategy. It is both multicultural and agonistic: a tool to communicate across historic divisions and suspicions while also opportunistically reinforcing them. Such symbolic use of cultural distinctions is, I've come to realize, a pervasive feature of American life.

In Chapter 4 lawyers recount war stories that convey, with humor and irony, the disconcerting unpredictability of their struggles to win trials. These stories reveal, with a candor necessarily lacking in official statements, lawyers' ambivalence about their role in the search for justice.

There is much that this study doesn't cover. By fixing on performance—the point of production, so to speak, in the trial process—I give short shrift to other phases of the lawyer's work. Anyone familiar with the occupation knows that preparations for major trials are all-consuming. But there's scant reference in these pages to the pretrial investigation, the depositions, the construction of a theory of the case, or the motions before the judge. All of these constrain the stories lawyers can tell. But to have included them would have made the book more technical and unwieldy, and they're not part of what the jury hears.

Likewise, I don't consider how jurors in particular cases weigh what they hear. Jurors actively construct their own story from the stories lawyers present to them.[21] My interest here, though, is in the lawyers' side of this meaning-making equation—in their conduct and mentality, their efforts to shape jurors' responses. Most believe that they sway jurors far more than jurors (who tell themselves they decide on facts alone) realize. Like many types of performance specialists, lawyers count for their effects on their audience's lack of knowledge of the craft.

So, too, I don't discuss judges' influence on deliberations. I hardly mention the views I heard them express, or the views of witnesses, police, or courtroom staff, even though all parties to a proceeding have their own takes on it and the attorneys. Nor do I dwell on clients and their families, the people whose lives are shaken, even shattered, by trials, and whose needs and concerns lawyers may—or may not—understand. This book is about the lawyers' standpoint. But others matter, too.[22]

Finally, and most importantly, I say little directly about the economic and political realities that structure trial practice. Nonetheless, it is vital to my critical purposes for readers to remember that these factors are always operating at or close to the surface. Money, of course, drives the legal profession. This was a stark lesson about the justice system that the public absorbed during O. J. Simpson's criminal case. Compared to defendants like Simpson, clients of limited or no means are far more likely to be represented by attorneys who are overworked, inexperienced, incapable, or overwhelmed by the other side's resources. Access to skilled, adequately funded advocacy is as class stratified as are other benefits in American society. The right of criminal defendants to have a lawyer may now be mandated by law, but that's a far cry from guaranteeing that the results will be well crafted.

What does this wildly varying quality of representation mean for the courts' claims to fairness? If lawyers are correct in saying that verdicts depend on the caliber of their performances, what responsibilities do they, and we, have to persons who seek justice from disadvantaged positions? I look at such moral questions connected to craft tradition in the conclusion of the book.

My method of study is ethnographic.[23] For a year I observed lawyers in court and elsewhere, listened to them in conversation, and spoke to them and to others about them. In the following chapters I describe what I saw certain attorneys do in specific situations and how they themselves explained what they did. I neither skewer nor apologize for them. I try to interpret their actions and to hazard some conclusions about the nature of their work.

My documentary approach is to include a lot of textual material (like many folklorists, I savor "texts") in order to depict—in light of my interests and limitations, of course—lawyers' words and deeds and a sense of the contexts in which they occurred. Jury trials are exceedingly complex; my choices of moments to write about, very constricted. Still, texts can convey something of the richness of the activity being reported. They let the reader hear lawyers' voices alongside and in counterpoint to mine. I hope the ample texts will encourage you to make interpretations of your own.

I've tried to write in plain English. In these times, when academic discourse is often perversely detached from everyday language and when readerships dwindle down to fellow professionals and captive college students, many scholars could take a cue from skilled trial lawyers, who know how to reach their audiences. This book is intended not just for lawyers and students in cultural studies, but for anyone interested in the justice system and story's persuasive powers.

I can't say whether lawyers who read this book will find secrets of the trade they haven't yet learned. But I hope they, and others, will find grist for thinking about the hidden ways in which stories permeate our institutions and guide all of our lives. Justice in American society is pursued through competitive performance. The need for stories in court is akin to our need for stories in other spheres. Paradoxes of the jury trial—Is it a rational undertaking or storytelling combat? Does it turn on evidence or on skill?—fall into place once we recognize that to discover truth, in public life as in our imaginations, we rely on art.

DRAMA

Chorus:
The augur has spread confusion,
terrible confusion;
I do not approve what was said
nor can I deny it.
I do not know what to say;
I am in a flutter of foreboding . . .
> —Sophocles, *Oedipus the King*[1]

The trial resolves a mystery. There has been a charge of wrongdoing. Is the defendant guilty? Is the corporation liable? At the beginning no one can say for certain. But at the end the matter is finished so far as society is concerned.

How do jurors get from posing to solving the mystery?

Consider how mysteries are solved in crime fiction. The detective sifts evidence, questions people, follows leads, pieces together possible versions of what might have happened. A double narrative unfolds: the present story of the investigation and the past story of the crime. The detective, driven by desire to learn the truth about the crime, ultimately discovers it, and at that moment the two narratives, present and past, converge.[2]

Jurors are like detectives—only silenced and seatbound. While the proceedings unfold before them, they try to reconstruct the chronological sequence of events and to discover cause-and-effect relationships that can explain them. They weigh scenarios, test hypotheses, form tentative conclusions. Finally they deliberate. They settle on a story. They match it to the best-fitting verdict among the choices the judge has given them. Their verdict inscribes the present on the past.

This movement toward judgment is propelled, as we shall see, by drama. The lawyers compete to induce dramatic responses within the jurors that will shift the way they frame the story. This dramatic potential is intrinsic to the trial form.

Two Decisive Hours

Let's return to the case of *Commonwealth v. LaRue Blaylock* described in the Introduction.[3]

The crier, you will recall, began the proceedings. Then Roger King made his opening statement, telling for the first time of the hideous murders the jurors had been called on to judge.

When King sat down, John Guilfoy, the defense counsel, announced that he would waive his opening statement.

King's first witness was Rupert Blaylock, who said he was the father of LaRue Blaylock and the father-in-law of the victim Donald Jones. King asked him if he had witnessed an argument between the two men the evening before the murders. "Yes, I seen them arguing, yeah." That was all King asked. Guilfoy had no questions, and Rupert Blaylock was gone so fast you could have missed him—except that he'd left a hint of a motive that might implicate his son in the crimes.

Now King called Mrs. Ellen Jones to the stand. She was wearing a black dress with a red vest and tie, and a small pearl pendant. He began:

> *Mrs. Jones, were you related to Marci Jones?*
> Yes.
> *How were you related?*
> She was my oldest daughter.
> *How old was she?*
> Eighteen.
> *Were you related to Audrey Jones?*
> Yes. She was my youngest daughter.
> *How old was she?*
> Sixteen.

Donald Jones, what was your relationship to him?
He was my husband.

There was something chilling to me in these simple statements. Ellen Jones was outwardly calm. She spoke crisply. King immediately began to lead her through her recollections of Monday, December 19.

She had left for work at an insurance company downtown about 7:30 that morning. Marci, who was home from school that day, called after 2:00 P.M. to tell her that Uncle L—Ellen Jones's stepbrother, LaRue—was in the house. Mrs. Jones asked what he wanted, and Marci replied that he'd come to pick up his tools. She asked Marci if he was angry.

Mrs. Jones was worried because she'd hired somebody else to finish the living room ceiling, which LaRue had been working on, and she didn't know how he would react to seeing that the repairs had been done without him. She had warned Marci not to let him in, because she wanted to be there when he first saw the ceiling. But Marci *had* let him in, and when Mrs. Jones asked her if he was angry, Marci grunted on the phone in the way that kids do, which indicated that he likely *was* angry. She asked her daughter to call her when he left, and Marci did in the next half hour.

Mrs. Jones arrived on her street at 8:30 that night, but instead of going directly home she went down the street to her mother's house, so she could hide the Christmas presents, pants for the girls, she'd bought on the way. At this point in her testimony she began to cry.

Guilfoy suggested she take some water or a break. But she recovered and went on, emotionally describing the conversation she'd had with LaRue at her mother's home.

LaRue didn't actually step inside the door of her mother's house, which struck Mrs. Jones as unusual. He stood there fidgeting, saying he had come to pick up some stuff. When she said Marci had told her he'd already gotten his tools, LaRue said no, that he'd decided not to mess with them until she, Mrs. Jones, got home. He'd just been down to her house, he said, but nobody had answered the door. So Mrs. Jones went over there with him. When she saw his tool bag she was surprised it was empty, except for a blowtorch. He took it, and the next thing she knew he was gone.

Standing on the enclosed porch, Ellen Jones noticed that the front door had swung back farther than usual. The bikes, the sofa, and the work table had all been pushed back so they weren't blocking the door, like they had been. Tools were neatly piled, one on top of another, on the floor. Except for a lamp in the living room, the house was dark. Marci was supposed to be out shopping with her friend, and Audrey, sent to the house earlier by her grandmother to turn out a light she had noticed burning in the basement, must have stopped on the way back at *her* friend's. So Mrs. Jones went again to her mother's house.

At 10:00 P.M., assuming that the girls would be home by this point, she returned. There was a football game on the television. She changed the station and sat down on the sofa. She could hear a faint voice coming from the porch, and when she went out to look she found Marci's radio, which was unusual, since it never left Marci's room. Back in the living room she saw that a ceiling tile was out of place, and, thinking that one of the cats had crept into the space created by the dropped ceiling, she went to the top of the stairs to check.

There were clothes hanging over the banister that hadn't been there before. Her sewing machine was no longer in the hallway. She turned on the light in Marci's room and saw that the dresser drawers were all pulled out and that clothes were everywhere. Audrey's room was also in shambles, and the bed had been knocked down. Something was blocking the door to her own room; she had to force her way in. The light on her nightstand wouldn't work, and when she tried to turn on her son's television to get some light, it was gone.

She was scared. Somebody had ransacked the house. Leaving the room she tried to open the bathroom door but it wouldn't budge, and she saw a messy smudge on it. Mrs. Jones went downstairs and called her mother, telling her that the house had been ransacked, that she couldn't turn on the light, and that she should bring over the flashlight. When the older woman arrived they used the flashlight to go into the basement, since the switch at the top of the stairs wouldn't work. They found a bulb in a socket, turned it, and it came on.

At this point, for the first time in his questioning, Roger King sat down.

> *When it came on, was your attention directed anywhere in that basement?*
> Yeah. There were things—we had bags, storage bags and sleeping bags and tents and stuff down there. And all of this seemed to have been pulled out. But in the corner of the basement it looked like things had been piled up in a semicircle like, and my mother asked me what was that for. And I told her I didn't know, that I didn't put it there. And

there isn't a light back over there, so she used the flashlight and we went back over, and—

She did not go on, until King asked:

> *When you went back over, did you see any bed clothing from any section of the house?*
> In the middle of the—behind—even by the table and stuff that had been piled up there, it looked like one of the girl's quilts.
> *So what, if anything, did you do?*
> I reached down to pull the quilt up, and it wouldn't come up. So I pushed the things back that were around it and I tugged at it real hard. And when it came up one of the girls was there and she had—the tape was all over. Her face and her hands and her neck were tied.

Ellen Jones broke down, sobbing. The courtroom seemed suspended beyond time. Jurors were visibly moved. It was the climax to which her testimony had been building. Although everyone knew it was coming we did not know when or how, or what she would discover. Her recounting of the mundane events of the day, with the little discordances whose sinister meaning she could not grasp, and finally this flailing in uncertainty and fear, had created painful suspense, which now was supplanted by horror.

The silence could have lasted longer, but King broke it, asking the court to mark an item for identification as evidence. Judge Stout quietly rebuffed him: "Suppose we just wait a minute and let Mrs. Jones compose herself."

King asked for a bench conference. By the time he got the item marked as "Commonwealth Exhibit One," Mrs. Jones was ready to continue:

> *How was the tape on the face of your daughter, and could you use your face to indicate?*
> The tape was wrapped around her head. It was covering the left eye, coming across her mouth. Just a little bit of her nose—her nose didn't seem to be completely covered, but it was around her mouth and wrapped around the head.
> *Was anything else around the face area other than the tape?*
> The wire that seemed to be wrapped around her neck.
> *Where were her hands?*
> Her hands were up near her neck. They were like up here. The wire around her neck seemed to be wrapped around her hands as well.

When you saw this, did you hear anything?
I thought I heard her. I really thought I heard her moan. And I reached
down to turn her over and there was blood everywhere. And I couldn't
move her and I couldn't get the tape off by pulling it. So I ran upstairs
and I got a knife.
What did you do with the knife?
I gave—when I got back, my mother was at her head and she took the
knife and cut the wire off. It seemed like—just seemed like she was—
like she was moaning. I thought I would get the tape off she would be
able to breathe.
So did you take the tape off?
Yes.
Did you cut her hands free?
Yes.
Then what did you do?
All I could think of was that she was hurt, she was hurt bad, so I went
to get—to call an ambulance.

King showed her Commonwealth Exhibit One—two sketches of her
daughter's naked body, drawn by the police with her assistance. The defense
counsel protested when King wanted to circulate the drawings to the jury,
but the judge overruled him. When the jurors had looked at the drawings,
King returned to the scene in the basement:

*Mrs. Jones, after you made the discovery of your daughter in the basement,
could you at that time identify which one of your daughters that it was?*
No.
Why couldn't you?
Her face was covered with the tape and the only thing that was showing
was one eye. And it looked like the tape was holding that eye open. I
really thought it was Audrey because when I touched her her skin was
kind of rough and Audrey has eczema and it was all over. And I thought
it was Audrey because she was supposed to had put the light out.

Upstairs, Mrs. Jones was unable to call the ambulance because she was too upset to hit the right buttons on the phone. She went to a neighbor's home to
make the call. When the officers arrived, she went back to her house, where the
police told her to stay in the living room. She waited, noticing more damage:

While you were in the living room, did you receive any information from a police officer concerning your other daughter?

Yeah. They asked me who was the girl upstairs in the tub. I told them I didn't know. I didn't think anybody else was home. I remember I kept asking my neighbors where Marci was, if anybody had seen her, and when they said that there was a girl upstairs in the tub I thought it was Marci because she was home.

Did they tell you what condition she was in who was in the tub?

No.

Did you have an occasion to be in your enclosed front porch when a body was discovered?

Yes.

How much of the body did you see?

All I saw was the feet. When the feet were uncovered, the officer told me not to touch anything else, to go back. Then they asked me who was the male on the porch and I told them I didn't know.

Did there come a time that you identified the three people found in your house?

The first time I got a look at my youngest daughter and my husband was at the morgue.

The person on the porch, later did you find out who that was?

Yes.

Who was it?

My husband.

Donald Jones?

Yes.

The girl in the tub, at the morgue did you find out who she was?

Yes.

Who was it?

Audrey, my youngest daughter.

The girl that was in the basement that you thought was Audrey, who was that?

It was Marci.

With this litany a circle was closed. Ellen Jones was again identifying the dead, as she'd done at the start of her testimony, only now it was at the moment when she knew their fates. The re-creation of her trauma was finished. It was the single line of questioning King had followed since she'd taken the stand.

He shifted to minor matters. First he asked about money missing from the house. Mrs. Jones collected coins, and perhaps a hundred dollars' worth had been taken, along with five or ten dollars Marci had been saving for Christmas and twenty dollars Audrey had been given for transit tokens. Then he began introducing exhibits and reviewing them with the witness. There were sketches of the house layout, and photographs of the rooms and articles of clothing, showing bloodstains and disarray. There was the comforter Marci was wrapped in—the plastic bag containing it was left unopened—and the hammer, awl, and shears that had been kept on the porch.

Other exhibits remained to be covered when, at 12:35, King suddenly shifted the topic of questioning to the conversation Ellen Jones had had with LaRue Blaylock when they were being driven to the police station to make statements. She had asked LaRue what time he had been at the house and what time he had left:

> *Was there anything unusual about his mannerisms at that time when you were questioning him?*
> When they brought him up to the car and he got in, he never once even looked at me. He never even once turned around. He never once said anything other than to answer what I had just asked him.
> *When you told him that you knew that he was there at three o'clock, what exactly did he say?*
> He started to stammer and he never really got a complete answer out.
> *Did he usually stammer?*
> No. Usually he just spoke normal. He never stammered about anything.

At this point King suggested to Judge Stout that it was an opportune time to break for lunch. Court recessed.

The trial of LaRue Blaylock would continue for three more days. The defense would have its chances. No solid evidence had yet been introduced linking the accused man to the crimes. Yet I left the courtroom feeling, without knowing why, that Roger King had already gone far toward sewing up the case.

Momentum

King, I later discovered, thought he had made great progress too. When I interviewed him after the trial, he said he'd felt the odds shift decisively in his favor at the beginning:

> My technique of trying cases is a persistent, pressurized approach. It's designed to make you think if you're the defense attorney, make you think if you're the judge or jury. And if you apply enough pressure on the typical defense attorney, he'll make a mistake. And at that level of the practice, dealing with life and death situations, the first person who makes a mistake is subject to lose the case.
>
> *Mistake*—from the defense attorney's standpoint. In the face of a strong opening, you got to stand up and say something. Take five minutes. Say: "Just remember they're just allegations. Remember, you got to decide this case with your head, not your heart. And remember, *they* have the burden of proof, beyond a reasonable doubt. And even with their so-called eyewitness, and their so-called circumstantial evidence, we will create doubt."
>
> Okay, when he declined to answer, let's hit him with a blow that he can't recover from. Let's bring on [Blaylock's] own natural father.

Many attorneys would agree with King that it's a mistake to forgo one's opening statement.[4] But why should the cameo by the defendant's father have been such a heavy a blow to the defense? King thought, furthermore, that the mother's testimony had sent Guilfoy reeling. "His spirits were broken after Ellen Jones. He found himself in a desperate situation." If King is right, why did the defense prospects deteriorate so fast?

I was stuck on this question for months after the trial. Eventually I came to this conclusion: what occurred was a movement of many in the courtroom from one way of framing the story to another. When the jury began they were neutral (or trying to be); soon they had taken on the prosecutor's view of events. They had been carried along by a momentum that had grown incrementally through a series of revelations. Such progression toward judgment is what skilled lawyers want jurors to experience. And perhaps in trials like this one, where the matchup is lopsided, such movement stands out in unusually stark relief.

The progression is a dramaturgical process. We can get a sense of how it works by recalling the earliest staged murder mystery in Western tradition, Sophocles' *Oedipus the King*. The drama scholar Francis Ferguson proposed that this play (and the other Greek tragedies) follow a three-part movement. They begin, he thought, with a Purpose, a seemingly rational search for an answer to a mystery. Then they pass through Passion (or Suffering) as the players make unexpected discoveries that force them to confront unwelcome truths. Out of this turmoil comes Perception, the resolution of the mystery accompanied by new awareness about human life. This change of awareness organizes the play as a whole; it is also repeated again and again during the play, setting up a rhythm that the audience enters, a movement that gains cumulative force.[5]

In *Oedipus the King* the mystery is who killed King Laius. The movement begins when Oedipus, taking the role of district attorney, calls as his first witness the blind seer Tiresias. Their conversation starts with Oedipus's straightforward purpose of finding out any facts Tiresias might know, but soon their passions are aroused: Tiresias darkly suggests that Oedipus was involved in the crime, and Oedipus attacks Tiresias's credibility. The chorus—our jury—is shaken. Something is out of kilter. For the first time they realize that Oedipus himself may be the guilty party. They're far from sure of his guilt at this point, but they've already been moved from one way of framing events to another, and are softened up for further revelations of a similar kind.

The opening scenes of the Blaylock case can be read in light of this schema. When the crier administers the oaths and recites the charges, he states the Purpose of the trial. This gives way to Passion as the prosecutor, tautly depicting the murder scene, makes jurors feel trapped in a situation that's worse than they'd imagined. (Roger King told me that his opening statement was calculated to make the jurors feel anguish, to think, "Oh my God, what am I into?") Then Blaylock's father appears, providing an initial Perception of Blaylock's guilt.

In dramatic terms, the jury's outlook may well already be subtly altered. They may see the potential of Blaylock's guilt more readily than they had before. The danger for the defense counsel in passing up his opening statement is that he lets the prosecutor establish unimpeded momentum. The impact of the father's testimony is intensified because it comes undelayed, on the heels of the prosecutor's shocking depiction of the crime.

Then, by choosing not to cross-examine the father, Guilfoy unintention-
ally lets King's momentum continue to build.

Next Ellen Jones takes the stand, and King puts the jury through a
most powerful Purpose-Suffering-Perception sequence. Initially, the audience expects she will tell factually what she knows about the crimes. But
then we are pulled along with her into hell. We go through the progression
as she reenacts the events with the prosecutor: first the questions about
what has happened in the house; then the awful discoveries; finally, the
recognition of her stepbrother's guilt.

What King does just before lunch, when he gets Mrs. Jones to testify
about her stepbrother's strange behavior during the ride to the police station, is more than eliciting a damaging bit of evidence: he's completing the
turn of the screw. Having just moved with Mrs. Jones through her suffering, the audience is at a peak of receptiveness to her view of the crimes. Her
identification of the perpetrator is cathartic.

When Guilfoy's turn came he *could* have cushioned the impact of Ellen
Jones's testimony. Or so King insisted to me: "Line on Mrs. Jones: 'You
were upset, weren't you? Even that night, you had no idea that your stepbrother did this, did you? In fact, even at the preliminary hearing, you were
unsure. How much of a role did the DA play, how much of a role did the
police play, in getting you to take the position you're taking?' End of cross-
examination. You could care less what the answers would be—but you got
a basis to argue." In other words, hit the discrepency between what she is
saying now and what she said before, and get out quickly. Guilfoy did neither. He questioned Mrs. Jones at length that afternoon without casting
doubt on her account.

In fact, King told me, Ellen Jones had believed LaRue Blaylock was
innocent. She thought he was innocent at the time of the murders and
continued to think so long after. King said that she had covered up for him
during the preliminary hearing, testifying that she wasn't aware of any fric-
tion in the family, although she knew fully well LaRue hated her husband
and that the two men had to be kept apart when they were once in the
same prison.

King had been assigned the case after the preliminary hearing. On first
meeting Ellen Jones, he told me, he'd said to her: "There's nothing you can
do, nothing you can say, to help him. His fate is in the hands of twelve people. And all I want you to do is tell me to the best of your ability. What you

know. And it's not going to be you pointing the finger—it's going to be a group of people collectively pointing a finger. . . . You were less than candid with me, Mrs. Jones. And you won't be at trial. I can assure you of that. For everything that I have a question about, I already know the answer."

Ellen Jones loved her stepbrother. King had to undermine that love. He did it by showing her that LaRue was not who he appeared to be, that he had deceived her—not about these murders, which she couldn't consider rationally, but about his past. LaRue Blaylock had been convicted of murder once before, as a teenager, for stabbing another youth repeatedly in the neck in a gang fight. At that time he had convinced her that the police were framing him. Now she thought they were framing him again. So King read her excerpts from the hearing transcript of the earlier case in which LaRue admitted his guilt and gave his account of the slaying. This was a turning point for Ellen Jones. She saw he could lie—and kill.

When King described the scene, I imagined the two of them sitting on folding chairs across the table from each other in the cramped, shabby room the Homicide Division uses for questioning. They were forming a bond. Once they had, she wouldn't need to be coached on how to tell her story. When he led her through it on the witness stand, she would instinctively cooperate to build suspense and locate her suspicions to suggest that she saw the defendant's guilt right away, without a hint that she'd undergone a change of heart.

When I asked King why he had seemed to rush her at the keenest moment of her grief—to me, the one jarring note in his performance that morning—he replied, "Because there are cases that it's prosecutorial misconduct to prompt or to elicit or to choreograph emotion." How does one draw the line, I wondered, of what is or isn't prompting emotion? Choreography seemed just the right metaphor for their sustained exchange.

The reworking of life in a trial is the lawyer's handiwork. King presents the mother to the jury as a pure bearer of truth, just as he presents the Joneses as a close-knit family. She and Donald Jones were, in fact, separated. Such sidestepping of inconvenient information is not an outright lie but rather a streamlining of character and action. Ellen Jones communicates persuasively because of what she has endured. She evokes the audience's deep feelings about what it is to be a mother and what it would mean to lose one's family, to suffer in such a way. According to Aristotle's well-known dictum, it's in the nature of drama that she be elevated, since tragic characters are exhibited as being better than they really are. And having misjudged her stepbrother, she even bears a tragic protagonist's responsibility for the calamity. As a witness she transcends limitations of personal identity, embodying the worst disaster that can befall a human being.[6]

Ellen Jones leads the jurors, through their vicarious experiencing of her emotions, to adopt the prosecutor's framing of the crimes. But how different things would have been if she'd clung to her belief in Blaylock's innocence. Or how diminished her impact would have been if King had delayed bringing her to the stand until later in the trial, or if her story had not followed the chronology of that day. By changing her allegiance, King, we could say, shapes the content of the enactment, and by deciding when she should appear and how the questioning should be ordered, he shapes its structure. What the jury finally hears is the result of many choices laden with dramatic implications, the realization of which is a matter of craft.

A key task for the lawyer—it's an overarching concern in dramatic art— is to fit actions together in a convincing whole. There's a story to tell the jury: evidence has to be selectively turned into a believable plot. The presentation of this story also has to be plotted, because the way it unfolds affects how it's received. As in other forms of theater, audience attention has to be held to achieve cumulative effects. Ideally, each scene will disclose some piece of the story that the audience needs to learn at that point while furthering their expectation of what will come later.[7] Much depends on one's ability to mold the progress of the action—something Roger King accomplished through such means as placement of witnesses, economy of questioning, and timing of revelations, a control of pacing that his opponent was helpless to stop.

My argument boils down to this: each lawyer tries to move jurors towards his or her framing of the story by setting them up for successive revelations, moments that lead to recognitions. At these moments dispassion gives way to feeling; feeling, perhaps, to new understanding. If the lawyer succeeds at such moments, at least some members of the jury recalibrate their reading of events. The opposing lawyers' use of these dramatic effects pulls the jurors in opposite directions. In well-fought trials one side gains, then the other. Each has successes that retard the other's momentum and generate its own. In closely matched trials jurors' sentiments remain fluid, and the mystery stays alive until the end.

The Blaylock trial wasn't a close match. Once Ellen Jones had testified I, for one, no longer expected the defense to be persuasive. Questions remained, but for me the case had lost its sheen of mystery. It felt more like a rite that had to be undergone to put the stamp of Cain on a killer.

Easy to overlook, at least for me, during the parade of Commonwealth witnesses who followed Mrs. Jones—the police, medical examiner, grandmother, and three witnesses who saw Blaylock on the Jones's porch—was the circumstantial nature of the DA's evidence. In our interview afterward, King was intent on showing me that his case had had potential weaknesses. He took Guilfoy's part: "Is all the Commonwealth coming up with a pair of semen-stained undershorts, the defendant's blood, people who did not see him do anything but be in the house, and one person who claims he saw him strike the first victim [on the porch]? *It's not enough!* Make them prove it." King himself regarded as "window dressing" the underpants, the blood, the other witnesses who saw Blaylock, and the testimony of the medical examiner, who produced three Styrofoam heads to show exactly where the blows had been struck: "Did you find anything in your examinations of these three bodies that would indicate to you that LaRue Blaylock committed the three killings? Answer: No. In your examination, did you find *one shred* of evidence connecting LaRue Blaylock to these three murders? No. *No further questions.*"

In his running commentary on what Guilfoy *could* have done, how he could have "taken the wind out of the Commonwealth's sails" (enough, anyway, to "have sent us scrambling a little bit, to hit him with something else"), King engaged in a what-if kind of anticipation that prepared him for the worst. Like a writer contemplating effects that different twists in the action might have on the plot, he imagined the contest as a seesaw.

Why *was* the matchup so uneven? During the proceedings a police detective took me aside and explained. He seemed sheepish about how easy it was for the Commonwealth to prove its case. John Guilfoy was overwhelmed, the detective said, because he was a general practitioner with relatively little trial experience involving serious crimes. The rule in Philadelphia courts was that indigent defendants in homicide cases were represented by private attorneys, not public defenders. The fee wasn't lucrative, but the system served, the detective said, to provide extra income for attorneys who needed it. If you wanted such cases, you submitted your name to individual judges, each of whom decided if you were qualified to get on the "wheel" for random assignments of the homicides that came before them. That was how Guilfoy had gotten this case.

Nailing Things Down

The matter of blood can stand as an example of how hard it was for John Guilfoy to frame his story. Although the bit of Type A blood found on Audrey's clothes was a link in the Commonwealth's chain of evidence, Guilfoy wanted to use it to point to the weakness of the state's case. But he didn't challenge King's inference, when the medical examiner testified, that this was LaRue Blaylock's blood. Instead, Guilfoy waited until his closing argument, when he said:

> Now, what else does the Commonwealth show you to say that LaRue Blaylock, the accused, did it? Bring in the comforters, clothing, the water samples, the pubic hairs, the head hairs, the nail clippings, the blood samples, and they have two areas of blood on Audrey's clothing.
>
> Who else has been in the bathroom that night? Officer Byrne, Officer McGrath, Officer Ricci, maybe the mother. I don't think she was, but it's your recollection.
>
> Of all this blood that the Commonwealth witnesses testified to, two drops. Minuscule. Two cc's. Whatever it is, it's less than an ounce. Nothing else.

This attempt to throw doubt on the source of the blood is vaguely worded. Instead of saying the blood could have come from one of the officers or the mother, Guilfoy has only implied it. Why mention the mother, who testified that she hadn't gone into the bathroom? What is gained by emphasizing that the quantity of blood found was minuscule, when it's not the amount but the source that matters? And calling attention to the Commonwealth's evidence might in fact help the Commonwealth, for although Guilfoy is trying to say it amounts to much less than it seems, he does so indirectly.

The defense wasn't entirely bereft of strategy. Guilfoy made perhaps his most forceful point in cross-examination, when he asked the detective who had taken Blaylock's statement at the police station to identify the jacket and sweatshirt Blaylock had worn the night of the murders. With a flourish Guilfoy held each garment in front of the jurors, asking them to pay particular attention to the collar area. In his closing statement he explained his reasoning: the grandmother had testified that whenever LaRue took a bath he used a lot of talcum powder, and the Commonwealth claimed that LaRue had bathed right after the murders to get rid of the blood. Yet there was no sign of powder on the clothes he'd worn.

That was Guilfoy's approach: wait until the closing, then point to those things that the DA had not mentioned or fully explained and claim that they, taken together, amounted to reasonable doubt. Guilfoy was incredulous that Gary Green, the witness King claimed had seen Blaylock strike Marci on the porch, could have walked away from such a scene, and as proof that no violence had occurred there he said:

> You heard Doctor Fillinger describe Marci's injuries. Where was the testimony about the pool of blood in the corner of the porch where she went down when she was hit? It's not there. Nobody testified to that because there is no blood in that corner. And you heard the severe injuries that Marci received.
>
> Isn't it in your common experience as reasonable individuals if what Green said is true there's blood in that corner?

When it was King's turn for closing, he didn't respond to the talcum powder argument. He explained that Green had ignored the beating on the porch because he subscribed to "the ghetto code": "I didn't see anything, I don't know anything, don't bother me, I don't want to be involved." As for the blood, he said:

> Mr. Guilfoy in his remarks mentioned blood, ladies and gentlemen. As I said, those photographs speak for themselves. And in the clinical atmosphere of this courtroom, if you noticed, none of the officers called blood blood. They called it stains because in this courtroom we are so caught up in not trying to alarm you. But how can we say don't be alarmed when you are told in very vivid description what happened to three human beings?

King told me that he'd been lying in wait for Guilfoy to refer to blood. The Commonwealth had been euphemistic, he said, not as a gesture of consideration but as a precaution against an appeal of the conviction on grounds that they'd sensationalized the crimes. This restraint now became a weapon.

Since Guilfoy had raised blood as an issue in a way that questioned its presence, King felt free to indulge in mentioning blood as much as he liked. "Mr. Guilfoy wanted blood," he said, showing the jury the photograph of Marci's nightgown where it had been found on the floor of her mother's bedroom. "Look at that. Is that not a river of blood?" Seconds later:

> Mr. Guilfoy wanted blood in the porch, ladies and gentlemen.
> Well, we take you to that very same bedroom, and going out
> of the bedroom, how much blood is on the wall?
> How much blood is on the floor?
> How much blood is on the sheets?
> Is this blood from the deep vaginal incision that Doctor Fillinger told you about?
> I would submit to you that it is.[8]

"Mr. Guilfoy-says-we-didn't-give-you-blood" became the refrain of King's summation, tinging his other references to blood at the murder scene with the idea that the defense denied the blood's ubiquity and was trying to escape it, but could never wash it off.

The change of stains into blood was one chord in "the crescendo" that King said he strove for in his closing argument. If we think of the summation as the culmination of a lawyer's efforts to build momentum, the last turn before the jury writes the end of the story, we can see how this speech tries to achieve recognitions that clinch all that has gone before. This is the lawyer's chance to unveil the story's meaning: to prove it to be inwardly consistent and true, and to open it outward so it becomes a parable that sheds light on the mystery of the human condition.

The main transformation that John Guilfoy attempted in his summation was to turn the testimony of the three eyewitnesses who saw the defendant on the porch into a suggestion of conspiracy. Maybe another trial had been "conducted on that street," Guilfoy said, where it had been decided to provide the Commonwealth with any evidence it might be lacking. Logically, this tack could have led to an impassioned plea against the scapegoating of an individual, which would make the case a parable for the rush to judgment that often appears so tempting when human beings are in tragic circumstances and under pressure to find a guilty party. The tragedy, Guilfoy could have argued, would only be compounded if the ac-

cused were convicted. But the closing never reached a higher plane of
meaning, an expectable failure since a basis wasn't laid for it during the trial.

Meanwhile, King had an ambitious metaphor for the jury to contem-
plate. He began his speech with imagery of home:

> You have seen, you have heard of a traumatic event which oc-
> curred one year and one day ago.
>
> You didn't hear, but it was implied, that our traditonal greet-
> ing last Christmas was not a "Merry Christmas" in the Jones
> household.
>
> And speaking about households, I need not remind you of cer-
> tain clichés connected with the home.
>
> "Be it ever so humble, there is no place like home."
>
> I need not remind you of the Biblical quotation "In my fa-
> ther's house there [are] many mansions," nor the cliché "Home is
> where you go and they have to take you in."
>
> Need I remind you about living behind walls and living be-
> hind locks and all of those things can be traced to one thing:
> Home.
>
> When we talk about the Bill of Rights, we talk about a per-
> son being safe and secure in the comfort of his own surround-
> ings.
>
> Ladies and gentlemen, I'm mentioning home in this position
> because home is where this scenario started and where it ended.
>
> Home, in that when Ellen Jones decided that the old ceiling
> was not good enough, that I need a new ceiling— that set in mo-
> tion this tragic scenario.

He then evoked once more the pain of Ellen Jones's discoveries. He reviewed the evidence against Blaylock, stressed the resolve the eyewitnesses
had shown under cross-examination, reconstructed how Blaylock might
have apportioned his time during and after the spree, and suggested how
premeditation must have gone through his mind. Near the end he recited
two poems, one by Maya Angelou and the other, its inspiration, composed
a century before by Paul Laurence Dunbar.[9] He asked the jurors "to analo-
gize this to those people who live behind closed doors and behind double
locks who try to keep the other world out":

The caged bird sings
with a fearful trill
of things unknown
but longed for still
and his tune is heard
on the distant hill
for the caged bird
sings of freedom . . .

"Maybe Marci Jones was thinking of freedom," he told them. "Maybe she decided to open the cage door to let in what she thought was a friendly figure. But it didn't work out that way."

Later I asked King why he had chosen this metaphor. It was disconcerting to me, because it hadn't squared with my idea of what the trial had been about. How was Marci Jones in a cage? Hadn't she come and gone as she pleased? And her murderer was no intruder breaking into a barred house, but a family member.

King answered by describing how he'd come to understand the defendant. The fact that Blaylock was a repeat offender was "the red light" for a prosecutor. King had looked into the earlier murder, and into Blaylock's relationship to each of the victims and to other members of his family. He'd studied how Blaylock treated his common-law wife, his son, and his stepmother, and his father. One word kept surfacing: *violent.* This was a man, King felt, who craved control and never had learned discipline. The one area over which Blaylock knew he could have control was his family. He liked Ellen the best, which is why he didn't kill her. He wanted to get back at her, to take something from her, to punish her and the rest of the family, who in rejecting his work had rejected him.

But none of this could King put before the jury. The only information touching on motive that he was able to present during the trial was evidence that, on two previous occasions when people were dissatisfied with home repairs LaRue Blaylock had done, he had responded with threats and violence. One of these outbursts was against his own brother. The broad pattern of behavior King saw wasn't admissible, yet he felt the need to offer the jury a solution to the mystery of motivation. In his mind, using the symbolism of the caged bird was an apt substitute for speaking directly of the man's simmering rage.

The jurors would respond to the metaphor in their own private ways, of course. Its effectiveness, like that of all cultural symbolism a lawyer employs, doesn't depend on its logical consistency or on whether it evokes the meanings it has for the lawyer; it depends, rather, on whether it draws jurors along certain paths of interpretation favorable to the lawyer's story.[10] Angelou's words fit the fate of the victims:

> *But a caged bird stands on the grave of dreams*
> *his shadow shouts on a nightmare scream*
> *his wings are clipped and his feet are tied*
> *so he opens his throat to sing.*

By associating the scream with life being taken, the nightmare with Marci being tied without chance of escape, listeners may dwell on the meaning of lives frustrated, longing for freedom. In choosing poems by Angelou and Dunbar, the prosecutor foregrounds—for those aware that they are African American—the narrowed chances so many black youths contend with as they grow up in this country. Marci and Audrey, compelled by circumstances to live where double-locked doors are needed as protection, were not safe from evil that came from within. The closeness of the danger made their freedom an illusion, their dreams of the future a mockery.

King achieved a heightening of effect by placing Angelou's poem first, following it with Dunbar's earlier version, and ending with the fourth verse, where Dunbar declares:

> *I know why the caged bird sings*
> *   When his wing is bruised and his bosom sore,—*
> *When he beats his bars around he would be free;*
> *It is not a carol of joy or glee,*
> *   But a prayer that he sends from his heart's deep core,*
> *   But a plea, that upward to Heaven he flings—*
> *I know what the caged bird sings!*

King made sure his listeners caught the reference to caroling by commenting, "The voices that could have sung last Christmas are not singing anymore, and you are not here to decide *that*." He did not elaborate on the image of praying to God, of pleading for life, but by evoking what the victims might have done as they were being murdered, he was anticipating the sentencing hearing that would follow conviction, when he would ask the same jury to give Blaylock the electric chair. He was already urging them to suspend the Christmas spirit that the killer had trampled one year and one day ago. From the heightened Passion of poetry he swung in the very next lines to his final claim of Perception, a cry of condemnation:

You are here to decide what to call *this:*
>whether you want to call it an assassination, an
>extermination,
>whether you want to call it butchery,
>whether you want to call it man's inhumanity to man,
>>I ask you to call it one thing:
>>I ask you to call it *murder*
>>>in the first degree.

King had no doubt of their answer. When he was done court adjourned, and in the hallway I heard him say to two admirers, "All I need now are the nails and the juice."

King was exultant. The jury had yet to begin deliberating, but he told the police—and me—to come back the following morning for the sentencing hearing to hear the rhetoric raised "an octave higher."

In the sentencing hearing the next day, the defense counsel asked jurors to recall that Jesus brought a message of love during this season. He pleaded with them to bring back a verdict of life in His name.

They showed no mercy.

CHAPTER 2

STYLE

Style is the principle of decision in a work of
art, the signature of the artist's will.
—Susan Sontag[1]

To persuade a jury, lawyers must imprint their will on their story. This, as in every art, is a matter of style.

Style involves consistencies of choice and action. Each lawyer has characteristic ways of appearing before jurors, striving for drama, conceiving of plot, questioning witnesses, delivering a summation. These techniques follow codified craft practices—shared knowledge of the tried-and-true set forth in manuals and courses on trial advocacy and learned from on-the-job observation and instruction. But the approaches are *grounded* in the performance style the lawyer forms out of his or her personality, past experience, habits of thinking, and manner of being in the world.

This chapter explores how style shapes lawyers' stories, and above all how—and how well—it equips them to meet the moment-by-moment demands of performance. A style's flexibility, we shall see, can be its most critical attribute. How capable is the lawyer of adapting to varied adversaries and responding to unpredictable turns of events?

We begin with an account of the next trial on Roger King's calendar after he defeated John Guilfoy; this time he faced Robert Mozenter, a formidable foe. In their battle of wills we will find elements of style that underlie all lawyers' craft.

The Trial

Arctic winds blasted the city.[2] Drafts steeped steadily through the windows in Judge Lisa Richette's courtroom. The few spectators kept their coats on.

By order of Mayor Wilson Goode, the City Hall heat was switched on only twenty minutes every hour. The judge, recovering from a cold, grew periodically incensed. "Court officers, are you cold-blooded?" she shouted. "Don't you realize there's no heat in here? . . . Let the mayor get rid of some of his bodyguards if he wants to save money! . . . We can't conduct a homicide trial under these conditions!"

Most of the roving jurors were eager for the trial to begin. Robert Mozenter—"Bobby," as he was known around the courthouse—was one of Philadelphia's most streetwise, flamboyant defense attorneys. They described him as "feisty" and "fiery," qualities some attributed to his height (five foot seven). Before entering private practice Mozenter had been in charge of drug prosecutions for the DA's office. The city police, who regularly testified against his clients, had recently retained him as their chief counsel—a high compliment to his skill.

The trial was for the first-degree murder of John "Muscles" Fisher—a drug execution, roving jurors said. Rumor among them had it that the defendant, Greg Brady, was the mastermind of a string of murders and that this was the first one for which the DA's office had enough evidence to go to trial. Brady, an African American in his late twenties, looked comfortable, even studious, in court, wearing a dark suit and glasses. The roving jurors figured he had to have big bucks to afford Mozenter.

The mood was amicable, as it often is during jury selection. The attorneys and the judge were old acquaintances. During delays in the questioning of prospective jurors, they bantered.

After King used a peremptory challenge to prevent selection of an animated grandmother by the name of Cohen, Mozenter wisecracked, "Counsel is prejudiced against Jews, your Honor. He's striking all Jews from the jury. All one." Mozenter is Jewish; Cohen had been the first Jew considered.

A bit later, when the judge commented that she couldn't promise jurors that the trial would be brief, Mozenter added, "Not with the Commonwealth, it won't be."

The judge replied, "You should take Mr. King to lunch for that re-mark."

King chimed in, "A good black is hard to crack."

To which Mozenter said, "That is, a *good* one."

Maybe the ethnic repartee was tied to the lawyers' preoccupation with the backgrounds of prospective jurors. Jury selection—voir dire—is tedious as well as dangerous, since it forces lawyers to make snap deci-sions, with potentially fateful consequences, from fragmentary informa-tion and visceral impressions. Eager to minimize risks, they resort to rules of thumb of their local legal community that are really nothing more than stereotypes.

Every criminal attorney in Philadelphia, for instance, knows the maxim that when the defendant is black, the defense should keep whites from South Philadelphia off the jury. South Philadelphia is a mosaic of working-class ethnic neighborhoods. According to stereotype, no matter how open-minded prospective white jurors from this area may appear—even if they have college degrees, which, according to another rule of thumb, indicates defense leanings—they're racially prejudiced and will side with the prosecution. Another warning with African American defendants: beware of blacks from Germantown. Much of the Germantown section is middle class and integrated, and the stereotype runs that black people who live there are upwardly mobile and unusually paranoid about crime.

Mozenter followed these truisms when he struck some white males who lived in ethnic enclaves without bothering to ask them a single ques-tion. Following other prosecutorial rules of thumb, King used peremptory challenges to get rid of people like Mrs. Cohen, who appeared to be "women's libbers" or "independent thinkers" of other stripes. These were the types likely to inject their own ideas into jury deliberations. All it would take is one of them "overintellectualizing" in the jury room, he believed, to cost him the case. They were also the ones, he knew from experience, most likely to be "turned off" by his aggressive style. He was watchful, too, for African Americans who might be prone to identify with the defendant as a brother or a son.

(As for me—Jewish, came of age in the sixties, fresh out of graduate school—King would've bounced me in a flash, I knew.)

A coarse strainer, rules of thumb detect reasons for one side or the other to worry about nearly everybody. Those who get on the jury tend to overlap stereotypes in ways that hold attractions for both sides. Consider some of the people picked to be jurors in the case of *Commonwealth v. Greg Brady:*

• A young African American man who had been raised in the Richard Allen Projects, in the heart of the North Philadelphia ghetto, and who was an ex-Marine. His early background was like the defendant's. On the other hand, his military training appealed to the DA.

• An older white banker from center city. Conservative by profession, he was well educated and lived in one of Philadelphia's most liberal neighborhoods.

• A young white man who used crutches. The difficulties he'd had to overcome could predispose him to support either side.

• A young African American woman, college educated, married, with children. Her background was favorable to the defendant, but family concerns could make her sympathetic to the prosecution.

• An older woman, Jewish and heavyset, whose husband was a salesman. She was talkative, but not in the politically tinged way Mrs. Cohen had been.

• A carpenter from Manayunk, a white enclave, who answered with quiet eloquence when the judge asked if he could decide the case impartially. Hesitating, Mozenter conferred with his client, who seemed impressed by the man's demeanor. Mozenter accepted him, but then, visibly uncomfortable, muttered loud enough for spectators to hear, "*He* wanted him, I didn't."

In the hallway during a break near the end of the selection process, the two attorneys swapped cautionary tales with each other about choosing juries. Mozenter confided that he feels best about his prospects when he uses all twenty of the peremptory challenges. King replied with a story about a DA who used his final challenge when one alternate juror still remained to be picked. The defendant was a Muslim. Who should the next prospective juror be but a Muslim-looking guy with short hair? Right there the DA's case slid from first- to second-degree murder.

Roger King gave a harsh opening statement about the death of Fisher, shot seven times from both sides by .38 special revolvers. Mozenter, he knew, ordinarily waives his opening until he presents the defense side of the case. King hoped that accusatory words might lure Mozenter to respond and overcommit himself at the start. He was probing what he saw as one of Mozenter's weaknesses, his "hot temper." King ended his opening statement with vehement language he usually saves for summations:

> We will present medical testimony that would indicate to you that this act was willful, deliberate, and premeditated.
> We will also show that the killers had time
> [*softly*] to ask the question, "Shall I kill?"
> [*shouts*] ANSWER that question, "YES, I WILL,"
>> select the weapons,
>> select the part of the body in which to use the weapon
> on.
> We will show that *this* man was the leader of those three.
> We will ask you at the end of the testimony to return a verdict of guilty of murder in the first degree.
> We will ask you to put an *adj*ective to it:
>> whether it's an assassination,
>> whether it's an extermination,
>> whether it's a slaughter.
> But we will ask you to find that this was
>> a willful,
>> deliberate,
>> and premeditated act.

Mozenter didn't rise to the bait. Uppermost in *his* mind, he told me, was the disadvantage he labored under because he didn't know the full list of Commonwealth witnesses. King had persuaded Judge Richette to issue a protective order keeping their identities secret on the ground that they might be murdered to be prevented from testifying. Mozenter smelled a "mystery witness" waiting in the wings. He was determined to be cautious.

The next morning King led off with Officer Gunter, the first policeman to arrive at the murder scene, the park at Twentieth and Ontario streets. The officer said he'd heard shots fired while his car was on patrol a block away, with the final shot coming just as he reached the park. On cross-examination, Mozenter cited police records indicating the officer had been informed of the shots by the radio dispatcher. Didn't that mean, he asked, that you yourself didn't hear the shots? The policeman was befuddled. Mozenter zeroed in: Gunter had been on the force for thirteen years and was frequently a witness in court. Was he nervous today?

Mozenter used winsome humor to temper the self-described "abrasiveness" of his style. Asking the officer how far he'd been from the victim as he searched the park, Mozenter made himself the measure: "Let's say that I—God forbid—am the body. Now you tell me where to go—not figuratively." Jurors smiled.

By the time Mozenter finished, Gunter agreed it had been too dark to see when he first got out of the car and said he'd known the deceased as a big-time dealer who had taken to using his own drugs. In the hallway Mozenter told me that Gunter's "embellishing" of the events surrounding the shots is simply the way memory works. It was unintentional, but he would use it as part of his strategy to show how prosecution witnesses were "shading" their testimony.

Mozenter stayed on the offensive with the next witnesses, the detective at the scene and the medical examiner. Their dry testimonies weren't incriminating to Brady. On cross, he made them expand their references to syringes found on the victim's body and quinine found in his blood. You could feel their reluctance to say anything that might help the defense.

"Sometimes you have to be nice, sometimes you got to bite their balls off," attorney Russell Goldman commented about Mozenter's strategy. "In a bad case like this, you really jump on it. Bobby don't lay down for nobody. You get the drug evidence out—it makes them look like they're holding back and you wonder what else they're holding back. You want the jury to think, 'What the hell, [the dead man is] scum.' "

The next day King suffered two embarrassments. When he entered the bullets into evidence, he discovered that the DA's office hadn't yet brought them to the courtroom. Then he called his first key witness, Ian Goodwin, but Goodwin wasn't there. While police searched the halls, King, who prides himself on the coolly systematic way he builds a case, stood scowling next to his counsel table, quietly kicking it with his foot.

Five minutes later, Goodwin appeared. A small young man with a faint voice, he wore baggy pants and a wool jacket with gold chains around his neck. He sank into the depths of the witness box, quite in contrast to the confident demeanor of the defendant. King began by establishing that Goodwin had known the principals in the case for many years. Goodwin had just started to relate how he'd seen Muscles Fisher walking down the street at 11:30 on the night he was murdered in the company of one Martin Willams, when Mozenter flipped from a normal tone of voice into rage: "*You'd better tell this witness to get himself a lawyer, your Honor! He's in SERIOUS problems with regard to perjury in this case. SERIOUS trouble!*" The explosion grabbed the audience's attention and caught the judge off guard:

JUDGE: Mr. Mozenter! [*pauses while thinking how to respond*] That's a very irregular thing for you to say!

MOZENTER: Well, this is a very irregular case, your Honor.

JUDGE [*still disconcerted*]: I'm SORRY! Now don't answer back, let me finish.

MOZENTER [*affecting contrition*]: Yes, your Honor.

To outward appearances Judge Richette was restoring order as an impartial referee. But Mozenter and this judge have close rapport, and he likely expected that she'd give him leeway to carry on at the margins of permissibility. After her rebuke he remained standing and continued to interrupt King, acting confused about what the witness was saying, until King objected:

KING [*stoically*]: Your Honor, may Mr. Mozenter be told to sit? He's distracting—

JUDGE: He's sitting, he's sitting.

KING: —the witness when he's standing.

MOZENTER [*to King*]: Who am I distracting, him or you?

JUDGE: All right. Let's not bicker!

Although she had said he was sitting Mozenter was still standing, moving slowly toward his seat. The judge, without intending to, was speaking on Mozenter's behalf.

Showing forbearance, King pursued his own calculated, if pained, strategy. Given Judge Richette's affection for Mozenter and her reputation as a "rabid liberal," he felt he was trying the case on unfriendly turf. He related to her deferentially, dutifully. He thought his best hope to persuade her that Brady was guilty, a menace to society, was to show he was as committed as she was to a fair trial. He would bend over backward to be fair. At the same time he wanted the jury to see him as a straight-arrow DA working doggedly against a smart-ass defense attorney. Mozenter had been a protégé of the legendary Cecil B. Moore, whose extremely aggressive style had featured periodic outbursts. Standard prosecutorial wisdom for handling Moore and his successors was: stay cool, don't get into a fight with the man, argue your own case.

Ian Goodwin testified that he was standing by his house across the street from the park when he heard Muscles Fisher being called into the park. Goodwin then heard a loud argument, heard Fisher say, "I had nothing to do with it," heard him laugh, and then heard six or seven shots fired rapidly. He saw one man, Cliff Townsend, leave the park. He didn't see the defendant, Greg Brady, but he did see Brady's car at the scene.

Mozenter's cross-exam was pummeling. He began by showing that Goodwin had told a lie. This is a common technique, one that Cecil Moore favored: put the prosecution witnesses on trial. Unnerve them, then undermine their credibility:

> *Mr. Goodwin, you testified on direct examination that you never have been convicted of a crime. Is that correct?*
> Yes.
> *Do you remember pleading guilty before Judge Collins on the charge of unlawfully carrying a firearm, theft?*
> Yes.
> *Well, what is that called? Is that a conviction?*
> It wasn't a conviction.
> *Well, you pleaded guilty to it. Is that correct?*
> Yes.
> *Well, what else did you plead guilty to that time besides carrying this firearm?*
> What else did I plead guilty to?
> *Yes.*
> I don't remember.
> *You can't remember, when you were convicted of a crime?*
> I wasn't convicted.
> *Well, you pleaded guilty. You said you were guilty, didn't you?*
> That's what my lawyer said.
> *You didn't say that?*

No.

Oh, so you pleaded guilty because your lawyer told you to plead guilty, not that you WERE guilty. Is that right?

That's right.

Groundwork laid, Mozenter went to the crux of his attack: inconsistencies between Goodwin's present testimony about the night of the killing and what he'd said at the preliminary hearing the previous May. Now Goodwin was saying that he hadn't been drunk. Previously he'd said, "I was drinking rather much," and "I was high at the time." Goodwin's first response to questions about the discrepency was that he couldn't remember ever saying he was high. Then he made several attempts to qualify it: he'd been a little woozy. He'd been feeling "nausey." He'd had just one beer that evening. He'd been drinking slowly all day. Mozenter saved the best thrust for last. Now Goodwin was claiming to have seen Cliff Townsend leaving the park after the shooting. But at the hearing his words were, "From the distance *I couldn't see.*"

As court recessed for the weekend, Mozenter said Ian Goodwin had been "a disaster" for the Commonwealth. King conceded that Goodwin had been "bloodied," but he liked the way the kid had kept coming back, sticking to his story, taking Mozenter's best shots. The roving jurors thought King was on thin ice.

On Monday downtown Philadelphia was deserted. Solitary figures, hands hiding their faces, braved the distances from one sheltering entranceway to another. With the wind chill it was a record-setting fifty below. I was amazed to find that the core group of roving jurors had materialized as usual. They greeted me with news that because the mayor had ordered the water in City Hall turned off over the weekend, the bathrooms had frozen. Many judges were canceling court, but not Judge Richette.

Kevin Adams, whom Mozenter derisively referred to as "the Commonwealth's *star* witness," seemed eager to tell his story. At ten o'clock on the night of the murder, he said, he had gone to a craphouse, a gambling spot known as the Motorcycle Club, on Germantown Avenue. There he saw Greg Brady, Cliff Townsend, and Reggie Green talking with Isaiah Gorton. "What's happening?" Adams asked. Townsend said they were going to kill this guy named Muscles. Brady said that he didn't want to *talk* with Muscles, but that he was going to *get with* Muscles. They showed their .38s. Brady's was in his belt, and Townsend borrowed one from Isaiah Gorton. They talked on about how they were going to kill Muscles. At 10:30 they left.

Then Kevin Adams went to Sid's Bar, where he stayed a couple hours, dancing but not drinking. At 1:30 he went back to the craphouse. Isaiah Gorton was still there. Fifteen minutes later the others came back with their guns out. For a second Adams thought they were going to rob him, so he threw his money on the table. But they didn't. Townsend told Gorton they'd killed the motherfucker. Brady said the dude named Muscles was dead. Green just held his gun up and didn't say anything.

Why, asked Roger King, hadn't he gone to the police when he heard this? "Because I was scared." Why did he go to the police later? "Because they broke my legs and gave me thirty-two stitches in my head and they took five hundred dollars from me."

Infuriated by this allegation, Mozenter called for a mistrial. (Cecil Moore, it's said, did this every five or ten minutes.) Judge Richette took over the questioning. Do you have proof that your leg was broken? she asked. Adams produced an admissions slip from Temple University Hospital. The day they broke his legs, he said, he had just won $1,300 at the craphouse. Five patrons of the Motorcycle Club beat him with a lead pipe, while Greg Brady watched from a distance.

King asked Adams what he'd been convicted of in the past. Possession of eight bags of marijuana and a gram of cocaine, and theft of a bicycle, he said. He denied that he himself had ever used drugs—Mozenter laughed loudly at this—and denied that he'd come forward to get the police to drop the charges still pending against him. Then why, asked King again, had he come forward? This time he answered, "They killed my brother."

Mozenter renewed his call for a mistrial, charging that King was bootstrapping the case and didn't have a credible witness. The judge told Mozenter to stop giving speeches and told the jury to disregard what Adams had just said about his brother.

Mozenter cross-examined Adams with the same dripping sarcasm he'd brought to bear on Ian Goodwin. He reviewed Adams's drug arrest record, which was longer than Adams had admitted. He ridiculed Adams's claim that the murderers had plotted the deed in his presence. "Here we are, Mr. Adams. We are gonna kill somebody today. Everybody show Mr. Adams the gun." He pointed out that Adams had said nothing at the preliminary hearing about his legs being broken. And he pressed about why, if he'd gotten out of the hospital in January, Adams hadn't made a statement to the police until April.

Adams answered that he *had* come forward in January but that the police had refused to believe him. Mozenter pursued:

> *The police didn't believe you in February of '84, did they, because there's no*
> *statement in February of '84, is there?*
> Somebody believed me.
> *How about in March of '84, did you go to the police then and tell them*
> *what you knew about Muscles Fisher?*
> Yes, sir.
> *And nobody believed you then either?*
> Yes, sir, somebody believed me.

At this moment Mozenter committed what many lawyers call (at least when it doesn't work) a cardinal sin of cross-examination: he asked a question to which he didn't know the answer:

> *Who believed you?*
> I got on my knees and prayed to God.

Mozenter ignored this, but it was music to King, who nudged Adams back to the point at the end of his redirect:

> *Do you still gamble, Mr. Adams?*
> No, sir.
> *Do you still involve yourself with drugs and the sale of drugs?*
> No, sir.
> *Why?*
> After my brother got killed, I prayed and I told God I would never
> touch none of it no more in life.
> *Does that account for why you are here today?*
> Yes, sir.

King struck the same chord with Kevin Adams that he had with Ian Goodwin. Instead of treating them with disdain, as prosecutors often treat their own witnesses when they have criminal records, he was supportive. He told me he hoped the jury would perceive "a metamorphosis" in his key witnesses "as their initial fear was set aside." I sensed he wanted to stand before them, symbolically, as a protector, ready to shoulder responsibility for their safety, pledging that with their testimony he'd put Brady away. Maybe his stance emboldened Adams and Goodwin in their retorts to Mozenter.

Tuesday morning King called a police officer who knew Kevin Adams and testified to his credibility. Then he called Sarah Jennings, the deceased's common-law wife. She wore a multicolored ski cap. We could barely hear her.

On the night of the murder, she said, she had answered the phone, and it was Martin Willams calling for Muscles. After the call Muscles left. Later Willams called again to say he'd heard some shots in the playground and thought Muscles had been hit. She had been living with Muscles for six years and had a daughter by him, two months old when he died. A week after the murder she sought out Cliff Townsend, whom she'd known all her life, to ask what had happened. "I wanted to know who killed my daughter's father," she said. He told her he knew. He told her he was there.

Mozenter asked no questions.

"Your Honor," King said then, "I think I have gone about as far as I can go." He did not look well.

"I think you've been very noble, Mr. King," Judge Richette said. "Mr. King is not feeling very well," she explained to the jury. "I'm sure he's not the only one in this room who is battling all kinds of viruses and what-have-you." She recessed.

Leaving, Mozenter for the first time was openly optimistic with me that he could win. He didn't think Kevin Adams's testimony had been enough to convict. His plan was to put his own case on quickly and get the record closed.

That afternoon the judge held a hearing on the issuance of a bench warrant for Bud Scott, Jr. Scott, it now was revealed, was the Commonwealth's mystery witness. Unfortunately for the Commonwealth, he had dropped from sight. The prosecutor subbing for the stricken King tried to persuade the judge that Scott had been properly served with a subpoena. But the judge, unconvinced, refused to approve a warrant for his arrest.

Wednesday morning Mozenter arrived to an empty courtroom. King had called in ill, but the clerk had forgotten to notify him. "He's not sick, the asshole," fumed Mozenter to the judge. "He's stalling. He's waiting to find some bum to testify. He's not sick, he's a grown man."

King remained indisposed Thursday, so it wasn't until Friday that Mozenter got to put on his case. He called Isaiah Gorton, the man Kevin Adams said had listened in on the murder plan at the craphouse and supplied one of the guns. "I shouldn't fucking put him up there," Mozenter said to me, "but I've got to."

King said, "I can't believe he's giving us a shot at this guy."

Isaiah Gorton was a bear-like, bearded man with a bass voice. The craphouse on Germantown Avenue, he testified, was a place where guys in the neighborhood got together to watch TV and gamble, not a place where anybody would bring guns. He himself gambled against Greg Brady there, and he knew Kevin Adams well. Adams had a daughter by Gorton's wife's girlfriend and had slept at Gorton's house. Gorton knew for a fact that Adams regularly used angel dust. Smoked angel dust as regularly as you smoke cigarettes, Gorton said, all day and all night, often as he could get it. It made him delirious and playful. The unfortunate day Adams got his legs broken he'd been high on angel dust and had argued with somebody over gambling. Gorton didn't know the guy's name. Instead of running, Adams had just stood there and let the guy hit him with a pipe, saying, "He can't kill me." The attacker was no friend of Greg Brady's, and Brady hadn't been there when it happened.

Mozenter treated Gorton as a good fellow. King insinuated an easy familiarity as he began the cross:

> *Mr. Gorton—*
> Yes, sir.
> *What is your nickname, sir?*
> They call me [*pauses*] Devil.
> *Do they also call you Satan?*
> Devil.
> JUDGE: What?
> Devil.
> *How long have you been known as Devil?*
> A couple years.
> [casually] *Now Mr. Gorton, has anyone told you that you could be arrested and charged with murder, conspiracy, and possession of an instrument of crime in the killing of John Fisher?*
> MOZENTER: Objected to.
> JUDGE: Sustained. The jury will ignore that.

King used Gorton's nickname to impeach his credibility. Devil—better yet, Satan—was an earned reputation, he implied. He went on to suggest that

Gorton had lied when he said that Kevin Adams was high when his legs were broken and when he told police that he didn't know Muscles Fisher or Sarah Jennings. He asked Gorton whether he was only a passing acquaintance of Brady's or whether they were close, and when Gorton answered, "We all right," King made him admit that that meant the two men were "tight."

When Gorton stepped down Mozenter tried to close the record. King demurred. Now, he said, the Commonwealth had to call two witnesses to rebut Gorton: the detective who'd questioned him about the murder, and the doctor who'd treated Kevin Adams in the emergency room. Testimony would have to be carried over into the following week. "I don't know who he's going to browbeat and intimidate between now and Monday," Mozenter said to the judge.

Over the weekend Mozenter's fears were realized: the police located Bud Scott, Jr. Still, Scott was a wild card. No one knew what he would say. He hadn't appeared at the preliminary hearing. At one point he had made a statement to the police implicating Brady in the murder, but later he'd signed an affidavit recanting his words. Now, on the advice of his lawyer, he was refusing to speak to King. This was supposed to make King ponder whether it was worth the risk to put him on the stand.

The spectator section was unusually full Tuesday, when action resumed. King called the nurse who'd treated Adams in the emergency room (the doctor wasn't available). But when he tried to get her qualified as a witness, Mozenter put up stiff resistence. The judge complicated matters by asking King to specify which parts of Adams's treatment the nurse had actually handled. When King said, "We'll get to that," Mozenter cut in sarcastically, "*When are you going to get to it, today or next week?*"

King shot back, "*Whatever time it takes, you turkey!*"

Mozenter spun to face the judge: "*He called me a turkey, your Honor. I never called him any names!*" She warned them to restrain themselves, but King would not stop.

"I'M SORRY, YOUR HONOR," he shouted, "BUT I'VE HAD IT UP TO MY EYEBALLS WITH HIM!"

Mozenter shouted, "WELL I'VE HAD IT UP TO MY HAIRLINE WITH YOU!"

Now King was moving toward him, menacingly: "LET'S GET OUT IN THE STREET AND GET IT ON!"

Mozenter did not back away, but his voice did: "*I went to law school, not boxing school!*"

All this transpired in a few seconds. Furious, Judge Richette cleared the courtroom.

The mood in the hallway was jubilant. The crowd mingled freely. People jabbered at each other. Unexpected pleasures of the courthouse!

A few minutes later Mozenter emerged, smiling, and joked with us. "I'm the injured and innocent party here. . . . I won the first round. . . . It'll cost you five bucks to see the second." King was closeted with the judge. When we were readmitted she announced that he had apologized to Mozenter and the court for his "extremely improper outburst."

Cecil Moore, Bobby Mozenter's mentor, used to make an art of antagonizing opponents until they raged with threats to punch him out. The nerve Mozenter had hit was King's supposed malingering. As King explained it to me, Mozenter's scornful remarks about hiding at home to buy time had been relayed to him. He had warned Mozenter when they'd met that morning in the judge's chambers: "Look, Bobby, we're decent enough friends out of court. I heard what you said, but let me tell you something that maybe you didn't realize: that's a very sore point with me." It was sore because King is so zealous about his work that he attends court in the worst personal circumstances: when his wife had life-threatening surgery, when his father had a heart attack, when his mother-in-law died, when his grandmother died. He hadn't taken ten sick days in eleven years with the DA.

He also admitted that, even so, his flare-up had not been guileless. He wanted the jury to see that, as "low-keyed" as he'd been during the whole trial, he could "revert" to the same "street-type" behavior Mozenter had used to attack Ian Goodwin and Kevin Adams. It was a risk. He didn't know how jurors would respond.

The nurse testified that Kevin Adams hadn't seemed disoriented when she treated his broken legs. If he had, she would have noted it on her report. Mozenter pointed out that she had no recollection of Adams independent of her report and hadn't actually tested him for drugs.

Now came Bud Scott, Jr. He had known the defendant since childhood. King proceeded gingerly up to the crucial moment in his testimony when Greg Brady told him to come with him for a ride. Scott got into the back seat of Brady's car. There were two others in the car already, Scott said, and while they drove the talk was about drugs. Brady said he had "to take care of business" with Muscles. They parked, and while Scott stayed in the car the others walked in the direction of the park at Twentieth and Ontario. Scott heard three shots. Brady returned alone, got in, drove away, dropped him off.

Scott had told this to the police in January. Then his father sent him to see the lawyer, and he'd signed an affidavit recanting his statement—because he was afraid.

Cross-examining, Mozenter established right off that Scott was a convicted car thief and heroin user who had been in violation of parole when the police picked him up in January for questioning about Fisher's murder. When the detective *first* asked him what he knew about it, Scott had answered, "I don't know nothing about his death." But after taking his statement, the police hadn't let him leave. He was detained in an interrogation room with two detectives for four more hours until he produced the information that implicated Brady. Hadn't he fingered Brady, Mozenter asked, because he was afraid he himself might be indicted for the murder? Or that the police would revoke his parole? Didn't he just want to get back on a corner where he could snort all the coke and heroin he liked?

On redirect, King read the beginning of the latter part of Scott's statement, in which the detective had said, "I understand that you would like to add something to the statement you made to us." Scott had replied, "Yes, I want to tell you the *truth*." King stressed the word "truth."

Mozenter then called two rebuttal witnesses. Andrew Perkins, who had drawn up the affidavit in which Scott recanted his statement, testified that Scott assured him that he hadn't been intimidated into changing his story. Then Scott's father testified that he had taken his son to see Perkins after the young man had informed him that the police had "told him which to say."

King's cross-examination of the elder Scott consisted of just two questions:

> *Mr. Scott, did you not talk to your son just before he went on the stand today?*
> Yes, sir.
> *And what did you tell him?*
> [*with a touch of pride*] I told him to go ahead and tell the truth.

Lightning quick, the exchange reminded me of the one a month before with LaRue Blaylock's father. As it happened, King had managed to overhear

Scott, Sr., speaking to Scott, Jr., in the hallway. When the father confirmed the words of advice he'd given his son, the voices of prosecutor and father rang as one.

King then called, on rebuttal, his final witness: David Darby, a lawyer whom Bud Scott, Jr., had approached for help in avoiding having to testify, before his father sent him to see Perkins. King made a single point with Darby: that it was not Scott himself who had made the appointment, but Susan Rand Brady, the defendant's wife.

The courtroom was mobbed. Busy lawyers showed up, along with courthouse personnel and police peripherally involved in the investigation. Joey Grant, a homicide DA, sat in front of me. It's an opportunity, he said, to see two of the best lawyers in the area go head-to-head. He'd never seen Roger King give a closing. The challenge for King, from what he'd heard, was that the evidence to convict wasn't strong.

Lillian Torrance, the roving juror who idolized King, had admitted her doubts. In the corridor King had asked, "How are we doing?", and she'd replied with a dour shake of the head. Now, she leaned over and advised me to watch for Mozenter to make references to the Bible. "It's a gimmick the defense attorneys have," she warned. "They read from the Bible like they're religious."

Gesticulating occasionally with his glasses, pacing freely back and forth before the jury, Mozenter made his initial remarks and then launched into his main theme:[3]

> You see that Bible that they put on the witness stand? I've thought about this for twenty years now, I've been doing this.
>
> Isn't it funny that when people put their hand on that Bible and swear to tell the truth, sometimes you wonder,
>
> [*looking skyward*] Is the roof going to open?
>
> [*rising to fierce intensity*] Is the lightning going to come down in this courtroom and strike everybody dead?
>
> I was concerned for my welfare in this case.
>
> I was concerned about YOUR welfare in this case.
>
> Because I had the SMELL OF MENDACITY FROM THE FIRST WITNESS TO THE LAST WITNESS in this case for the Commonwealth.

I've never SEEN
so much lying
in
my
life.
      KING: I'm going to object.
I've never
seen
so much inconsistency.
            KING: I'm going to object à la the ABA Canons of
                   Ethics, your Honor.
            JUDGE: Well. I think you can temper that a bit by
                   stating what you mean by inconsistencies.
            KING: Thank you, your Honor.
You know, this courtroom to me is a holy place. I unfortunately spend more time in this courtroom than I do in my living
room.

And this place is church-like, if you will. Because in an
American courtroom,
        the truth
        and justice
        allegedly prevail.
And what we read in the newspapers or hear on the television
and see on television is a lot of nonsense, because *here,*
        in this holy place [*points to the floor*]
        is where the truth is to be gleaned.
This is not Starsky and Hutch.
This is not Perry Mason.
This is everyday life [*strikes hands together*]
and you're everyday people.
And in our system of justice, when a man is accused of a crime,
he's presumed innocent until proven guilty beyond a reasonable
doubt.
    Legal mumbo jumbo?
    A phrase that lawyers conjure up to set ourselves apart from
the rest of our community?
    Or is it STEEPED

in history

and human experience?

*

In the old days, they used to stick them in the Tower of London and just lock them up. And in some societies in this world, unfortunately, in South America and in Russia and in Nazi Germany and Fascist Italy during the reign of Mussolini, and even in some allegedly democratic countries like France, a person is locked up, and he has to prove himself innocent.

But that is not our system of justice. Our system of justice is that a man is presumed innocent until proven guilty beyond a reasonable doubt.

And for that reason we have a trial.

For that reason you sit in the jury box and determine from the evidence from that witness stand,

NOT from the mouth of the lawyer,

NOT from the mouth of the judge,

but from the *mouths* of the witnesses who testify.

And the Commonwealth has the awesome responsibility of chipping away, taking that cloak of innocence off of Mr. Brady's back.

And they have to do it by credible evidence.

*

He said, when he was called before the bar to plead his case,

"How do you plead, Mr. Brady?"

"Not guilty."

"How will you be tried?"

"By God and my country."

An old English phrase coming down—

I like that—

coming down from medieval times.

It gives me chills up and down my spine.

Mozenter reviewed "common sense" standards for judging credibility. Then he attacked the testimonies of Scott, Adams, and Goodwin. He reminded the jury how he had demolished Goodwin on cross-examination:

It took me twenty minutes. Used my scalpel, you know.

Cross-examination is a scalpel in the hands of a lawyer.

What we do is cut away the falsehoods [*cuts with his hand*] to get to the truth, by our questioning, or that's what we attempt to do. Sometimes we can do it, especially when we have an individual who has made prior inconsistent statements, either under oath or not.

He testified six different ways in this courtroom.

He offered jurors his metaphor for the concept of reasonable doubt:

I always tell the same story, but I haven't found anything better.

Suppose you and your husband or wife or your friend want to buy a house. Probably the most important decision you got to make in your life, the way the prices of houses are. You got to not only determine whether the house befits your standard of living, you got to determine whether the neighborhood is okay, is safe for you to live in, whether or not the school system is good for your kids to go to school and get a good education. A lot of things to consider.

You go to a real estate agent, and he or she takes you to an area, a neighborhood. You like the neighborhood. The school system's good. He takes you to a home to look at. The house is for sale. He takes you through the house—you, your spouse, your friend. He takes you through the house, and you look at the rooms. The rooms are lovely. The house is in good repair. There's a bathroom or two. The kitchen is adequate, and the *price* is right, and the mortgage arrangements are fair.

You walk outside this house, with the real estate person and you stand on the curbstone, and he says to you, or she says to you, "What's your answer? You like the house? You want to buy?"

You look up at the house.

And you see

a shingle that's loose.

You hesitate.

You don't say, "Yes, I want the house."

Ladies and gentlemen, that is reasonable doubt.

If you [*snaps fingers*] hesitated about anything that was said in this courtroom that pertains to this case, you must find the defendant not guilty.

Even if that real estate agent later on explains to you that that could be fixed, your hesitation, based on what you saw from that subject matter, that house—that is an important decision for you to make—your hesitation is reasonable doubt. Common sense.

*

I'm going to tell you what this Commonwealth is trying—this house they're trying to sell you.

This house doesn't *have* a roof.

They took you through a house with four walls,
        no roof.

And that's what they're selling you.

With one last claim about the tainted character of the Commonwealth witnesses; an apology, if anything he had done "in the heat of battle" had upset the jurors; and a warning for them to be "colorless and color-blind"; Mozenter presented this conclusion:

This man is on trial for first-degree murder. The Commonwealth is attempting to prove its case beyond a reasonable doubt with the type of testimony that was handed down in this courtroom.

Not one, [*jabs with his finger on each line*]

not one,

not one witness,

not one witness
        was a direct evidence witness.

All circumstantial.

All witnesses who have said prior inconsistent statements, who have lied on the witness stand either today or yesterday or before.

And all having motives to testify.

The judge called a recess.

Prosecutor Joey Grant turned around in his seat and uttered one of the trial bar's most popular aphorisms: "They say if you have the evidence, you argue the facts. If you don't have the evidence, you argue the law. If you don't have either, you just argue." Mozenter, in Grant's opinion, had just argued. It hadn't been one of his best performances. The defendant, Grant remarked, was all smiles, cocky in a way that proclaimed to everybody, "Look at what a smart lawyer I have." Grant volunteered another bit of wisdom: "You can read all the books and think up all the arguments, but you never learn what stacks up unless somebody comes and kicks your ass."

Then it was Roger King's turn. He moved continuously, fluidly, as if he were stalking prey:

Ladies and gentlemen, I would like to think that over each door of each courtroom in Philadelphia the following inscription is there:
Enter this room
with ALL of your shortcomings,
with ALL of your misdeeds of the past:
we will lend you an ear.
And that's all that I asked you in my opening remarks:
Please lend us an ear.
While listening to Mr. Mozenter, a play came to my mind, done by Melvin Van Peebles back in the late seventies, called *Don't Play Us Cheap*. I thought about that. And I thought about a very popular phrase by the Bell Telephone System: "Reach out and touch someone." Or: "Reach out and grab something."
Mr. Mozenter, in his remarks, harped on criminal records, prior inconsistent statements. He harped on ALL of the reasons not to believe a person. But ladies and gentlemen, he did not tell ya that the term "Common Pleas Court" [*walks toward the jury, running his hand along the bar*]
had its beginning with common people,
people who had criminal records,
streetwalkers,
peddlers.
Common Pleas Court was where common people could come and have their hearing in court.
Mr. Mozenter talked to you about countries where tyranny

reigns. You don't have to go outside, ladies and gentlemen, this country, to find tyranny.

For tyranny comes in all forms!

Tyranny comes in the form of neglect.

Tyranny comes in the form of being in the wrong place at the wrong time.

Tyranny comes in the form of fear.

OH, YES, we can talk about codes: we can talk about the Morse code, which is a code, and we can talk about the remorse code, or the code of the ghetto.

"I didn't see anything,"

"I don't know anything,"

"I *don't want to be* involved."

Let's talk about *that* kind of code, that kind of code that when you are brought in, the first thing that's out of your mouth is, "I didn't see nothin', I don't *know* nothin'. Don't make me get involved."

No thought is given in that circumstance, ladies and gentlemen, and Mr. Mozenter didn't address himself:

unlike those cheap novels,

unlike those plays that you have seen,

I DON'T HAVE the luxury of reaching out and touching six or seven or eight Roger Kings,

as articulate,

with *my* background,

with my insight.

NOR do I have the ability to stand up here and direct like a director would do in a play,

like a director will do in a TV show.

I make no apologies for my witnesses. . .

IF this had occurred on Rittenhouse Square,

or at one of the Hyatt Regencys

or on the Main Line,

we would have gotten residents from Rittenhouse Square,

Center City.

If it had happened on the Main Line

you'd a got *preppies,*

you'd a got people with Ivy League education,
you would a got a person with no insight on what goes on at
    Twentieth and Ontario.
BUT it didn't.

    Ladies and gentlemen, we didn't choose the cast of these char-
acters. We didn't pick Ian Goodwin. If you believe the testimony,
I would submit to you that the people involved in this conspiracy
did.
    For Mr. Goodwin's *only* problem was that he happened to be
out on the street that night, and happened to see and happened to
hear something.
        Do we condemn him for that?
    Kevin Adams, gherri curls and all, REBORN, he has now
seen the light:
        Do we condemn him for that?
    Bud Scott:
        Do we condemn Mr. Scott for being a car thief?
                For snorting heroin?
        I would submit to you that we do not.
    Dr. King once said, ladies and gentlemen, that the only way
someone can ride your back is if ya bend your shoulders and give
him a chance to get aboard.
    Mrs. Roosevelt said back in the thirties, and I quote her di-
rectly: "I believe that anyone can conquer fear by doing the things
that he fears to do, provided he keeps at them until he gets a record
of successful experiences behind him."

    I would submit to you, ladies and gentlemen, that Ian
Goodwin, *for the first time,* walked into this courtroom, sat
down and told you his story. If you want to believe him, believe
him.
    Kevin Adams, the same.
    Bud Scott, the elusive Mr. Scott, who had to be brought in in
handcuffs. But *you don't think about what preceded* that, ladies and
gentlemen. Think about what ya heard from [*points*] *that* witness
stand.

King assessed Isaiah Gorton: "He has the biggest motive of all! You think he's going to get up and 'fess up to being a part of a murder?" And he defended the Commonwealth witnesses:

> Now, in all his remarks when he tells you about his scalpel that
> he uses on cross-examination, you saw Kevin Adams.
> Did he attack him on prior inconsistent statements?
> Did he weaken his testimony on cross-examination?
> I would submit to you, no.
> Fall.
> Match ends.
> The decision to Mr. Kevin Adams.
> "I was there.
> "I heard them.
> "I saw the guns.
> "They were .38s."

*

> I would submit to you, ladies and gentlemen,
> if you believe Kevin Adams,
> if you believe Kevin Adams,
> I would submit to you that that,
> in and of itself,
>   is not only the floor,
>   not only the four walls,
>   that's a domed stadium.

He delivered the last words of his summation almost as an afterthought, an aside:

> And by the way, ladies and gentlemen: I will leave you on this
> note of irony.
> Mr. Mozenter was questioning Kevin Adams, and Kevin
> Adams looked at him when he asked the question: "Why wouldn't
> anybody believe you?" And Mr. Adams said the following:
> "I got down on my knees
> "and I talked to Jesus.
> "*He* believed me."

Isn't it ironic that the defense's witness used to contradict Mr.
Adams had a nickname [*whispers*]:
of Devil?
Satan?

Joey Grant was beaming. "Look at the defendant now," he said in a low
voice. "The smile has been wiped off his face."

The jury deliberated Wednesday afternoon and was sequestered that
night. Some jurors, who had trouble sleeping, woke around the same time,
3:00 A.M., resolved about what they had to do. In the morning the jury's
mood was much less emotional than before.

The verdict came that afternoon: guilty of murder in the first degree.

Mozenter asked to have the jury polled. As they were, he stood incred-
ulously. "I DON'T KNOW WHAT EVIDENCE THEY WERE
LISTENING TO," he said loudly, "OR WHAT COURTROOM
THEY WERE LISTENING IN." Out of the judge's hearing, as the
jurors exited for the last time, he called them assholes.

Some jurors were angered by both attorneys' behavior. Two of the
younger women asked me if I'd heard Mozenter swear at them, if I'd seen
the shouting match, and if these sorts of things happened in other courtrooms. They praised Judge Richette for her evenhandedness.

While the jurors were waiting for their checks, Roger King assembled
them in a conference room. He wanted them to know that they had done
Philadelphia a great service by nailing the man who is the head of "The Family," one of the major drug rings in the city, trafficking in close to half a million dollars worth of cocaine a week. Greg Brady, he told them, had at least
ten murders to his credit. The first, to King's knowledge, was a man who had
stolen something from Brady's mother. Brady killed him in the presence of a
friend, whom he threatened to kill too if he ever talked. Eventually the friend
told the police. He left the area, but when he returned they blew him away
on his porch. "Once they started killing," a police officer interjected from the
back of the room, "it got easy." Witnesses to their crimes were afraid to come
forward. This time, Sarah Jennings was slated to be killed along with Muscles Fisher, but she hadn't gone to the park. What you have done, King said
to them, is to cut the head off. With the head gone, the body will die.

The jurors were pleased, relieved to know they'd done the right thing.
When King commented on the need for patience and subtlety in trying a

case against Mozenter, a juror expressed satisfaction that King had called Mozenter a turkey. Others agreed. If moments before some were putting a pox on both lawyers, now they sided with the prosecutor.

He gave them phone numbers where he or the judge could be reached twenty-four hours a day, if any of them were threatened. The jurors had been making lists of their phone numbers so they could stay in touch, maybe have a reunion. But with this note of warning, the group's spirit faded into self-protectiveness. Several jurors asked to have their numbers taken off the lists. Then all passed their lists to the foreman, who tore them to bits.

King's face glowed with relief as he headed to the next hearing, a detective by either side. The African American detective said about the defendant: "He turned white while he was standing there waiting for the verdict, and that's tough for a black man."

Poetics of Identification

The stances lawyers take toward participants in a trial—toward witnesses and defendant, opposing counsel, jurors and judge—are a matter of style. Much is at risk in how they enact these stances, since they have to work with, through, and against the wills of all these persons to get their story told.

We can think of these enactments as staged dialogues. When Roger King adopts a respectful tone toward Goodwin, Adams, and Scott, for example, he is confirming their worth as human beings and the truthfulness of their testimony. When Bobby Mozenter cross-examines them in a derisive tone, he's labeling them scum, their testimony lies. Relationships are staged not just through words, but also through expressiveness of gesture and intonation of voice.

These stances carry potent cultural messages. King, during his examination of Goodwin and company, portrayed himself as a role model for those errant youths. Mozenter styled himself a hard-boiled realist who had penetrated their evil minds. As skilled lawyers, both turned their interchanges with trial participants into opportunities to position themselves as bearers of moral value in the story they were telling about the nature of life in this place and time.

Such stance-taking is ubiquitous in human communication. All speech is "dialogic," as the literary philosopher Mikhail Bakhtin declared. It is pervaded by shadings of agreement and disagreement, deference and parody, desire and distance, an ever-shifting array of sentiments from the human emotional palette by which we express attitudes toward each other and the world. We draw near to some people and away from others when we accept, qualify, or oppose their words, and when we reject what they say or affirm their sentiments as our own.[4]

Lawyers in performance *elevate* these everyday poetics of identification. They orchestrate a whole series of relationships within their complexly layered story, and they call on the jury to identify with their stances, to see the story as they do.

Let's look at how King and Mozenter staged their encounter with each other. In his summation Mozenter chose to show restraint toward King. He attacked weaknesses of King's case, not King directly. But King, taking advantage of his position as the second speaker, condescended to Mozenter.

King openly derided Mozenter's reference to the scalpel: *Now, in all his remarks when he tells you about his scalpel that he uses on cross-examination. . . .* The tone is sarcastic. This is the same tactic King had employed against John Guilfoy's use of blood in the Blaylock summation: seizing a word favored by his adversary, he made it a refrain that exposed the other's weakness and his own strength. Mozenter dared proclaim himself a success discrediting Commonwealth witnesses? Well, then, the jurors should compare their skill. At one point in his closing King said: "What did the father tell [Bud Scott] to do, in spite of the first four pages of the statement? Remember those resounding words? Because I only asked one question. *I was into my scalpeling then.*" In this sidelong boast, he equated skill with truthfulness: *I* accomplished more in a flash than *he* did in hours wielding his so-called scalpel.

King also parodied Mozenter's image of the house. In the Philadelphia courts house-buying is a well-worn metaphor for the concept of reasonable doubt, with the house proving to be unsound or sound depending on which attorney is using it. King figured Mozenter would resort to the image because it's a trademark of his (as Mozenter remarked to the jury, *I always tell the same story*). Playing on Mozenter's references to house parts and shingles, King trumped him, saying, *That [believing Adams], in and of itself, is not only the floor, not only the four walls, that's a domed stadium.* The sharply honed retort was calculated to vitiate the long analogy, to land a counterpunch where predictability made his opponent vulnerable.

King anticipated, from past encounters, that Mozenter would praise English law and decry tyranny. *Even in some allegedly democratic countries like France, a person is locked up.* . . . King countered with an account of the humble democratic origins of the court where the trial was actually being held. *Common Pleas Court was where common people could come and have their hearing in court.* If Mozenter invoked a grand English past, King would top him with living local tradition.

So while King appeared to be making his own points, his words were actually locked in hostile dialogue with his opponent's. With the scalpel he directly appropriated a word. With the domed stadium he aced a metaphor. With Common Pleas Court he subtly inverted a whole line of argument. In the following snippet King's retort is still more oblique, but just as antagonistic:

> IF this had occurred on Rittenhouse Square,
> or at one of the Hyatt Regencys
> or on the Main Line,
> we would have gotten residents from Rittenhouse Square,
> Center City.

> If it had happened on the Main Line
> you'd a got *preppies,*
> you'd a got people with Ivy League education,
> you would a got a person with no insight on what goes on at
> Twentieth and Ontario.
> BUT it didn't.

At first glance these words may seem inapt. Of course the murder didn't occur amid the wealth of downtown Rittenhouse Square or the suburban Main Line. So why say it? I take the cultural argument embedded here to go something like this:

> If you jurors think my witnesses cannot be believed, you fall prey to class and race prejudice. The same stereotyping that tempts you to dismiss their testimony tempts you to believe witnesses who are well-educated, well-off, white. Don't be fooled. The rich are no more virtuous or insightful than the poor. People are conditioned

by their stations in society to be what they are and know what they know. My witnesses, inarticulate as they seem, are experts about their own reality. I vouch for them. (*I don't have the luxury of reaching out and touching six or seven or eight Roger Kings, as articulate, with my background, with my insight.*) And I am in a position to speak with authority about what goes on up and down the class scale, in the street at Twentieth and Ontario *and* in the opulent homes of the Main Line. Where, jurors, do you stand? With the Ivy League's condescending view of common people, or with hard truths about American life?

King was trying to draw jurors into the web of affinity he'd displayed for Goodwin, Adams, and Scott, and into his disdain for Mozenter. His means at this moment was the discourse of class relations. His intonation uttering the word *preppie* was a clipped sneer. Mozenter, no elitist, never suggested that the Commonwealth witnesses were liars *because* they were lower class. Yet King infers that such an attitude was implied by Mozenter's argument, in effect planting words in Mozenter's mouth. The so-called Ivy League mentality, walled off from the real world, is for King a surrogate for the vacuousness of Mozenter's story. Throughout his closing King pitted the authority of his experience against the authority of Mozenter's. His message to the jury: decide which of us knows whereof he speaks.

What relationships did King and Mozenter stake with the jury? Lawyers do more than engage in dialogue with jurors as a group; like Michael Tigar in the Nichols trial, they often siphon words to individuals. King told me that during closing he had singled out three jurors he believed would be leaders in the deliberations. The man on crutches: "I want to talk to him because of his plight, what he had to overcome; he's a person who can appreciate effort one way or the other." The banker: "Lifestyle of the defendant—subtle hint of income, '83 Lincoln Continental, high-priced defense attorney." And the ex-Marine, whose selection King regarded as "the coup of the trial": "He knows it when he sees it, he grew up around it, he probably sees it every day—the flashy cars, the cockiness, the arrogant aspect of it."

To my great surprise, Mozenter tagged these same three jurors as the ones who did him in. His worst mistake, he said, had been to go with the Marine: "too stiff, too straight; he looked at me like, 'You got it, jerk, I stuck it in your eyes.'" During the trial Mozenter had told me he liked the feel of the jury. Afterward he said he believed he would have won the case except for his mistakes in voir dire.

"I don't think *Cecil* would have picked the jury I picked," Mozenter said disgustedly, referring to his teacher, a recognized master of jury selection. Mozenter hadn't been willing to drag out the selection process by using all of his peremptory challenges, he said, because he felt rushed. He knew King was looking for that mystery witness. He had no idea it was Bud Scott; he thought it was Martin Willams, the triggerman who had escorted Muscles Fisher to the park: "I *knew* Martin Willams would *kill* me. My client wasn't worried about Martin Willams, because he probably knew where the hell he was."

Which brings us to the lawyers' dialogic relations with the defendant. For King, Greg Brady was an object of scorn. King fueled his contempt by looking at the police photographs of the victims. He liked to imagine how he would cross-examine a Greg Brady or a LaRue Blaylock if such a man dared take the stand in his own defense. He saw the confrontation in African American cultural terms, as a form of intimate insult. "I would have stood up," as he said of Blaylock, "got in his face, questioned his masculinity, and said a bunch of things that would have gotten him *most* upset."

King had monitored Brady's reactions during the summations, noting how he gloated as Mozenter spoke and how he turned to beam at the audience when Mozenter finished. Brady's confidence inspired King. He took pleasure watching it disintegrate as he spoke. "Five or ten minutes into my closing, there was a very strange look of concern. Fifteen minutes into my closing there was a look of desperation. There was active communication between the two [*Brady and Mozenter*]. And I'm feeling this—I'm not hearing it but I'm feeling it—and I'm feeling it with the movement behind me, and I'm going to make the jury look at what's going on back there." Brady's mother was a barometer: "About halfway into my speech I glanced over at her, and she gave me a look of 'We're in trouble.' And if she was reacting that way, then I knew he had to."

Mozenter had trouble identifying with his client. "A guy like Brady," he told me, "I don't especially like as a human being. He was just there. I didn't have any empathy. The *challenge* was there. It was a challenge to me."

The problem is a common one, especially for criminal attorneys. The American Bar Association's *Model Code of Professional Responsbility* states that a lawyer should accept "his share of tendered employment which may be unattractive both to him and the bar generally." A lawyer should not take a case if "the intensity of his personal feeling . . . may impair his effective representation of a prospective client." Otherwise, the assumption is that nothing stands in the way of the lawyer fulfilling the duty to "represent his client zealously within the bounds of the law."[5]

But can one always mask one's feelings? Michael Tigar stood behind Terry Nichols's chair at one point during his summation, hands on Nichols's shoulders, and said, "I tell you, this is my brother. He's in your hands," while Nichols, face flushed and chin trembling, looked down. Bobby Mozenter's stance toward Greg Brady was different. Their interactions at counsel table hinted at cool cordiality. Mozenter never took on Brady's voice directly, never used his own voice to convey Brady's words or thoughts except when he cast him in the role of a generic defendant asking to be judged *by God and my country*. Their relationship was marked by a telltale lack of warmth.

As Mozenter's ambivalence suggests, the enactment of relationship isn't a simple matter of creating any impression one chooses. One's ways of identifying are rooted in the past, in affective experiences from childhood onward with significant persons and situations. Lawyers' reactions to the people they deal with in court are thus more than volitional. They feel respect, hostility, camaraderie, and the like as we all do, for reasons that often transcend the circumstances at hand. The job requires them to channel their reactions so emotion and strategy coincide. Sometimes repugnance has to be swallowed, or a flicker of feeling fanned into a flame, or delving done to find a way of relating that will fit. The stretching has limits. Any lawyer is accustomed to adopting certain interpersonal stances. Others feel forced. Like other aspects of courtroom style, the display of identifications depends on habits of acting in the world.

Repertoires

Turn now to the source from which lawyers generate their authority in performance: their repertoire. This consists of the patterns for action the lawyer can summon to meet the emerging courtroom situation. As in any craft, one's repertoire is the result of previous learning, most of which has, through repeated use, sunken into one's unconscious, where it's immediately available when needed. Craftsmanship is based on this husbanding of effort. The dancer could not dance the dance and the batter hit the pitch if they had to "think" about their moves. The greater the mastery, the more comprehensive this unconscious skill will be.[6]

To show how lawyers' repertoires work in closer-grained detail, I'll focus on parallelism, a central feature of many types of oral performance:

> I told you, don't expect Boy Scouts.
> You will hear from drug dealers;
> you will hear from drug users;
> you will *hear* from people with criminal records.
> They might SOUND a bit different,
> they might look a bit different,
> but listen.
> *(From the Brady closing)*

You will hear is a formulaic expression of Roger King's. Usable in a number of contexts, it works as formulas often do in oral performance: it triggers access to appropriate language so he can fill in the "slots" as he composes. The phrase *You will hear from* _____ is completed with the names of various types of deviant people (drug users, criminals, etc.). The phrase *You will hear about* _____ (or, *You will hear that* _____) is completed by describing the steps in the commission of a crime. Formulas such as these organize the speaker's thoughts and delivery under the second-by-second demands of performing. They also guide the audience, who rely on redundancy to follow comfortably what's being said.[7]

Undergirding the use of particular phrases is the lawyer's own style for generating parallelism. With King, a repeated word can be enough to get it rolling:

> . . . of all the cheap novels that have been written about the courtroom,
> ALL of the plays that may have been a hit or may have been a flop on Broadway,
> all of the hodgepodge of TV shows that solve a crime in thirty minutes or that have lawyers who are impeccable in their dress and impeccable in their style,

NONE of those things prepared you for
      what you experienced in the *Commonwealth of Penn-*
sylvania versus Greg Brady.

                        (*From the Brady closing*)

King also uses rhythmic repetitions of stress, pitch, and syntax to create parallelism:

> . . . the term "Common Pleas Court" had its beginning
> with cómmon people,
> péople who had criminal records,
> stréetwalkers,
> péddlers.

What's formulaic in a repertoire, then, are not just specific phrases, but also the underlying syntactic, intonational, and metrical structures for producing them. For example, in a summation four months after the Brady conviction, King employed the exact structure of his Rittenhouse Square bit but inverted the social stratum:

> IF this had happened in prison,
>   you would have gotten inmates,
>   guards
>   and maybe even a warden.
> If it had happened in a whorehouse
>   you would have gotten prostitutes
>   pimps
>   and johns.
> BUT it didn't.

The same principle holds for other aspects of the repertoire: a lawyer has a ready-made supply of things to use and has templates for composing new things of a similar kind.

    Bobby Mozenter, too, relies on parallelism:

We're not mathematicians;
we're not scientists.
We're human beings.
The witnesses that get on the witness stand are human beings.
The defendant is a human being.
The victim *was* a human being.

(From the Brady closing)

Here and elsewhere, Mozenter uses parallelism to give cumulative weight to a point by piling up examples. By making a list of what human beings are and are not, he underscores why we should judge evidence by common sense. Likewise, he shifts into parallelism to argue about how we assess credibility:

When you walk down the street and you talk to somebody, and he tells you or she tells you a story, you make a decision, don't ya? Subconsciously, even consciously at times, whether or not that story makes sense.

Whether or not that person is telling you the truth.

Whether or not he has a motive for saying what he's saying.

Whether or not he has made an inconsistent statement on a prior occasion.

Whether or not he told you a different story on a prior occasion, now he's telling you another one.

(From the Brady closing)

This stringing together of parallel constructions to make a point repeatedly is common in oral performance. King does the same thing. But for King parallelism often has a further rhetorical effect, one consonant with the African American sermon tradition he imbibed growing up in Tuscaloosa, Alabama, where his father and uncle were preachers. King employs parallelism as a tool for persuading by means of syllogisms. That is, he uses it to set up certain premises, and once the audience accepts these premises, he leads them to a conclusion of a different sort. When King reminds the jury, "I told you . . . you will hear from drug dealers; . . . from drug users; . . . from people with criminal records . . . [who] might SOUND a bit different, . . . might look a bit different," he is setting out premises we easily agree with; the conclusion "but listen" follows with deceptive ease. He makes a more daring argument in this sequence:

> For Mr. Goodwin's *only* problem was that he happened to be out on the street that night, and happened to see and happened to hear something.
>> Do we condemn him for that?
> Kevin Adams, gherri curls and all, REBORN, he has now seen the light:
>> Do we condemn him for that?
> Bud Scott:
>> Do we condemn Mr Scott for being a car thief?
>>> For snorting heroin?
>> I would submit to you that we do not.

Yes, we won't condemn Kevin Adams for being saved, but why shouldn't we condemn Bud Scott for being a thief and a junkie? Why wouldn't a law-upholding DA condemn him? The parallelism ties the three prosecution witnesses together; by contagion it spreads the magic of Adams's salvation onto the others, coaxing us toward the counterintuitive conclusion that their criminal records don't make them unworthy, that all three are believable and may well be on the road to redemption. The syllogism has the sound of logical reasoning, but it entails a leap of faith.

This technique of King's is found in church preaching. Here is an excerpt from the opening of a sermon delivered by Bishop E. E. Cleveland, pastor of Ephesians Church of God in Christ in Berkeley, California:

> For your hands are defiled with blood
> Your fingers with iniquity
> Your lips have spoken lies
> Your tongue have muttered perverseness
> None call for justice
> Nor any pleads for truth
> They trust in vanity
> And speak lies
> They conceive mischief
> And bring forth iniquity.
> And you know what the Lord said?

I want you to repeat after me
The fault
Is not in the Lord
You are just not ready[8]

After a series of parallel syntactic constructions, which set forth humanity's crisis of sinning, the line "You are just not ready" leaps to a resolution, an answer to the riddle of why the world is in dire straits. As folklorist Gerald L. Davis explains, "You are not ready" encapsulates the theme of Bishop Cleveland's speech, and the pastor will return to this core at strategic points as he develops his "argument."[9] Roger King is doing something similar in segment-ending lines like *Please lend us an ear* and *I would submit to you that we do not:* he compresses into a few words the theme of his story, and circles back to it in different guises in the course of his closing.

Circularity, Davis argues, is an organizing principle of African American performance aesthetics. The performer makes an initial core statement and then moves innovatively outward, returning to the core at intervals—like jazz. A feature of this aesthetic, prevalent in sermon tradition, is that endings are open-ended. Recall how Roger King ends his summation not with closure but with a final twist on his theme: *Isn't it ironic that the defense's witness used to contradict Mr. Adams had a nickname of Devil?*

So Mozenter and King have different orientations toward parallelism. One favors reiteration, the other transformation. Similarly Mozenter relies on the use of rote material, while King, who is looser, prefers improvisation and riposte. Do these differences represent an order of patterning that animates many aspects of each lawyer's behavior? Are they instances of a basic contrast in styles?

Let's look at what may have been Bobby Mozenter's riskiest strategic decision: whether to put Isaiah Gorton on the stand. If he ditched Gorton, he had no witness to rebut Kevin Adams's testimony about premurder plans and postmurder boasts. Adams *might* be enough to convict. If he went with Gorton, he *might* give the police enough extra time to locate Bud Scott, Jr. Mozenter, gambling that he could handle Scott if it came to that, plunged ahead with Gorton.

It did come to that. And when Mozenter finally faced Bud Scott, he questioned him in the same key he had sounded in his cross-exams of Ian Goodwin and Kevin Adams. He was unrelievedly high-pressured, his tone accusatory and mocking. This manner had worked effectively, I thought, with Goodwin. But against Adams it seemed less compelling, maybe because he'd already used it once. The third time, with Scott, it felt predictable. Its constructed quality showed. What I'd first regarded as a stinging style now struck me as stylized, with Mozenter's unvarying voice a caricature of itself. The effect was to increase my own doubt about whether all three men were the reprobates he claimed.

King fastened on Mozenter's repetitive tone, afterward, as a vulnerability. Part of the plan, King asserted, had been "to use his forward momentum against him. . . . We floated Ian Goodwin out there, and [Mozenter] really, really went after him. We threw him out early enough so the jury could get a real view of [Mozenter] at his aggressive best." Mozenter, King claimed, "shot his wad" early, on Goodwin. Meanwhile, King himself kept playing it low-key: "We laid back on him, and waited until it really counted."

By ceding center stage to Mozenter for much of the trial, King wanted to embolden him, to tempt him to overreach. King's strategy was to move the jurors in his direction *eventually*, taking control with his summation. Passivity was a ploy to entice Mozenter to underestimate him. And King's case *was* shaky. With Bud Scott in hiding, the story lacked validation. Only Scott could account for what had happened between the time Adams had heard the murder being planned and the time Goodwin had heard the shots. By passing up the chance to close the record before Scott could hurt him, did Mozenter slip into King's trap? Having dominated the courtroom throughout the trial, Mozenter wasn't ready to shift gears, to disengage from his stance of control and, simply, stop.

The repertoire gives you what you need to perform at a given moment as part of an overall plan. Each moment in the flow of a performance poses both oppportunities and pressures. At one moment you must decide whether to put on a witness or close your case. At another you must combine certain phrases, intonations, and bodily gestures to take your questioning down a chosen path. The way you handle the moment is conditioned by your larger plan. Certain parts of this plan may be so crucial to your theory of the case that they're unalterable. Much else remains unfinished, open to adjustment and development as the trial evolves. Clarity in grasping the trial's trajectory, resilience in responding to it, and boldness in shaping it are all repertoire-based skills.

How repertoires are marshaled to meet moment-by-moment demands can be seen in "set-pieces." These are segments that are loosely memorized (through key words and associations) so the speaker can reel off the whole piece at the right time. You may have noticed that when Roger King, in his opening in the Brady case, said:

> We will ask you to put an *adj*ective to it:
>> whether it's an assassination,
>> whether it's an extermination,
>> whether it's a slaughter.
>
> But we will ask you to find that this was
>> a willful,
>> deliberate,
>> and premeditated act,

he was pretty much saying what he'd said in his summation in the Blaylock case:

> You are here to decide what to call *this:*
>> whether you want to call it an assassination,
>> an extermination,
>> whether you want to call it butchery,
>> whether you want to call it man's inhumanity to man,
>>> I ask you to call it one thing:
>>> I ask you to call it *murder*
>>>> in the first degree.

The two renditions, while far from identical, are conceptually equivalent. They start by asking the jury to give the crime a name, then propose what that name should be, and end by offering equivalent definitions of the crime. In the terminology of folklore studies, these are two "versions" of the same "item" in King's repertoire.

The item has a specific role to play at a specific juncture in certain kinds of trials. This doesn't mean that King has always used it in the same way or that it will indefinitely keep its present form or niche. Like all set-pieces, it's been formed through multiple occasions of performance. Over time elements of one's repertoire shift. An item may be a staple of performance for months, years, or the duration of a career; it may merge with other items, be superseded, go inactive for a while, disappear. And because of the accretive process that brings it into being, it will bear marks of its author's style.

Here is the niche I think this set-piece has for King: it comes near the conclusion of either a closing or an opening, in trials where he's decided to depict the crime as an execution. Legally, its purpose is to stress that this is first-degree murder with no mitigating circumstances and no room for a compromise verdict. Rhetorically, it provides a climax to his speech by hurling a harsh accusation. In style it's like much of King's oratory: the language is terse, poetic, symbolically thick; parallelism, repetition, and rhythm enhance its effects.

Like all set-pieces, this one contains a worked-out solution to a recurrent need. Probably it originated as a means of dealing with a moment in a particular trial, and no doubt many jurors who hear it assume it has been newly minted for *their* trial. They hear an elevation of diction, a poeticizing designed to enhance the authority of the speaker's words.

So set-pieces have the appearance of inspired spontaneity when in fact they're portable, usable again and again. They function—like other parts of a repertoire—to promote economy of effort. Armed with a polished, reliable way of handling a problem, one is freed from having to figure out how to cope with the situation in the heat of performing, and thus freer to attend to quirks of the immediate moment and to the overall plan.

Economy operates, too, in framing the story as a whole. The lawyer approaches each case as belonging to, or at least sharing features with, a category of cases already in his or her repertoire. The kind of victimization in the Blaylock case, for instance, led King to treat it, mythically, as a tragedy of Home. The Brady case fit King's already formed take on Intimidation and Redemption, and Mozenter's take on Lying.[10] Themes are tied to personas. Redemption suits King as preacher; Lying, Mozenter as tough guy. And themes overlap: the story of Home and the story of Redemption share symbolism. Thus set-pieces are often usable, with tinkering, in a wide variety of cases.

The recycling of set-pieces and themes from trial to trial is an inevitable result of the American dependence on the jury system. The performance of repertoire would be much constrained—and the stories told therefore quite different—if verdicts were in the hands of judges who knew the lawyers rather than jurors who had never seen them in action before.

There is no sure connection between retention of past learning and attainment of craftsmanship. You can learn inadequate as well as adequate patterns for action—or patterns that work well in some contexts but are off-key in others. Awareness of what you need to know and of what action belongs in what context represents a distinct order of learning. This is the part of the repertoire that shapes the acquiring and use of what's in the repertoire. The more flexible this mechanism for learning is, the less you will take for granted and the better you will be at sizing up what's going on.

Strains in Performance

Unpredictability tests craftsmanship. Skill can be measured by the resilience of the response.

Consider what happened to Roger King's story in the second trial for the Muscles Fisher murder, which took place eleven months after the first one. With Greg Brady's conviction in hand, the DA was prosecuting the others believed to have committed the crime with him. The defendants were Cliff Townsend, Reggie Green, Isaiah Gorton, and Martin Willams, each of whom was represented by his own lawyer. Consider the following from King's summation:

> It happened down beneath those things that the general population seems to be indifferent to.
>
> And what is that?
>
> That's the hustling world of cocaine.
>
> This is a thing that we talk about when we say somebody else can take care of this problem. Right in the shadows of City Hall you might want to ask yourselves, how this particular crime could have happened.
>
> The defense took pains to go through the pathetic might of some of the Commonwealth's witnesses.
>
> You have some of the witnesses in this case accused of being drug pushers and drug sellers.
>
> You saw Bud Scott, who, at twenty-five, before he opened his mouth and before he sat here, you would have said maybe he looked like the boy next door. But you saw him stutter through—
>
> ONE OF THE DEFENSE ATTORNEYS: Objected to.

JUDGE: Go ahead. Proceed.
—the spelling of his name.
And somewhere, somehow, you twelve members of this community must take a stand.
You must do what you must do.

The story has thus been reframed. In the Brady trial, the fact that the Commonwealth witnesses were testifying in life-threatening circumstances signified that, whatever had undermined their human potential, there was still hope for them. Quoting inspirational words of Martin Luther King, Jr., and Eleanor Roosevelt, King had implied that Goodwin, Adams, and Scott could even aid in the rehabilitation of their community. In the second trial a seachange in meaning occurs. The men are no longer protagonists. They're not even worth defending:

If they are dredges, if they are rogues, they were associates of the defendants.
Because if they weren't, they wouldn't be involved.
And okay, sometimes it's necessary, I would submit to you, to go to the bowels of the earth in search of the truth.
We put those witnesses up there for twelve people to say: I believe or I don't believe.
And we didn't put them up there for you to think about inviting them home for dinner or showing them off as some group of people that we are proud of.
What they are represents a great deal of what is wrong with how we live and how we prosper.

This is no longer a story about Intimidation and Redemption. The theme has instead become Apathy and Responsibility, and the jurors themselves have become the protagonists:

You can't shift the weight here.
It is all here and now.
We want all of it, right here.
We don't want it next week.
We want it now.

We don't want it when you get together with your neighbors and talk about what is not being done and why does this situation exist.

And one other irony, ladies and gentlemen, the defense again and again went back to: Isn't it a strange commentary that regardless as to the amount of drugs that the Commonwealth's witnesses were caught with—

DEFENSE ATTORNEY: Objection.

—no one went to jail.

Is there a toleration?

If not a toleration, an acceptance?

It does not affect me.

It does not affect my family.

Therefore, maybe the thinking is, that they only kill the public.

And maybe, as I sit down before you now, maybe, as the defense would say, it's just another junkie shot in the head three times—

ALL FOUR DEFENSE ATTORNEYS: Objection!

Ladies and gentlemen, it may not have been a great sense of loss to society as a whole.

It was a loss to humanity.

He was alive.

He was not what he could be.

Maybe he wasn't what he should be.

But, he was.

He had life.

He was somebody's son.

Somebody's baby.

In the Brady closing John "Muscles" Fisher was a nonentity. He wasn't mentioned; what mattered was the regeneration of the living. Here, in sharp contrast, his death is invested with pathos. King suggests it will only have meaning if the jurors meet their obligations, if they don't turn their backs on the conditions that led to his fate. In the earlier trial war was being waged in the inner city for the souls of troubled youths. Here it's waged in the city at large for the hearts of its citizenry. King summons the jurors to become partners with him in the work of saving the community:

I would submit to you that it's up to you now.

The police have done everything they can do.

The stenographer, police officers, lawyers, and the judge will soon put it in your hands.

Don't sit back there and create doubts.

Don't sit back and say I need more.

You don't have any more.

That's all there is.

Deal with it.

And if you need courage, look for your own convictions.

What is right,

what is wrong.

If you need strength, reach out and touch somebody's hand.

Touch the person next to you.

Stand up and be heard, because that's the only way.

There has been a systematic realignment in the roles of the dramatis personae. The placement of mythic significance has shifted, but without any loss of meaning.

What happened? Evidence and witnesses, while largely the same in both trials, played out differently in each. The first time, a misstep on cross-examination led Kevin Adams to say that God believed him; a witness who might not have testified had the nickname Satan. From such seemingly thin threads King wove a protective symbolism around his witnesses. Both points came out in the second trial, but without the same potential for foregrounding. The four defense attorneys' combined attacks on the character of King's witnesses, and the combined impressions they made *as* witnesses, persuaded him to abandon the plan to uplift them in favor of a more promising mythic tack.

Before trial an able lawyer sees alternative paths of interpretation that may be open, but the choice of the one to follow often awaits the unfolding of the case. The story needs to be designed to accommodate this uncertainty, without large gaps that might weaken its appearance of truth. (The story can persuade without accounting for motive. In the first trial, motive was never addressed in open court.)

Can highly accomplished lawyers *always* create the appearance of truth? Or are there limits to the circumstances where skill can prevail?

Three months after Roger King won convictions against all four defendants in the second Fisher murder trial, he stumbled into a quagmire. He was before Judge Juanita Kidd Stout, trying Greg Brady, Cliff Townsend, and Reggie Green for the first-degree murder of Vinton Scales, a drug addict.

It had been a vexed prosecution. An eyewitness to the crime who had inadvertently revealed her identity when she entered the courtroom during the preliminary hearing was murdered. Another eyewitness recanted his testimony on the stand. By the end King had called twenty-seven witnesses, only two of whom claimed to have seen any of the defendants commit the crime—and both of them had dubious credibility. Robert Bud Marshall, shot along with Vinton Scales and paralyzed from the neck down in the incident, admitted under oath that he'd done robbing and shooting in his time. The other, Ann Enlow, admitted under questioning by Bobby Mozenter, who was again representing Greg Brady, that she had smoked marijuana and drunk beer before the shooting. Here is the windup of King's closing:

> We went inside of the beast.
> We went inside where the deals are made,
>   where they talk with the hustlers
>   or the hustler-type mentality.
> "How much can I make,
> what can I blow it on."
> You heard that kind of testimony;
> you saw those kinds of people.
> And as Peggy Lee would say, "That's all it is."
>
> Now, if you want to let the defendants walk out of here, do so.
> If you want to look at Robert Bud Marshall and what he says, and why this came down to be what it is—
> You know, that is a heck of a combination, John Ferris [*a Commonwealth witness*] and Robert Bud Marshall. Do they corroborate each other's testimony?
> Ann Enlow.
> Can you imagine mixing Ann Enlow, John Ferris, Bud Marshall, and Larry Smith [*a Commonwealth witness*] and still come out with the same conclusion?

I submit to you that you saw it.

There sits the shooters of Vinton Scales and Robert Bud Marshall, if you believe the Commonwealth witnesses.

I'm not going to ask you to believe.

I'm going to tell you that's all there is.

If you want to let them walk out of here—

      MOZENTER: Objected to.

      JUDGE: Sustained.

Fine.

We'll make it easy.

We'll ask you to return only one verdict:

guilty of murder in the first degree.

Guilty of murder in the first degree, because

      how cold,

      how callous,

      what lack of regard for others was shown.

Crowded street,

hot summer night.

Vinton Scales paid.

Bud Marshall, he still is paying.

You talk about the number of witnesses.

This is my case in a nutshell:

two pages.

You got IDs,

and you got people giving you the reasons

for what they said

and why they said it.

That's all there is.

That's all there is.

You are familiar enough with Roger King's style to sense that this is subpar performance for him. It lacks his customary verve. The terseness of his way of speaking here lapses into indefiniteness. Details are referred to without anything being made of them. His usual balance between exactitude and evocativeness is off. His set-piece on cold-blooded murder, for example, is truncated. His attitude toward his own witnesses (*a heck of a combination*) seems dismissive. The refrain *That's all there is* is repeated until it sounds like an unintended admission of weakness; the challenge *if you want to let the defendants walk out of here, do so,* like an unintended invitation. It's as if King has internalized the voices of the opposing counsels and is unwittingly confirming their accusations.

Mozenter, in his closing, had already given the jury a metaphor for the weakness of King's position:

> If you recall my opening speech in this case, I said that the Commonwealth is going to be like the quarterback who calls for the ball from the center, fakes it to the fullback, and drops back for the pass.
> Everybody's eyes are on the fullback who doesn't have the ball.

As is his style, Mozenter returns to this image repeatedly in his summation, always to make the same point: when you look at how King keeps trying to tie Greg Brady to this piece of evidence or that piece of testimony, you find there's no connection. The seventh time, he completes the metaphor:

> Another innuendo, another fake handoff: this time to a halfback.
> But he's still dropping back to pass.
> And he has no receivers.
> There is nobody there to catch that ball he wants you to catch.
> But you are not going to catch that ball because there is nothing there to catch.
> He doesn't have the ball in his hand.

Just as Mozenter finishes his house metaphor by stripping off the roof, here his twist is that the quarterback is playing without a ball. The quarterback fake has special aptness as a tweak at King. This is how King responds in his closing:

> Mr. Mozenter told you that I was a football player.
> Yes, I was a football player,
> played out in the California sun,

played at that school with the white horse that runs around
the track,
    where everybody had a tan beauty on their arms
    and cheered ninety thousand strong on Saturday.
    But even that Camelot has changed now,
    because everybody now,
    even those paper-thin heroes of yours,
    had nosegays from cocaine.

This is startling imagery, conveying King's feelings of marginality in an idyllic, overwhelmingly white middle-American scene, and calling it to account for the moral rot subsequently disclosed there. Yet the imagery dangles. It's not germane to his larger story, nor does it answer the accusation in the quarterback-fake metaphor, much less turn the metaphor against Mozenter. King's response is overpersonalized, on the defensive, off his game.

Mozenter's metaphor captures the trouble King is having connecting the defendants to the crime and—not coincidentally—the evidence to his plotline. King falls back on personal and professional authority to command belief from the jury. But to claim that all the needed links are present, even to specify what they are, is no substitute for an argument solidly linking them. Although King is convinced he is on the side of the angels, he can't quite pull off his story. The tentativeness of his closing betrays the weakness in his case.

Such wobbling under the tremendous pressures of courtroom performance happens more often than you might think. In *A Civil Action*, Jonathan Harr's popular account of the lawsuit brought by families of leukemia victims in Woburn, Massachusetts, against two large corporations, we find the plaintiff's attorney, Jan Schlictmann, suffering the same indignity as he undertakes his summation at the end of an extremely debilitating trial:

At the counsel table, Nesson [*Schlictmann's co-counsel*] turned in his chair so he could watch Schlictmann, who stood to his left and behind him. But after a few minutes, Nesson turned away. He picked up his pen and began writing quickly in his trial notebook. *Jan is a bit shaky. Trying to remember. Pauses that are not for effect*

but rather to remember what to say next. A memorized speech. . . .
Why can't I look at him? Why does his argument embarrass me instead
of engage me?

Schlictmann confided to the author the inner turmoil he felt:

> Facher's [*the lead opposing counsel's*] objections had thrown
> Schlictmann further off-stride. He was having trouble remember-
> ing his speech. It was long and detailed, and for a moment he had
> the terrible, nauseating fear that he had lost the jury's attention.
> He tried to shut that thought out of his mind and concentrate on
> what he wanted to say next. He felt an overwhelming fatigue. He
> paused for a long moment to gather himself, to order his thoughts,
> and all the many things he wanted to say came to him in a jum-
> bled, disorderly rush.

At one point Schlictmann cited dates related to contamination of the wells
that were supplied by one of the corporations, instead of by his own expert—a crucial error the judge promptly corrected. Then Schlictmann said
to himself, "All right now, I can't make a mistake," in words loud enough
for the whole courtroom to hear. And near the conclusion of his speech, as
he warned the jury not to be confused by all the complicated evidence, his
voice took on a pleading tone.[11]

Neither King nor Schlictmann simply self-destructed. (When Schlictmann's jury deliberated, the initial vote was, in fact, four to two in favor of
the plaintiffs.) But their summations could not generate the momentum
they needed to make their framing of events stick. Despite all their ability,
preparation, and desire to win, they faltered.

"Jurors are very perceptive," King said to me after the Blaylock trial.
"If they sense that *you* feel that there's a weakness in your case, they'll pick
it up. And all they need is one small tear to make a gaping hole." It happens even to highly skilled lawyers. But why should inability to make as
strong a case on the evidence as one wants or expects shake one's eloquence?
Why can't a top-notch lawyer always remain impervious to the other side's
advantages and to bad breaks?

Lawyers at trial are moralists. Their role requires them to act as stew-
ards for a code of conduct by which human beings ought to live. They bring

these values to bear on the case. This is more than a matter of making moral arguments or projecting moral character. The lawyer's *entire* performance is a moral statement, in the same sense that art can be seen as an inherently moral act. Art is moral not primarily because of its content, but because it's an achievement of expressive coherence that can be experienced by others; because the maker, through skill, has imposed gratifying pattern on the chaotic world. The aesthetic of what is created nourishes our consciousness. We respond to it because it communicates the rightness of being we seek in life.[12]

Because the truth of the events being contested in court can't be apprehended directly, jurors depend on appearances. The importance of finding the truth makes them *more* dependent on appearances. This is, as Erving Goffman observes, a central paradox of human interaction: "the more the individual is concerned with the reality that is not available to perception, the more must he concentrate his attention on appearances."[13]

Jurors instinctively infer signs of guilt and innocence from the caliber of each side's performance. Their response depends on the performance's attainment of aesthetic qualities such as intelligibility, vitality, harmony, and wholeness. The lawyer tries to create a multilayered consistency of appearances, a complex redundancy that will withstand jurors' scrutiny so that wherever they turn, they will find confirmations of soundness to earn their trust.

In the trial of Greg Brady for the slaying of Muscles Fisher, Roger King achieved this consistency. King's manner of identifying with witnesses, their mutually reinforcing testimonies, his preaching voice, his choice of theme, the flow of the trial, his engagement with his adversary, the composition of the jury: these all validated one another, creating a plausible universe whose parts were roughly in balance. But for Bobby Mozenter balance was more elusive. The damaging testimony of Bud Scott, Jr., threw him. His closing argument was laden with generalities. Jaggedness was detectable even before the trial, when he let his client persuade him to pick a juror against type and then said perturbedly, "*He* wanted him, I didn't."

Inability to seize the moment—to grasp its potential or turn aside its dangers—is a hazard endemic to performance. Performers are responsible, as long as they're on stage, for bringing off the role in a way that meets the audience's expectations. To do this creatively they need to be in the proper relationship with the projection of themselves that they put forth. This identification is what actors accomplish when they merge with the part they play, what authors accomplish when they perfect a vision and point of view. But compared to actors, who rehearse, and authors, who rewrite—compared to performers of most kinds, who can count on stability in their material and the contexts of its performance—trial lawyers are in a precarious spot. The evidence, witnesses, client, and judge have obdurate existences. The other lawyer pushes a counterreality. The situation in which they perform is constantly in flux.

Given the uncertainties besetting their performances, trial lawyers are, I think, unusually vulnerable to ruptures of identification with their projections of self. They take the posture of moralists, but the trial may pose a set of circumstances, or turn in a direction, that frustrates their attempts to create coherence. Barriers and discouragements in making a well-formed presentation to the jury put strains on their ability to act to their full capability in their role.

They claim to be moral, but they can't always construct a transparent, intelligible universe. The contradiction can cut the ground out from under them. If they succumb to these adversities they slip to a less inventive, accomplished standard of performance. Through lapses of one sort or another—misfirings or insufficiencies of unconscious skill—they send the jury unintended signals of their own actual view of the situation. Their style, however imperceptibly, weakens. They lose their authoritative edge.

The quest, as Gregory Bateson said about art, is for grace. Attainment of grace requires integration of "the diverse parts of the mind," of consciousness and unconscious, of "the reasons of the heart" with "the reasons of the reason."[14] The master trial lawyers are the ones best able to realize this integration. If free to choose their cases, as many are, they play to their strengths. But whether they can choose or not, once involved in a case, however unwieldy the evidence, they make whatever they're dealt seem as if it nearly all fits. In the widest range of circumstances they sustain clarity, focus, and intensity. They prove the story, and themselves, whole.

These abilities are not, ultimately, verbal or cognitive. They are qualities of mindfulness, outward manifestations of inward grace.

A LEGENDARY LAWYER

I first heard about Cecil B. Moore during the desultory jury selection for the Brady trial. I noticed Bobby Mozenter swapping stories with Judge Lisa Richette's clerk about Moore's prowess. Then I heard Roger King telling tales about him to a homicide detective. Dead six years, Moore was still a hovering presence in the Philadelphia criminal courts. I wanted to know why.

In the privacy of his office, King dubbed him "the infamous Cecil Moore." He said it with mixed feeling. I sensed he was alluding to the hostility the city's white community felt toward Moore and, at the same time, to a discomfort that clouds his own admiration of the man. Moore routinely gave the DA fits, and he traumatized King in *Commonwealth v. Crenshaw,* which King regards to this day as the most perfect case he's ever tried.

It was in 1977, close to the beginning of his career in the Homicide Division of the DA's office and the end of Moore's as a defense attorney. King fancies that the ten-and-a-half week trial took so much out of Moore that it accelerated his downhill slide. The case was a gruesome murder. King was merciless on Crenshaw, keeping him on the stand for a day and a half until he literally convicted himself. But after more than three days of deliberation the jury came back with a verdict of not guilty.

"It took me two years to get over that," King said. "I think I have something like sixteen death penalties? I'd give them back, for that one."

"How did Cecil Moore win?" I asked.

"I made one mistake. One. The type of jury that I picked. I felt I could beat a legend with his strength. Hey, I'll give him his type jury! That's a form of arrogance. Although in this case it was by necessity, because the

Commonwealth, after the first day of jury selection, had used eighteen challenges."

King got trapped, he said, because every white person over the age of forty-five told the judge they couldn't give the defendant a fair trial since Cecil Moore was representing him. Nine blacks wound up on the jury. With his kind of jury, "he could beat God himself."

Studying Cecil Moore in the course of that interminable trial, King saw that "everything he did and everything he said in court he did for a purpose." That would become a cornerstone of King's own method.

King owed him an indirect debt as well, for Moore had made it easier for him, a newcomer to Philadelphia, to find a place and ultimately glory in the District Attorney's office. The older man had done much to create the atmosphere in which a younger generation of African American attorneys could flourish. By proving that a black lawyer could take on the legal system dominated by white prosecutors, white judges, and white police, outperform them, and consistently win, Moore struck a blow against racism in the courthouse.

Later I sought out Oscar Gaskins, who as a young defense lawyer had been an associate of Moore's. Like everyone I met who cared for Moore, he referred to him affectionately as "Cecil." He noted that Moore was influenced by Robert Nix, Sr., a black attorney who was already prominent when Moore began practicing in 1954 and who soon after embarked on a career in Congress. Moore copied some aggressive methods of cross-examining from Nix, Gaskins said, and also emulated him in combining law with politics. (Moore's first political foray, in 1958, was to run for Congress as a Republican against Nix, who thrashed him in the staunchly Democratic district.) Whereas the senior lawyer achieved success through mainstream channels, Cecil Moore was a nonconformist, perfectly suited to the improvisational openness of the sixties.

"He thought that all Philadelphians were handkerchief-heads—all black Philadelphians," Gaskins told me. "He just could not understand why they were so passive, how they could have let the system survive for that long without any real aggression or real challenge to it. He didn't have the kind of respect for white people that the average Philadelphia professional had. It was his view that this is the worst group of blacks in the world! They're just perfectly satisfied with the status quo."[1]

This kind of rhetoric antagonized middle-class professionals and clergymen who claimed to represent the black community. To anger them was what Cecil Moore wanted to do, just as he flustered his legal adversaries by baiting them in court. Let the elite disparage and fear him. To Gaskins and other young black intellectuals, and to many ghetto residents, Moore was the one who uttered truths no one in authority dared speak. And the one who proved he could turn talk into action.

Reading through old newspaper files, I found that Moore asserted an outsider's perspective on race relations in Philadephia. He had grown up in McDowell County, in the mining country of southern West Virginia. "We were so poor the rivers ran once a week," he'd say. But he also made it known that his father and grandfather were medical doctors and that where he came from Negroes wielded power, winning elections to judgeships and school boards so often that they could legitimately call the county "a free state."[2]

He had enlisted in the Marines in 1942 because, as he told it, he'd refused to lie down for a white man. He'd gone into a loan office in Georgia to ask for a loan, and the manager had called him a nigger and punched him in the mouth. Moore beat him unconscious and got to the recruiting office a step ahead of the lynch mob.

A sergeant major, he saw many comrades killed or wounded in the first wave of attack on Saipan. "You see, I made a living killing for this country," he told a reporter. "I was determined that when I got back, that what rights I didn't have I was going to take, using every weapon in the arsenal of democracy. After nine years in the Marine Corps, I don't intend to take another order from any sonofabitch that walks."

Transferred by the Marines to Philadelphia in 1947, Moore attended law school at Temple University at night. When his enlistment expired he supported his family as a whiskey salesman. He was admitted to the bar at the age of thirty-nine. With both his residence and his law practice in North Philadephia, a predominantly African American section of the city, he soon acquired a mammoth caseload and the reputation of being the one lawyer who could and would help anybody who was poor and in trouble.

It was from this base as a trial lawyer, with verbal gifts, tactical astuteness, and heedless determination to win honed in City Hall courtrooms, that Moore gained control of Philadelphia's civil rights movement. In 1962 he was elected president of the moribund local branch of the NAACP (National Association for the Advancement of Colored People). He soon launched a campaign of picketing and boycotts that attacked pervasive patterns of employment discrimination in the city. The ultimate result was the creation, by his estimate, of 175,000 jobs.

Of the many stories that still circulate orally about Cecil Moore's civil rights victories, here is one: Wanamaker's, the grand Philadelphia department store, refused to hire African Americans or to return phone calls from the NAACP. Refused, that is, until Moore called to tell them that they could either change their policies that day or he'd send the city's "biggest black mammas" into the store to try on their new dresses.

One threat from him was usually enough. What employer wanted to be confronted by the army that called themselves "Cecil's people"?

His strength was felt everywhere in the city in those days. It was he who organized a group of black attorneys (Oscar Gaskins was among them) to get an injunction against the Mummers Parade, the New Year's Day march up Broad Street staged annually by clubs from the ethnic communities, forcing them to cease the derogatory practice of wearing blackface. It was he who got youths from rival gangs to band together in a prolonged campaign of picketing and civil disobedience at Girard College, a school for white male orphans whose walled presence in North Philadelphia starkly symbolized the racist legacy of American institutions. During the riots along Columbia Avenue, while other leaders were meeting in emergency committees, it was he who walked the streets, coaxing people to cooperate with police and coercing speakers who were egging on the crowds into joining his appeal for calm.

Today, Girard College is integrated as a result of a lawsuit by Moore, and Columbia Avenue, one of North Philadelphia's main thoroughfares, has been renamed Cecil B. Moore Avenue. Since his death he has been apotheosized in the city at large for his role in the struggle for racial equality. However, there is irony in the praise, as Gaskins sees it, because Moore was hounded from his leadership position in the late sixties by a coalition of black leaders, "old-line Philadelphians" who used their connections with the national NAACP to split the local organization into four separate chapters. Chafing for power under Moore's autocratic rule, they took what he had made into "the most powerful and the largest and busiest and most productive branch of the NAACP in the country," and, according to Gaskins, wrecked it.

Despite all the politics Moore's trial practice never slackened, although another elite—the white legal establishment—kept trying to rein him in by forcing him to conform to their norms. There were recurring threats to censure or disbar him for unprofessional conduct, and byzantine maneuvers to limit the size of his caseload. But he was too clever to be controlled by apostles of order. A keen reader of laws and mores, he knew how far he could go.

Typical of the measures intended to muzzle Moore was an administrative court ruling that defense attorneys could carry no more than fifteen cases for longer than a year, at a time when he had a backlog close to four hundred. "Who died and made them God?" Moore complained to a reporter. "These guys are preaching fundamental democracy but practicing fundamental totalitarianism and repression. . . . I don't turn away any folks with no funds. I don't turn away folks who feel I can bring truth and justice to their cases. . . . And I still believe that people have the right to the counsel of their own choice and the right to a trial by jury which this ruling eliminates. The last time I read the state and federal constitution, that was still the law." He filed suit in U.S. District Court and got the ruling overturned. Two years later the administrative court tried again. He got it reversed again.

A lot of arrests were phony to begin with, Moore contended, and a lot of the judges had so much law-and-order in their blood that, although they were incapable of realizing it, the only possibility for defendants they ever considered was jail. Moore had an extraordinary knack for using whatever came to hand to equalize the odds. The sheer size of his caseload, for one thing, was a boon for delaying trials. He could always claim, without lying, that he was tied up in another courtroom on a pressing matter. Meanwhile, to the amusement of the defense bar and the consternation of the DA's office, witnesses would die off, get disgusted, or forget about the case; evidence would grow stale; the prosecutor would get jumpy; and when the trial finally came, Moore's chances of winning would be that much better.[3]

He never paid taxes. The Internal Revenue Service kept on his tail. Glumly. Because they garnished his salary when he was elected to the City Council in the 1970s, he was never paid for holding office. But that hardly compensated for the manpower, frustration, and uncollected monies he cost the government over the years. He eluded IRS agents by never keeping records of clients' payments.

Although his financial condition at times appeared precarious to friends, Moore cut a handsome, imposing figure. Tall, with a Marine's bearing, he dressed impeccably in fine silk suits, starched shirts, and gleaming accessories. He smoked six-inch cigars. And he drank, which eventually killed him. He drank constantly, according to Oscar Gaskins, but slowly. He'd sip a bottle of hundred-proof Old Granddad that he kept in the back of the courtroom, and, especially in later years, it could last two days. Alcohol lubricated his style. Judges would call recesses—so it's told around the courthouse—to get him to adjourn to their chambers with the bottle.

His clients were mainly women—an unending series of wives, girlfriends, mothers, sisters, and daughters seeking help for men who were in jail. "He had that black preacher approach to dealing with women," Gaskins said. "If you [a man] walk up to a preacher he shakes your hand, and if you're female he puts his arm around your neck and kisses you on the cheek, because he recognizes that 70 or 80 percent of his parishioners are female." Friendly and flattering to women in person, he was at the same time "the world's greatest male chauvinist," according to Gaskins, a misogynist who professed hatred of professional women. He sought relaxation in "masculine situations," with a single exception: he loved to be with Helen, his girlfriend who became his wife in his last years, after his first wife's death. She was the one person who could make this supremely self-confident man feel insecure. He had three daughters, but his wife raised them. He spent little time at home.

Moore's philosophy of trying cases, which Gaskins and others absorbed, was primal. He believed, Gaskins said, that you have to dominate and control the courtroom. That if you can't, you lose. That you have to make the jury forget the defendant and try the two lawyers. That you have to provoke the antagonism of the District Attorney. That you have to neutralize the judge. He believed "the courtroom is a stage," Gaskins said, and you act according to what you can get away with in the circumstances in which you find yourself.

Few prosecutors had the self-restraint to resist Moore's incitements to battle. "In that situation the juror doesn't know that the confrontation is being caused by the defense," said Gaskins, who still employed this technique:

> All he knows is that there's confrontation. He's got to make a choice. Most of the District Attorneys would take Cecil on. That was a mistake. He's more articulate than they are, he's better look-

ing than they are, he's better dressed than they are, he's clearly more knowledgeable than they are, he could command the respect of the court better than they could. So invariably, he was the winner. And he didn't always initiate the confrontation based on a frivolous question. I mean, he'd deal with it at a point when the issue is significant—as opposed to every time the District Attorney says something you argue about it, or you scream every time you make an objection.

Periodically, the District Attorney tried to reduce Moore's backlog by instituting a special "program," assigning a courtroom, judge, and prosecutor exclusively for Moore, to tie him down. As one wag put it, this was like giving Willie Mays his own pitcher and ballpark. Going against Cecil Moore on a daily basis was said to invite nervous exhaustion, ulcers, and the derailment of a career.

Bobby Mozenter, then a young prosecutor, was one who drew this assignment. Mozenter told me that he, like a lot of lawyers, had regarded Moore as "an arrogant bastard" based on what he'd heard. But he was fascinated by his reputation for beating up lawyers and intimidating judges, and when he had the chance he'd slip into the back of a courtroom to watch him in action. When the DA assigned him to Moore, Mozenter told me, he jumped at the chance with a novice's eagerness.

The first case they argued against each other was a rape. The evidence against the defendant was overwhelming. The victim had been brutalized so badly that she had jumped out of a third-story window and broken her back trying to escape. Moore had delayed the case for years. Mozenter got the victim to put her brace back on for her appearance before the jury. It took them two days to reach a verdict. Moore, who routinely won rape cases, lost. Mozenter recalls winning the second trial they did together, the third, and the fourth. Then, for the next year and a half, Moore beat him repeatedly, either by outright acquittals or by verdicts to lesser charges than the DA had sought. He beat him every time.

In one case, according to Mozenter, a witness on the second day of Moore's cross-examination turned her face upward and cried, "Oh, sweet Jesus, come and get me!" In another, Moore convinced the jury that the victim, who died after being stabbed a dozen times, was a jezebel because there was semen in her anus and thus deserved to die.

"Nobody could cross-examine like Cecil," Mozenter told me:

> Nobody. His closings to the jury were fabulous. But better
> than that, he was a master technician in jury selection. The guy
> had an uncanny feel for human nature. You'd get up there, he'd ask
> you five, six, seven questions, and he knew exactly what kind of a
> person you were. You couldn't beat Cecil because he beat you when
> you picked the jury. He had the jury he wanted *every* trial.
>
> And he knew about blacks better than anybody. He could tell
> by their accents and their speech what part of the South they came
> from. He knew that black people from North Carolina felt one
> way, and blacks from South Carolina, Virginia, feel another way.

Moore knew because he had traveled the South extensively as a young man.
His secret allies were people other lawyers saw as "ciphers"—to use Oscar
Gaskins's word—nonentities who could be counted on to go along with
the majority. All Moore needed to set up a win was to get a couple of ciphers seated on the jury.

"He knew which judge to push, which judge not to push," Mozenter
said:

> I used to say to him, "Cecil, you get along with some of these
> *real* redneck judges." He says, "I know how to handle rednecks."
> Like he used to get along with one judge, Irish guy, he was a real bas-
> tard. You'd shiver in your pants to go in his courtroom. You could-
> n't talk to him, the way he'd look at you. And he would win cases in
> front of that judge. You *knew* that this judge hated blacks—he hated
> blacks, he hated Jews, he hated everybody. Loved Cecil. He was a
> drinking man. Cecil got drunk with him a couple of times.

Mozenter went drinking with Moore many nights after their courtroom joustings. He'd stop by Moore's office around ten. Sometimes it was
still crowded with clients waiting to see him, folks who paid for his help
with fifty dollars, a hundred dollars, rings, watches, clothes (clients knew
his sizes and his preference for sharkskin suits), chickens, whiskey, whatever they had or could get their hands on. After Moore finished the two attorneys would take a stroll down the street. If they passed an IRS agent hid-

den behind a newspaper, Moore would shout, "Motherfucker!" in his face. They'd eat dinner, drink, and talk until two in the morning about the next day's cases, about law and legal tactics, about life.

Mozenter, who started to have a drinking problem trying to keep pace with Moore, became his student and almost his son. He was in awe of Moore's courtroom performances and the qualities that animated them: the charm, the lightning wit, the flawless memory, the superb knowledge of the law. Ninety percent of what Mozenter learned as a lawyer he credits to "the master." He copied his manner and "tricks of the trade" shamelessly. He took on his voice to such an extent that for years afterward he was known around the courthouse as "the white Cecil Moore."

From Moore, Mozenter learned such techniques as how to distract the jury by coughing, snoring, dropping a book, or jiggling a pocketful of change when his opponent was damaging his case; how to frustrate the opponent's witnesses on cross-examination by avoiding the questions they were waiting for, by asking the same thing five different ways, or by forcing them to stay on the stand until they had said what he wanted to hear; and how to berate the opponent in an undertone so the judge wouldn't detect it but so the remark had just the right amount of malice to hit a nerve and trigger a reply.

With Cecil Moore, such verbal insult ran close to the surface. On one occasion, still widely remembered in the local legal community, it boiled over into scandal. This was in 1967, at a tense hearing in which the Philadelphia Board of Education was seeking a court order to ban black power demonstrations in the schools. Moore was getting pushed around, Mozenter believes, because he was a criminal lawyer, out of his element in the civil courts. According to newspaper accounts, the incident began when the crier ordered one of Moore's witnesses to be seated when there was no chair to sit on. Moore called the crier a hack political appointee, and the judge told Moore to get out of the courtroom if he couldn't control himself. Then David Berger, the school board's counsel, accused Moore of wasting his time and the court's, and Moore shot back: "You're playing footsie with racist bigots. You and the rest of the Jews get out of my business!" In the ensuing disarray he hurled the insult again—"I said, Jew, get out of my business"—and challenged Berger to "give me your best shot."

Mozenter, who says he was able to slip a Jew onto a jury against Moore now and then because Moore had trouble identifying them, confronted him about it afterward:

He came out in the hallway and he said to me, "You mad at
me?" I said, "Yeah, I'm mad at you, you motherfucker." I said,
"You of all people, calling the guy a Jew." He said, "Well, don't be
mad at me, 'cause that's what he is, a Jew. And there are blacks that
are *niggers* and he's a *Jew*." I said, "That's bullshit, Cecil, that's bullshit."

Invective was crucial to Moore's verbal style. The young prosecutor
who hadn't served in the military was liable to find himself heckled in open
court by Moore as a "draft dodger" and cursed at under his breath as a "fag-
got" and "cocksucker." The rape victim might be repeatedly demeaned as
a "bitch." The hostile judge might be dismissed as "the best magistrate
money can buy" and challenged to a fight.

Moore could be just as bare-knuckled in the political arena. In the
space of a few minutes of an on-the-record interview, he could dismiss the
black middle-class as "upper-crust niggers," call the national NAACP
"conference-goers and tea-sippers . . . the greatest bunch of Toms I've ever
seen" (this in 1963, when he was president of the local NAACP), and slam
the city's liberals by saying, "I'd rather deal with any southern racist than
the unscrupulous bigots living in Chestnut Hill." At other times the insult
was not frontal but couched in exaggeration. Speaking in a packed session
on the topic of rape at the local bar-bench conference, Moore argued that
only a man who had himself committed rape was capable of representing
defendants accused of rape. Most men's first sexual experiences were rape-
like, he added; women who went to bars alone in "provocative" clothing
were inviting rape; and Women Organized Against Rape, the volunteer
group that offered counseling to local rape victims, "shaped" the testimony
these women gave in court. Judge Lisa Richette, who was on the panel with
Moore, kept shaking her head in disbelief.

Many white Philadelphians hated Cecil Moore and rejected whatever
he said. They tended to take his words literally and felt threatened by what
they thought he stood for. Most black Philadelphians heard his rhetoric differently. What he did, when he resorted to verbal excess to attack an individual or group, was rooted in vernacular forms of ritualized insult. Ritualized, because in traditional African American verbal dueling (known as
"sounding" and "playing the dozens"), the put-downs are performed in a
structured, competitive situation, the presence of which signals that they

don't need to be taken literally—although the most painful insults have barbed truth in them—but rather are moves in a game whose winning depends on the player's skill at verbally outmaneuvering the opponent, which is achieved when the opponent, responding to the attack personally, overreacts.[4]

Cecil Moore's power in the games of law and politics flowed from his consummate control of a whole range of African American verbal arts, from signifying to preaching. He was nicknamed "Preacher Man" on account of his spellbinding speeches. Yet his oral style, like his work in society, looked to the streets. Moore didn't condemn the sinner. He represented him. He led juries to see through the defendant's eyes, to sympathize with the desperation that went with the deprivation of liberty. ("I have learned," he once wrote about defendants in capital crimes, "that such a man feels himself to be the loneliest man in the world, without regard to feelings of guilt or innocence.") His stance as a lawyer was that of a person alone and defiant, voicing life's harsh realities. His stance as a civil rights leader was the same: he was often at odds with the movement's religious leadership, with Martin Luther King and local clergy, because his approach to action was individualistic and freewheeling compared to theirs.

On the record player in his council member's office in City Hall, he would listen to music by the likes of Billy Eckstine, Fats Waller, and Count Basie. He regarded himself as a "pro" like them, and like Congressman Adam Clayton Powell.

To his community Cecil Moore was a folk hero in the mold of others celebrated for their moral and physical strength—men like Jack Johnson, the heavyweight boxing champion who beat every Great White Hope who climbed into the ring and who defied segregation with his outspokenness, relations with white women, and opulent lifestyle. With Moore, the hero's hardness showed itself in his indifference to criticism and pressure; the hero's morality, in his obsession with winning freedom for the accused and equality for the community. Scandalizing the powers-that-be, he exposed their moral bankruptcy.[5]

Although there are some who vehemently dispute it, many in the legal community say that Cecil Moore was the most impressive criminal attorney Philadelphia produced in the middle part of the century. He was, reputationally, the heir to Chippy Patterson, who is remembered as the premier local defender of the teens and twenties. In some ways they were alike.

Patterson represented the poor, social and racial outcasts; he had a reputation for taking the cases of all who sought his help and an astounding record of success; he was habitually broke. Patterson's personal background fascinated the public because he was a renegade from the local aristocracy into which he'd been born. His magic touch with jurors came, according to his biographer, from "his simultaneous, contradictory identification with both Philadelphia's ruling class and the humble prisoner he was defending, so that the twelve felt they were imposing sentence not only upon the accused but upon counsel as well."[6] His style favored gentle irony over invective, quick wit over oratory.

But it was Cecil Moore's style, not Patterson's, that had lasting influence on many lawyers. I met a number of them who insist that Moore's way of performing changed the tenor of criminal practice in the city. Attorneys who had the disposition for it copied aspects of his approach. Just as Moore became mentor to Bobby Mozenter, who'd grown up in an Orthodox Jewish family with a father who loved verbal debate and a mother who was a quick judge of character, so he struck responsive chords with others in Mozenter's generation, particularly among those with strong ethnic backgrounds, Italian and Irish as well as Jewish and black. Through Moore, many say, the tone of advocacy in Philadelphia courts acquired an unnervingly aggressive cast.

The appeal of his style did not depend, I think, on race, nor was it felt only by lawyers who were consciously attracted to black culture. It lay more in how open they were to the culture of criminal defense. At the root of Roger King's discomfort with Cecil Moore, I suspect, is the orientation that has made King a career prosecutor, in contrast to most of Moore's protégés, many of whom cut their teeth in the DA's office but later went out on their own.

Roger King, with his sonorous voice, kinetic delivery, and charged rhetoric marking him as a preacher, remains, in court, a fundamentalist. He calls the defendant to account for his sins, summoning vengeance in the name of a higher moral power: justice, the community, and ultimately, God. It is that commitment that pitted him against Moore.

Putting it in mythic terms, we could say that prosecutors, like preachers, tend to be conservative, to seek to preserve the community by upholding order, while defense attorneys tend to have an anarchistic streak, to attempt to vindicate the individual (and thereby the community) by undermining authority's claims to be truthful and just. There are parts of Moore's style, in particular the anti-authoritarian "carrying on" he did much to popularize, that prosecutors, as defenders of order, can't comfortably imitate.

Still, King and Moore have much in common: their competitive edge (King attributes his to "the competitive nature of athletics, learning to identify weaknesses and exploiting weaknesses"); their love of African American language; their anger about racism that fuels their relentlessness in court.

The legendary stature of Cecil Moore suggests how a great trial lawyer can infuse a vernacularly based style into the work in a way that affects the ongoing practices of a local legal community. Moore didn't originate a style or set of strategies. Rather, like any accomplished trial lawyer, he drew on varied examples from his own past and from what he observed in court. His genius was his capacity to combine multiple sources of his experience in ways that armed him with everything he needed to meet the shifting demands of each new situation.

The hold he's continued to have on other lawyers lies, I think, in the virtuosity with which he met the test they all face. He made the crazy world reverberate inside the courtroom's walls.

IDENTITY

Here the most agonizing mystery sponsored by
the democratic ideal is that of our unity-in-
diversity, our oneness-in-manyness.
Pragmatically, we cooperate and communicate
across this mystery, but the problem of identity
that it poses often goads us to symbolic acts of
disaffiliation.

—Ralph Ellison[1]

Cecil Moore had grace in court. It didn't make him "nice" or save him from demon drink. It was a kind of mindfulness.[2] Moore was, much of the time, *fully* present: clear in purpose, attentive to all that was happening, attuned to his audience, tapping the right moves in his repertoire, fully in sync with his presented self.

We can think of the lawyer's courtroom self, his or her persona, as a mask. The act of masking is not an evasion. It can be seen, rather, as inherent to American life—in Ralph Ellison's words, as "a playing upon a possibility, a strategy through which the individual projects a self-elected identity and makes of himself a 'work of art.'"[3]

American identity is fluid. We have license to invent ourselves. Cecil Moore, Roger King, Robert Mozenter, Michael Tigar, and Gerry Spence have all created strong personas from a mix of given and chosen characteristics in light of their circumstances. In their self-fashioning, they're not different from other performers—writers, teachers, artists, politicians, ministers, police—who project heightened versions of their selves to prove their authority, their trustworthiness to lead, be listened to, or guide.

This chapter asks: what sources of identity do lawyers draw from to create their personas? And how do they use identity to authenticate their stories and themselves?

By this point in the book the reader, I trust, will see these as significant questions. I confess that during most of my research, I did not. When I saw how Roger King and Cecil Moore relied on African American oral traditions, I thought that their indebtedness to cultural roots was unusual, if not rare. I didn't realize that talented lawyers, whatever their background, have cultural anchors until I witnessed lawyers from around the United States on stage at the Festival of American Folklife in Washington, D.C., in 1986.

The participants I invited to the Festival were all renowned in their legal communities. I designed the program to stage head-to-head matchups between them, modeled on the case-file method used in trial-training workshops, where lawyers argue from stripped-down versions of evidence from actual or invented cases, balanced to give both sides ample ammunition to persuade. These demonstrations—a number of which will be descibed in the following pages—were brief, largely improvised displays of skill. They were a context in which lawyers could show in compact, unfettered ways how they conceive their craft.[4]

In one contest after another I found that lawyers possessed well-honed folk identities. They came before juries not as detached agents of the justice system or as synthetic Every Americans, but as men and women belonging to communities and bearing a history, a moral and even a spiritual address.

Why? For the lawyer's story to be powerful, it has to account for evil, adversity, and inequity, the underside of American life, in ways that reaffirm democratic principles, the American faith in the good. For this to occur the lawyer has to *live* the story, filter it through his or her own experience, and then create an angle of vision that jurors can imaginatively adopt as they make sense of the story for themselves.

The challenge, as Ellison described it for writers, is to "project this variant of the American experience as a metaphor for the whole."[5] To do so successfully is to bridge divisions of race, class, gender, and the like that separate the lawyer from jurors and jurors from each other. The lawyer uses his or her identity to move the jury toward unity and universals based on deep-lying aspirations all jurors can be presumed to share.

Yet—and herein lies a chief irony of American life—this bridging of differences with audiences very often has, as its flip side, the sowing of distrust about others. The need to cast doubt on opponents' stories leads the lawyer to stereotype *their* identities. This is usually done adroitly, subliminally, since stereotypes are volatile. If they are too blatant, they backfire. But they are powerful. They feed potent American mythologies. As the spectacles of the O. J. Simpson trial and the Clarence Thomas Supreme Court confirmation hearings attest, lethal images of race and gender that circulate through society fasten easily onto legal antagonists, with explosive results.[6]

We now leave behind the gritty world of actual trials for the scene of a mock courtroom in a big circus tent on the Mall in Washington. It is summer. Festival-goers jam the bleachers and mill around the edges of the tent. The witness stand, jury box, and judge's bench are made of plywood to signify the stage's distance from a real courtroom, its status as a space for reflection on trial art. The lawyers appear in their usual courthouse attire, sweating in the sweltering heat.

As they perform, some project the authority of experience grounded in their ethnicity, gender, or class; others, an authority based in the place they live, their age, a prior occupation, or the craft tradition itself. Many blend multiple sources of authority. Listen, and you can hear how vernacular identity centers them in their quest for grace.[7]

Sources of Emotion

A case file: Charles Bryant Gainer has been found guilty of murdering two elderly women while burglarizing their homes. The only question before the jury now, in the trial's death penalty phase, is whether he should live or die. To make their decision, the jurors weigh aggravating against mitigating circumstances. Under the state's death penalty statute, the facts that there were two separate murders and that each was committed during a felony are aggravating factors, which may justify execution. The facts that Gainer is "borderline mentally retarded" and was a heavy user of marijuana and crack at the time of the murders are mitigating factors. The jury can spare him if they decide that when he committed the murders he was unable to realize that they were crimes.

The evidence closely resembles an actual California case.[8]

The defense attorney is Roy Barrera, Sr., fifty-nine years old, from San Antonio, Texas.[9] Standing in place, he speaks rapidly, rhythmically, urgently, his pitch hardly varying. There is sorrow in his eyes:

How did he get here?
This is a young man
who was born in the state of Mississippi
out of an illicit relationship
that existed at that time between his mother and his father.
He was born out of wedlock.
Initially and at the outset, we have a bastard that has been
brought into the community
not by anything that he did
not by any desire on his part
but by the will or the lack thereof
of his would-be parents.
You have heard that at the age of four
his father, if you please, abandoned him
as you would abandon a puppy
or an animal that is no longer in service or of use.
And that he disappeared.
And that his mother thereafter took up with a man by the
name of Smith, a stepfather, if you please, for this young man—
again, without benefit of clergy, an association, a relationship,
which gave birth to *another* little bastard, if you'll pardon the expression.
It was on or about this time that, in keeping with the thinking that prevailed at that time,
not by his choice,
not by anything that he wished upon himself,
but by force of the adults that brought him into this world,
by force of the society that didn't see fit to remedy the situation at that time,
this young man,
this *boy,*
was given away
by his mother who didn't *want* him . . .

To his paternal grandmother. An elderly lady, who opened her doors, and he was with her, up until around the age of seventeen.

During the course of this time he did get himself in trouble, with cocaine, with crack.

You show me a youngster today

in *any* community

who doesn't have access to

drugs

notwithstanding paternal love and affection,

and I'll show you a community that is nonexistent in these United States,

certainly not in the state of California.

And he, like others, millions like him, was exposed to it.

*

What did those psychiatrists tell you? . . . "Persons of lowered intelligence would be more sensitive to the ingestion of drugs, and would be more likely to experience impaired judgment and behavioral controls."

Why do I call that to your attention?

Because we're looking to his behavior,

we're looking to see what was in his mind at the time that he *did* this.

Isn't it evident *to* you

that his judgment was impaired

when he went in and took a toaster, or a TV

at the force that he used upon these two elderly ladies?

Ladies and gentlemen, again:

Is his judgment impaired,

is he *lacking* in judgment,

is he incapacitated when the first witness that comes along he said, [*matter of factly*] "I did that."

And then it's read in the newspaper what allegedly he had done to the second lady, and he said, [*casually*] "I did that too."

Now is that the sign of a killer?

A man who should be gassed in the gas chamber?

A boy, if you please, because if his mind didn't grow with him,

notwithstanding that he has the physical stature of a man by force
of years, mentally he never grew.

And if he never grew, his judgment was impaired just as much
as that of a juvenile who is not put to death when he causes a death
or other grievous crime by virtue of the fact that he has not yet arrived at the age of reason.

*

I daresay, ladies and gentlemen, that if these two elderly ladies,
who God had blessed with a long, long life, in this community—
and certainly I don't say, nor do I suggest, that Charlie had any
right to terminate it—if they had *one more day* to live, he had no
right to terminate their lives; but in fact, if they were here, and capable of coming back and talking to us, I am satisfied that they
would be the first to tell you,
[*a tear runs down his cheek*] "Don't do it.
For Godsakes don't do it!
I've lived my life,
and I'm happy
with my Maker.
Don't do it!"
There but for the grace of God goes your grandson or someone else's grandson, in this community and in this state.

Prosecutor Roger King makes this response to Barrera:

If you follow what the defense said,
EVERY PERSON FROM A BROKEN HOME
should be out there killing,
should be out there pillaging,
should be out there looting.
EVERYONE who it takes a little bit *longer* to learn
has a license to hunt down
an eighty-one year old
a ninety-one year old.
I would submit to you, ladies and gentlemen, in the words of
Robert Louis Stevenson: "Sooner or later EVERYONE must sit
down to a BANQUET OF HIS OWN CONSEQUENCES."

And I would submit to you, that as he sits here now, in the clinical atmosphere of a courtroom,

DON'T look at him, and see your nephew,

DON'T look at him and see the boy next door.

HIS conduct put him here. . . .

I won't apologize,

I won't sympathize,

and I don't want you walking out of here with your head hung down.

You have done nothing!

In this society wherein it is popular:

When Johnny can't read, it's the teacher's fault.

When Johnny can't find a job, it's

                         YOUR
                         fault.

YOU are not at fault here.

YOU did not pummel,

YOU did not beat,

YOU did not squeeze the life out of those two victims,

        therefore

        you

        are

        not

        guilty

        of

        any

        thing.

[*softly*] He is.

And AS

he sits there,

as counsel said,

"This *boy*,

[*words dripping, head thrown back*]

this *puppy* that no one wants."

I would submit to you, ladies and gentlemen,

look at him as a dog,
look at him as a MAD dog. . . .

The defendant's fate, as is usual in death penalty hearings, turns on the responsibility he is seen to bear for his crime. This is the mythos of free will versus determinism: do we make our own destiny or do external forces shape what we—what some among us—become? Conventions for placing responsibility are rigid. The defense locates the impetus for the act in psychological or social forces beyond the murderer's control. The prosecution locates it in his or her character. The defense urges jurors to be compassionate, on behalf of society or the convicted one's family. The prosecution absolves them, so the defendant seals his or her own doom.

This is how Roger King reads Roy Barrera's intentions: "Your attention has been shifted away from the vicious acts of the crime into one of sympathy, and the defense attorney has gotten you . . . to point the finger at yourselves, saying, 'Maybe this is my fault.'" His own job, King says, is to "get you out of that sociologist's laboratory and onto the streets of reality."

How does Barrera use his folk identity to argue for mercy? He invokes the social compact. His plea is suffused with references to family, kinship relations, the fabric of community, God, vagaries of fate—all traditional Mexican American cultural concerns. Barrera fashions this symbolism into an image of right living in America, a communitarian ideal that can appeal to jurors regardless of racial or class background.[10]

At the outset we have a bastard that has been brought into the community, not by anything that he did. The defendant was born into a specific community. The world in which he's lived becomes an extended community, one that now includes the jury. It should be a moral community, Barrera is saying, in which every person is recognized as having instrinsic worth and particular needs. Gainer's community bore *some* obligation in the face of his neglect by his parents, his mental difficulties, the scourge of drugs. It can still act ethically now. When Barrera has the murdered women plead for mercy, he enlists them as the conscience of this community.

What makes Barrera's plea formidable—what guards it from attack as bleeding-heart liberalism—is his aura of authority. Barrera is legendary in the San Antonio Mexican American community as a great lawyer. He has an extraordinary victory rate, a penchant for high-profile cases, and influence in Texas Democratic party circles. His courtroom manner exemplifies traditional Mexican American stylistic ideals: integrity, dignity, modesty, toughness, emotion, irony, wit. Roy Barrera embodies—and capitalizes on—this world view.

He locates the affective sources of his approach to jurors in his ethnicity:

> I am of obvious Mexican American extraction. We are emotional people. I feel that *all* of us, reaching far enough into us, we will all be subject to acting and reacting out of emotion. We cry, we laugh, we joke, we show anger. All of these things are signs and characteristics that really are in all of us. Some of us will have to reach a little more. But I think that emotion is contagious. And if I can bring myself around emotionally to feel what I am saying—and I *must* feel it—then I think I can spread a contagion of sympathy and emotion.

Barrera insists that these feelings must *not* flow from direct identification with the client. "If a lawyer marries his client emotionally," he says, "then he is going to become that proverbial fool who represents himself." He could not represent his own son because, when "bound by our emotions," we are "unable to think clearly."

How, then, do lawyers "feel it"? How do they connect with their emotions so they can spread a contagion to jurors? Through the mediation of their moral stance. By making the particular case and the pain of those caught in it an instance of perennial issues in American society, lawyers buffer themselves from emotions swirling around the trial and tap instead into the affective core of their own cultural commitments. They tap into the authority of feelings and sentiments they've experienced in morally defining situations over the course of their lives.[11]

If Barrera gets his emotionally charged energy by taking a traditionalist stance, King gets his by assuming a conservative one. He delights in subverting race-based expectations. Equating the belief that society is responsible for Johnny finding a job with a lame apology for crime, he swipes at dominant black—and liberal—ideology about American democratic obligations. A white prosecutor who tried this Johnny-can't-read polemic against a nonwhite defendant would be vulnerable to charges of racism, but King's identity gives him authority to do it, acting as protector of the good for African Americans. His strict law-and-order outlook has a solid base of support in black communities. It runs deep in his experience. And it has obvious appeal to many whites.

From an unsympathetic perspective King could be accused of pandering by making an argument consistent with a racist game.[12] Yet he is keenly aware of ironies of race in his work. The DA's office has labeled—and confined—him as a prosecutor of black defendants. King alluded to this, indirectly, when he criticized the District of Columbia's prosecution of John Hinckley, attempted assassin of President Ronald Reagan. "Whether they had to beg, borrow, or steal," he told me, "they should have shaken the tree of their system and come back with their best black attorney. Brought him forth. Then you're creating ironies on ironies." Instead, King said, they chose a prosecutor who was "caught up in his Ivy League background, or his Little Three background," who "didn't relate to his jury," leaving them "completely mystified."

King's point was that someone like himself, well versed in combating insanity defenses and appealing to the mixed race and class composition of urban juries, would have possessed the requisite authority to hold Hinckley dead to rights. The ironies he alludes to entail reversal of racial stereotypes. A black prosecutor can become the most effective agent of justice against the white assailant who would rip society apart; a black man can be best positioned to tell the tale of the arrogant attempt to evade personal responsibility. (A biographical note: Roger King had intended to enter civil practice when he first arrived in Philadelphia, but was turned down, and turned off, by elite firms with their "Ivy League mentality." So he went into criminal law.)

Emotional tactics were prominent in another defense of Gainer—by Michael Tigar, forty-five at the time and teaching at the University of Texas at Austin. Tigar's moral stance is progressive, his background WASP. He has a slightly lumbering gait and an understated, colloquial manner of speaking, foils for his exceptionally polished rhetoric:

> Now you're going to get back in that jury room, and somebody's going to say to you, "Well, how can we decide this? How can we decide this?"
> And Judge Carrigan will tell you that you've got to consider whether or not these crimes, these terrible crimes, were committed while the defendant was under the influence of extreme mental or emotional disturbance.

You're going to have to consider his age—that he was nineteen years old at that time.

You're going to have to consider his mental capacity.

That's not something to be derided, members of the jury. That's a part of the majesty of the law, without the having of which we are ALL in the jungle world that Mr. Sharp [*the prosecutor*] SAYS that *he* deplores.

And the judge will tell you that you ought to think about those things.

But then some voice says to you, "Well, *my God, he beat those women to death*. Those unresisting women. Where did he learn to do that?"

Well, he's marginal mentally retarded, members of the jury. We know that.

His momma didn't love him. She moved in with another man, who used to BEAT HIM SENSELESS, when he wouldn't listen.

How did

that tree

get that way?

What wind

was it

that bent it?

What human hand

twisted it?

*

If you've ever driven down a foggy road at night—you probably have—if you drive over the bridge here, and when the land fog rolls in between here and Leesburg on Route 7, you can hardly see your way.

And one thing that you always say is, "Don't overdrive your lights! Don't go any *faster* than you can react."

Why am I talking about that?

Every year that goes by, members of the jury—

science, and what scientists do—

we stand on the shoulders, each generation,

ROY BARRERA, SR.

ROGER E. KING

TRIAL LAWYERS
AT THE FESTIVAL
OF AMERICAN FOLKLIFE

PHOTOGRAPHS © LYLE ROSBOTHAM

MICHAEL TIGAR

J. TONY SERRA

BOYCE HOLLEMAN

JAMES GOETZ

JO ANN HARRIS

PATRICK WILLIAMS

PENELOPE COOPER

JUSTICE R. EUGENE PINCHAM

JOHN SHEPHERD

DIANA MARSHALL

LORNA PROPES

RALPH LANCASTER, JR.

JAMES FERGUSON II

and we learn more and more and more about the possibility of human redemption in this life,

about the possibility of understanding why people go off the rails and commit crimes,

we learn more and more about those things.

We've learned a lot just in the last ten years about the management in institutional settings of people who surely should not be out in the street. Haven't we?

Well, maybe you'll say, "Well, golly, we haven't learned enough, I'm not confident enough about that."

Don't overdrive your lights, members of the jury, don't overdrive your lights.

What if, five years from now, you've signed this warrant, and somebody finds some new treatment, that within the walls of that facility he *can* adapt, even if you don't think he could now. Of what use then?

As a famous man said, "It would be the sterile regrets you'd accord to his vain shadows and insensible actions." How would you feel about it?

And then a voice in the jury room says, "Now wait a minute. We're free here.
    We can
    wreak
    vengeance.
    We can somehow embody the avenging spirit.
    We can toil up and down the blind alleys we imagine to be our own eternal souls and [*choking*] SCOUR OURSELVES IN THE BLOOD OF A MENTALLY RETARDED NINE-TEEN-YEAR-OLD!"

[*Slowly he makes a full turn. Subdued:*]
Members of the jury.

You notice that we don't let psychiatrists decide death cases.

We don't even let lawyers decide death cases, and we don't let prosecutors do it.

We get twelve people
from all walks of life
to make the really important decisions in our society.
As I remember, some such decision was made by the founder
of Christianity.

I'm gonna go home now. I'm done.
And I'm gonna sit at the dinner table, and my daughter's
gonna say, "Daddy, what did you do today?"
And I'm going to say, "Well, I tried to save the life
of one of God's creatures."
And members of the jury:
what will you say when you go home?

"Nothing lawyers do is original," Michael Tigar says. "It's a tradition.
. . . We're whittling the same old animals we always did, and trying to do
as good as somebody else did." Tigar, who is a legal historian, really means
this. When he was a boy, his father told him that if he wanted to be a
lawyer, he should be the kind of lawyer Clarence Darrow was. Tigar's mentor, the legendary Edward Bennett Williams, modeled himself on Darrow.

This demonstration is filled with echoes of Clarence Darrow's voice
from the death penalty phase of the famous Leopold and Loeb case. Nathan
Leopold and Richard Loeb, wealthy Chicago teenagers in search of the perfect crime, kidnapped and murdered the son of a prominent businessman.
Tigar's argument, like Darrow's plea in 1924, is an impassioned attack on
the premises of capital punishment. His reference to the jungle, for example, copies Darrow's words about human evolution: "If the law was administered without any feeling of sympathy or humanity or kindliness, we
would begin our long, slow journey back to the jungle that was formerly
our home."[13]

Tigar's questioning of how the tree got that way follows Darrow imag-
ining the thoughts Leopold or Loeb's mother might have: "How came my
children to be what they are? From what ancestry did they get this strain?
How far removed was the poison that destroyed their lives? Was I the bearer
of the seed that brings them to death?"[14]

Tigar's faith that society will continue to make progress in understanding criminal conduct is "stolen," he says, from Darrow:

Crime has its cause. Perhaps all crimes do not have the same cause, but they all have some cause. And people today are seeking to find out the cause. We lawyers never try to find out. Scientists are studying it; criminologists are investigating it; but we lawyers go on and on, punishing and hanging, and thinking that by general terror we can stamp out crime.[15]

Even his reference to "the founder of Christianity" is lifted from Darrow: "Let me ask this court, is there any doubt about whether these boys would be safe in the hands of the founder of the Christian religion? It would be blasphemy to say they would not."[16]

Words from Darrow no doubt echo in many lawyers' performances, the result of generations of study and subterranean oral chains of transmission. But Michael Tigar is likely unique in his careful emulation of this ancestor figure of his profession. Tigar's style combines the didactic sensibility and literary diction that were Darrow's stock-in-trade. This combination formed a thriving rhetorical tradition in the nineteenth century; it was a type of speechifying admired by the American public. Now it is rare, erudite, and could easily sound pretentious unless brought off by a lawyer whose personality somehow fits with it. Tigar's scholarly self-assurance (he was first in his law school class at Berkeley), leftist politics, poetic leanings, look of boyish wonder, and touch of noblesse oblige all fit. Through Darrow, Tigar gets what King and Barrera get with help from ethnicity: authentication as a worthy citizen and astute observer of the American scene. He recasts his white, male, advantaged class position by means of the oratorical glory and social consciousness of his craft's past. Darrow grounds him by giving him old—now fresh—perspectives on quandaries of contemporary life.

Michael Tigar, like Barrera, describes how he taps his emotions in an imagined situation such as the Gainer hearing:

I am opposed to the death penalty in all of its forms. I think it's savage and barbaric; I believe that. So it's pretty easy for me to imagine. And particularly when talking about the gas chamber, I can conjure up images that will get me going. I conjure the image of Albert Harris, Governor Ronald Reagan's handpicked prosecutor, standing in front of my client, Angela Davis, and describing for her benefit, as well as for all the onlookers in the courtroom, that he wanted her put to death. And how it was gonna happen. And she was gonna walk up to that room, and sit in that chair, and the cyanide pill was gonna drop. And my God, that was just at a pretrial hearing; he didn't even have a jury in the box!

Defending Angela Davis in one of the sixties' most politically charged trials, Tigar had at a young age his first chance to take the role in society that Darrow loved to play, the controversial role he would much later be called to take on behalf of Terry Nichols: that of representing a person whose life is at stake when the nation is caught up in the drama and when desire for vengeance runs high. He uses Albert Harris's emotionalism—the righteous indignation, the gut hatred that made him treat Angela Davis as subhuman—to illustrate the irrationality underlying the death penalty. Emotion, he claims, overwhelms reason.

Is he right? James Sharp, the lawyer who argued the prosecution side against Tigar at the Festival, said that *he* would have found it "unbecoming" for the government to seek execution in a case like Gainer's, although as a skilled professional he showed no qualms about doing it during his demonstration. Roger King, explaining how the District Attorney's office decides whether to ask for the death penalty in a given case, said, "We *say* we are objective"—his intonation signaling his knowledge that at times they aren't. The temptation for prosecutors to go for death, if they think they can make a good case for it under the statute, must be powerful.

Let's put the dynamics of the situation in dramatic terms: if you are a prosecutor entering the death penalty phase, the momentum of the trial may well be with you. But this momentum is driven by emotion. To move the jury to the ultimate act you need to stage a tableau of ultimate forces. Below the surface of reason you stir desire for retribution.

If you are the defense attorney you need to question the morality of state-sponsored execution. Not overtly—to be seated on a death-qualified jury, jurors have agreed to impose the death penalty if the facts warrant it—but as an ultimate question of conscience for each juror, faced with *this* ruined life. In the name of humanity's ideals, you beg.

Even in this most extreme of circumstances there is no recourse to truth except through storytelling. We tell ourselves the decision is based on reason. We need to believe that it is so we can believe we act morally in executing human beings.[17]

Local Inflections

A case file: John Diamond, a police officer, is on trial for first-degree murder in the death of his girlfriend, Trudi Doyle. She was shot in the vestibule of the Truck Stop Cafe, where she worked as a waitress. No one saw the shots fired, but witnesses heard them, and heard Trudi Doyle, just before the shots, say, "No." Taking the stand in his own defense, Diamond has claimed that it was an accident, that he was trying to persuade Trudi to leave with him to start a new life in California and that the gun went off by mistake when she grabbed it from his holster.[18]

J. Tony Serra, age forty-nine, defense attorney from San Francisco, represents Diamond. With long gray hair in a ponytail, ill-fitting suit, and psychedelic tie, he looks like an aging, unreconstructed hippie. He has a national reputation for pulling off unlikely victories, and specializes in politically radical and otherwise unusual clients. *True Believer,* a film starring James Woods, was modeled on his life; Gene Hackman studied him in preparation for his role in the film *Class Action.*

Serra's delivery of this summation is rapid-fire and impassioned. His torso is rigid; he gesticulates continuously. He stands directly in front of the jurors, leaning closer and closer to them as he goes on:

[W]ith regard to what was *in* the mind of my client when those shots occurred,
   you can't take the act in isolation.
You can't merely focus on what happened in the vestibule.
You have to know everything [*draws an imaginary circle with his hands*] that the evidence allows you to know about both parties.
What do you know about Mr. Diamond?
He is an EXEMPLARY HUMAN BEING!
He's a decorated war veteran.
He is a highly disciplined individual.
He is loved and respected by everyone in the community!
His sergeant came forward and told you that, with respect to his two years in the police force, that he was *heralded,* that he was commended for being a superior police officer.

You know that, with respect to his relationship to this woman,
    that he LOVED this woman:
    there was no violence,
    there was never argument,
    there was never any suggestion of altercation;
    that his entire relationship to her was one of
    compassion
    and beauty
    and feeling;
    that he wanted to marry,
    he proposed marriage.
    It was *she* who refrained from the decision.
    It was she who didn't want the responsibility. . . .

And so: he came that morning.

He waits for her. She doesn't come to him!

By that *negativity,* by the fact that *she* breeched the normal
routine, you can infer that there is somethin' amiss in HER perspective, not his. He has done what's routine; she has *failed* to do
what was routine.

Remember: two suicide attempts in the previous month. One,
where her life was almost taken.

We have an unstable woman,

a woman who couldn't care for her own child,

a young woman who was *bea*ten by her former husband, who
was a drunkard.

Recall that she, at this time, she had to make a large decision
in her life: whether or not to start *anew,* with a man who genuinely
loved her.

But how many cobwebs in her mind?

       How much *clearance* she would have to do in order
really to give herself in an honest relationship once again? . . .

She took the gun;

he *tried* to take it away from her;

at that particular time one shot rang out;

the gun fumbled;

he grabbed it again;
his fingers grasped the gun, holding it tremulously—
    after all, a shot had just rung out,
    the one he loved there was bleeding,
    she was probably folding—
and then the second shot came when he instinctually,
    through tremor,
    through noncerebral activity,
    through motion,
    just grabbed the gun,
    it went off two times. . . .

Recall what happens then.
He didn't run.
He didn't lie.
He knelt beside her, the woman he loved.
He *held* her *hand.*
He was *shocked,* and he was *frozen.*
He was *dazed.*
It was all of the attributes of one who a great misfortune has befallen, and one who, in the face of that misfortune, is just in a state of shock.
And as *soon* as that shock dissipated,
as *soon* as he could,
at the *earliest* time when he overcame the grief that rendered him almost paralyzed,
he told the story forthwith *exactly* the way it occurred.

Boyce Holleman, sixty-two, practices in Gulfport, Mississippi, where he was District Attorney for nineteen years. With bushy eyebrows and trim white mustache, grandfatherly demeanor, and touch of the curmudgeon, he seems an incarnation of the country lawyer of American lore. He is a revered figure on the Gulf: the road that runs by Gulfport's county courthouse is named Boyce Holleman Boulevard.

A stem-winding speaker, Holleman moves about the courtroom with grand, open gestures:

I was *amazed* to listen to distinguished counsel from San Francisco, who comes here to defend this man. . . .

What he didn't tell ya about this dear soul who he called a fiancée—

I thought, to have a fiancée, at least where *I* come from, the woman has to say YES—

THIS WOMAN SAID NO,
AND PAID FOR IT WITH HER LIFE.

Now let's look at the facts.

ON THE TWENTY-SEVENTH OF NOVEMBER, before this occurred, on December the first, he came home, and Trudi was in a state of comatose condition. She had overdosed on some sort of drugs and pills, and he took her to the hospital.

Now why did she do that?

[*full-blown sarcasm*]

All of this

    LOVE

        that he had for her?

This

    ROMANCE

        that they had going on?

This

    DESIRE

        to live together for the rest of their life

            that my good friend tells you about?

And THREE DAYS BEFORE, this young lady is attempting to take her own life.

But he responded!

With *care*

    and *tenderness*

        and *love.*

He took her home,

    and took out his pistol,

        and put it to her head,

        and said:

            "If anybody's going to kill you,

it's going to be me."

That's the evidence!

That's what he admitted! . . .

Now ladies and gentlemen, you were not

required,

when you came through the doors of the courtroom last Monday,

and his Honor swore you in as a juror,

YOU DID NOT TAKE AN OATH TO LEAVE YOUR
COMMON SENSE OUT IN THE JURY HALL, out in the room
where you were summoned.

Common sense is what makes the jury system work!

And if you can buy this

UNREASONABLE

UNLIKELY

ILLOGICAL

CHAIN OF EVENTS

incurred

and made up

and rolled into this lovely package

by Mr. Serra

from *San Francisco,*

YOU HAVE LEFT YOUR

COMMON SENSE

IN THE HALLWAY,

and the jury system will fail. . . .

Now what happened on the morning of the murder?

He walks into the cafe.

The cafe is long [*he waves to show its length*], the Truck Stop
Cafe, he comes in through the vestibule.

He goes to this end [*goes stage front*] and sits down.

She comes about behind the counter, and she sits down over
on this end [*goes stage back*].

His fiancée! His LOVER! His companion, counsel would say.
THE REST OF LIFE, ELECTS TO SIT AT THE OTHER END
OF THE CAFE!

LEAVES HIM SITTING BY HISSELF.

Why?

[*slapping hands together*]

SHE

was TRYING

to BREAK

AWAY from him!

SHE WANTED NOTHING TO DO WITH HIM!

She knew he was dangerous.

She knew he meant what he said when he put that pistol to her head and said, "If anybody's going to kill ya, it's going to be me."

She sat with her friends, her fellow waitresses, at the other end of the room, and he sat alone,

WATCHING her,

READY,

with that pistol stuck in his belt.

She goes out.

He sees her get up.

He goes out into the vestibule.

HE said he thought she was *leaving*.

Now you don't just casually get up in your waitress uniform and leave.

He knew where she was.

He knew what she was doing.

In his *anger* he moved for her, to the vestibule.

And she was heard to say: "NO!"

This fiancée.

This loved one that counsel would have you believe was his choice in life.

She gave him a final no. In a place she thought was safe. Her place of employment. Full, open view of her friends. She said, "NO."

No to what?

NO TO HIM,

NO TO LOVE,

NO TO CALIFORNIA,

NO, I'M NOT GOING WITH YA,

NO!
I SEEK TO ESCAPE FROM YOUR CLUTCHES
AND YOUR GRASP
AND YOUR PISTOL.
NOOOOO, I'm not going.
And what happened?
BAAAM!
BAAAM!
And she's dead.

Attorneys who work with or against Tony Serra say—and post-trial jury interviews confirm—that many jurors feel hostile to him at the start of a trial, but their resentment dissipates. The distaste is not for his want of professionalism: Serra is fiercely energetic, but he follows the rules impeccably. It's against his identity. His persona is a flagrant anachronism. As times changed most people went straight and grew into responsible adulthood. Didn't Serra? His presence may strike the unsympathetic as a rebuke to legitimate authority and the majesty of the law. Even jurors who identify with the counterculture—and in the Bay Area many, of course, do—may wince to behold it resurrected.

Because Serra's outsiderhood is self-willed, it irritates. But over the course of a trial he has ample chance to woo. His forensic skills are formidable; his manner, charming. So he builds from his initial acceptance by jurors who feel a kinship with him. As doubters come to respect him, they stop regarding his identity as an affectation and start recognizing in him the independence of a nonconformist. His place-based hippiness becomes a moral ground from which he—and they—can critique conventional moralism. He has brought off this shift of perspective with juries even in bastions of conservatism in the Deep South.

Serra's recent role in the nontrial of Theodore Kaczynski, the Unabomber, illustrates this critical approach. Kaczynski attempted to replace his very skilled court-appointed attorneys with Serra. They were determined, completely against Kaczynski's wishes, to argue that he was mentally ill. He instead wanted a political defense in which he could explain the antitechnology philosophy that drove him to mail bombs that killed and maimed people. Serra wanted to give him that opportunity.

"I have always served the objective of the client," Serra explained to writer William Finnegan. "A person has the right to defend himself in the manner he chooses, even if it means death, as long as he appreciates the risk." Serra was sure the jury would grasp Kaczynski's hatred of technology. "It's not crazy, and it's not difficult to understand," he told Finnegan. "And if the hole in the ozone opens and kills us all, he'll be proved right!"[19] Serra figured he wouldn't be able to present Kaczynski's actual story until the death penalty phase, but he thought he might then be able to persuade some jurors to spare Kaczynski's life. The defense team and Kaczynski's family abhorred the prospect of such a defense. They prevailed. In desperation, blocked from retaining Serra and then from acting as his own counsel, and facing the certainty that his lawyers would portray him as paranoid schizophrenic, Kaczynski was trapped into a plea agreement.

Tony Serra's capacity to enter Ted Kaczynski's point of view comes from a career of evoking contrary realities for jurors. Through his counter-cultural self, they experience his clients as complex human beings.

Serra's own deviance, which is voluntary in contrast to negative stereotypes based on physical attributes such as skin color and gender, throws into relief how skilled lawyers use identity to turn stigma to advantage. Subtly or overtly, these lawyers infuse their story with certain ways of seeing the world associated with their group. In the course of exposing jurors who are prejudiced against them to the cogency of their outlook, they also challenge preconceptions about the group's inferiority through the proof they provide of their own lawyerly competence.

Prejudiced jurors go through a reversal of expectations. Encountering a black, woman, or hippie attorney who disarms stereotypes, they find they enjoy the experience. They have pledged, after all, to be fair. By warming to the attorney's perspective, they prove their open-mindedness to fellow jurors and themselves. They may even offer a bonus of loyalty. As a colleague described Serra's way with jurors, "Once they are converted, they want to be generous to compensate for their original bias."

Such dynamics have become a staple subtext in the more realistic TV series about lawyers, beginning with the long-running *L.A. Law*, which portrayed black attorneys utilizing race; a midget attorney, size; women attorneys, gender; a gay attorney, homosexuality; usually with success. When I asked an attorney who is lesbian about the effects of homosexual identity on jurors, she said that women lawyers aren't hurt by it and often are helped. While she couldn't openly signify her sexual orientation even if she wanted to (she doesn't)—breadth of social acceptance does not exist, yet, for that—she believes some jurors pick up on or suspect her lesbianism, and its tacit presence ultimately adds to their sense of her independence and strength of character.

Back to Tony Serra's performance in the Johnny Diamond "case": his alternative view of reality is reflected in his idiosyncratic manner of speaking: *It was all of the attributes of one who a great misfortune has befallen, and one who, in the face of that misfortune, is just in a state of shock.* His syntax and wording abound with little tics. Sentences are convoluted. Word order and emphasis vary unpredictably. Legalistic and formal language coexist with poetic free-association. The effect is to stretch normal habits of listening. To follow what Serra is saying, jurors have to enter his point of view. At first the speech may sound odd, the story weird. Later they ring true.

The sixties' mythos that Serra injects into this case concerns equality in love relationships. Why do we assume that the woman must be the one who gives emotional care, that the man can't show feelings or carry the burden of sustaining the partnership? Why can't the range of private arrangements among lovers be admitted? Challenging traditional assignments of gender roles, Serra offers the jury a story of Manly Tenderness. He makes John Diamond the protagonist of Trudi Doyle's tragedy. Were this a real trial, my guess is that Serra would become Diamond's counterpart, his double. Serra's sensitivity, signaling *his* capacity to uphold a nurturing relationship, would come to stand for his client's supportive love.

It is against the plausibility of both the story and its bearer that Boyce Holleman launches his attack. At the crux of his closing is a joke told by indirection, a jibe at Serra's expense. Holleman sets it up with the casual remark about *distinguished counsel from San Francisco, who comes here to defend this man.* After gleefully satirizing Serra's version of Trudi Doyle's death, he delivers the punch line, asking *if you can buy this unreasonable, unlikely, illogical chain of events, incurred and made up and rolled into this lovely package by Mr. Serra—from San Francisco.* Holleman pauses briefly after *Mr. Serra.* The words *from San Francisco* come like an afterthought, and the offhanded emphasis rings bells—San Francisco, national symbol of flakiness, the kind of place where somebody would concoct this loony tale and suckers would fall for it. Tony Serra: San Francisco in the flesh. The invocation of the city makes the speech a caricature of group gullibility, a numbskull joke.

Holleman wages a war of one culture against another. The counterculture is fair game, and he abuses it with impunity, relentlessly twisting Serra's sentiments, turning Diamond's love into a parodistic refrain: *to have a fiancée, at least where I come from.* . . . Folks in Boyce Holleman's corner of the land aren't fooled when a small woman gets mowed down by a big man's gun. He poses the competing stories as a choice between the traditionally ordered way of living his own presence so reassuringly embodies and the tortured rationalizing his opponent represents, a product of the deracinating influences of modern urban life. Without openly acknowledging it, he engages in a moral diatribe of the South against the North.

Holleman's mellifluousness, humor, and panache partake of the intoxicating world of theater. His courtroom oratory, shaped, he says, by Elizabethan literature and the Bible, transports as it entertains. He's prominent in local theater and has played the role of Clarence Darrow in solo performances. Serra, feeling bested in the encounter, recognizes this power of Holleman's, and describes how he would try to combat it in court:

> In this particular exchange what we *all* did is rather come under the swoon of the prosecutor because of his personality. In a regular trial, I would have tried over and over every day—knowing that he has charm and wit—I would have tried to dilute that by bringing the jury to view him as a very artful and manipulative type of orator . . . to undermine the credibility of counsel because he is, in fact, so gifted.

Serra thinks he can break Holleman's spell if he can get jurors to regard him as an actor. He can estrange them from Holleman's performance if they see that it *is* performance, that Holleman—and by inference, his cultural doctrine—are just too good to be true. Serra would use his opponent's easy, prodigious authority against him: a craft jujitsu.

In another demonstration, James Goetz, forty-three, from Bozeman, Montana, defends Diamond. Tall and young-looking, Goetz speaks in a slow, carefully measured way, in a deep gravelly voice that sounds like it belongs to an elderly man:

> Ladies and gentlemen of the jury. We start by conceding what

I think is obvious in this case, and what you have seen in the evidence, and that is that John Diamond shot Trudi Doyle.

He *killed* her.

And it was *his* Mauser pistol that he did it with.

I say these things because they're obvious to you, and I think you would agree with me that Mr. Diamond has been forthright in his testimony, has *never* denied those facts.

And I say it because the prosecution has laid *great* emphasis on issues in this trial that I submit to you are nonissues.

The powder burns on Mr. Diamond's hands, testified to by the paraffin tests;

the fact that he had a Mauser pistol;

the fact that he had a pistol in his belt;

the fact that there was a shell in the chamber:

have you heard once Mr. Diamond or me suggest otherwise?

You have *not,* because those are obvious facts which are conceded.

Likewise, the testimony of the forensic pathologist.

There is no doubt in this case—tragically no doubt—that Trudi Doyle died that morning of gunshot wounds.

And I submit to you that those are not the elements or the facts in this case that decide whether Mr. Diamond is guilty or innocent, because those facts are clear.

The *facts* that we have to *look* at, however, are those which are absolutely consistent with Mr. Diamond's *innocence* in this case.

Now I want to tell you a couple things about the nature of the overall proof of the prosecution.

Number one: The prosecution has produced *no witness* who has testified that John Diamond deliberately shot Trudi Doyle.

Now it's not the fault of the very competent prose*cu*tion that the prose*cu*tion hasn't produced that witness. There *is* no such witness. They could *not* produce such a witness, because the facts just do not show that.

Instead, we have various witnesses in the Truck Stop Cafe, who saw things in a real hurry, which, when taken in a cumulative

way, the prosecution said, add up to guilt, from which you should
infer guilt.

And the standard in our criminal system, as the judge will instruct you, is a standard that the state must prove the defendant
guilty

beyond a reasonable doubt,

a concept *sacred*

to our system of criminal justice,

in our system that *all* defendants, before the majesty of this
court, are presumed innocent, until proven guilty.

And until proven guilty beyond a reasonable doubt.

Because of that very sacred presumption in our society, that
perhaps some

who *may* be guilty

should be let go

rather than lock up

someone

who is not guilty,

even though there is circumstantial evidence, of the type that
we see in this case, that may tend to point to guilt.

Jo Ann Harris, fifty-two, is Goetz's adversary. A former federal prosecutor in New York, she would later become head of the Criminal Division
of the U.S. Department of Justice in the Clinton administration. Harris is
tall and lanky. Her voice is low, even, and powerful, so well modulated that,
instead of raising it, she deepens it for effect:

Mr. Goetz is a very eloquent lawyer. He's a smart lawyer, too.
And he's doing the best he can for his client. And here he's done
*every*thing he can to avoid a lot of the really important facts in this
case for his client. Instead of offering a rational explanation for the
irrefutable scientific evidence—and I'll get into that in a second—
he's virtually asking you to take John Diamond's story on faith. . . .

His client said that Trudi Doyle, five foot, four inches high, a
hundred and twenty pounds, disarmed this expert judo man, this
police officer, this ex-Marine who had spent six years learning self-
defense.

Mr. Diamond came here and told you that Trudi Doyle disarmed him.

Then he said, you will remember, "As she *held* the gun at me, I took my hand and I hit it up, and the gun went *flying* in the air." Do you remember that? Do you remember when Mr. Diamond told you that, when he was on that witness stand?

And do you *remember*

that what he then said was,

that as the gun came *tumbling* down,

somehow

his finger brushed the trigger,

and the shot went off.

And that somehow, and he even, I believe, said that it was "unbelievable"—that's a word he used in his testimony, "unbelievable," that his hands *somehow* got on that trigger, and the recoil from the first shot sent another gaping hole into Trudi Doyle's chest.

Do you remember that? . . .

This is what the eyewitnesses and the earwitnesses saw and heard.

They saw Trudi Doyle out in the vestibule.

Diamond was blocking her way back into the vestibule, and they could not see a whole lot of her body.

But what they saw was—and I'll try to remind you what the autopsy report shows at the same time—what they saw was her right hand in the air with a pack of cigarettes. Miss Doyle was right-handed. Not exactly consistent, ladies and gentlemen, with reaching for a gun and dragging it out of a police officer's belt, at all.

So the hand in the air.

And then they saw her shake her head no.

And ladies and gentlemen, I say to you that she was shaking her head no because John Diamond had pulled his Mauser out of his belt at that point, blocked off from the people in the diner, and was aiming it at her, and she said,

[*quietly*] "No, no, John,"

and he fired.

And at that point, the first shot hit the left side of her chest, going at a downward angle, coming out on the right side over here, consistent with a right-handed shooter, which Mr. Diamond was.

And then, ladies and gentlemen, she took her right hand—dropping the cigarettes—and placed it over that wound, and started going back, when he shot again, the shot going through the band on her wristwatch, carrying [it] through the wound—and you remember that Dr. Pierce said he found pieces of that wristwatch in the wound—and carrying into her body where the shots lodged.

Finishing her summation, Jo Ann Harris confides that she is uneasy about this exchange. The reason: Jim Goetz's concessions at the beginning of his speech have pushed her into a change of strategy. Her plan, she explains, had been to start with a "very dramatic opening," which would have gone something like this:

This much we know absolutely:
Trudi Doyle,
twenty-three years old,
five foot, four inches high,
and a hundred and twenty pounds,
a mother,
a productive member of this society,
    is
    dead.
Brutally,
two shots from an ugly Mauser
ripped into her chest
the morning of December the first
in the Truck Stop Cafe.

John Diamond
over six feet
over two hundred pounds
    killed her.

He shot
that
Mauser.
Diamond says it was an accident,
that Trudi Doyle,
twenty-three years old,
five foot, four inches high,
a hundred and twenty pounds,
                    disarmed him.

The State says
it's first-degree
murder.
And here is why.

She had to jettison this rhetoric because Goetz made a point of conceding the fact that *John Diamond shot Trudi Doyle.* If she had dramatized the shooting she would have played into his claim that she was dwelling on nonissues. He had outflanked her. Her preference would have been to "begin at the beginning": first, the dramatic hook, and

> then, you begin the story. It's when she arrives in Warrington. And how they came together. And John Diamond's background as a ne'er-do-well until he gets into the Marines. And how guns really turn him on. I think you have to develop a chronological story or it just doesn't work.

Jo Ann Harris's focus on clear, well-ordered narration—a story that gives the listener a grasp of motivation—comes from her background in journalism. Like many women lawyers in her pioneering generation, she entered the profession late, enrolling in law school when she was thirty-six, after a productive career with *Time* magazine. Her cool, concise speaking style is a model of the reporter's craft. She creates a factual picture of the death scene, for example, by synthesizing a number of sources of information. Quoting Diamond's testimony, she takes great care to be accurate. Jurors won't know that she was once a New York journalist, but they've been weaned on the hard-boiled realism of the American popular press. Harris has storytelling resources of that occupational culture at her disposal.

Reportorial methods enhance her aura of competence, which is fostered too by her imposing height and voice—attributes that are, in her words, "intimidating," and that, "casually dealt by forces wholly out of my control . . . permit me to be my natural low-key self without doing great harm to my cause." These physical signs of commanding presence are conventionally associated, of course, with men.[20]

Like Jo Ann Harris, James Goetz stresses factual substance and puts himself in a modest role (unlike Serra and Holleman, who stress mythic concerns and bring themselves to the fore). He combines close control of material with straight-from-the-shoulder delivery. Goetz describes himself as "conversational, fairly intense but not rhetorical, not big flourishes." He grew up in the country south of Bozeman. His trial practice includes complex civil cases at the state level on behalf of Native American and environmental groups. He went to Yale Law School, but his persona is resolutely local.

Goetz speaks with an unadorned directness typical of old-time settlers' speech in the Far West. In this vernacular there is an aversion to exaggeration, a modesty that steers away from pyrotechnics and values spare evocation. Goetz relies for emphasis on cadence, not extended metaphor, as when he explains the concept of reasonable doubt. His colloquialisms—*they saw things in a real hurry*—are minimalist. In the absence of elaboration, he draws jurors' attention to the tightness of his reasoning. He buries his elite education in his hometown roots, making it serve rigorously practical ends.

Goetz's austerity is based in a populist outlook, but it's quite different from Gerry Spence's lyrical brand of populism, and different again from the boisterous populism of Patrick Williams of Tulsa, Oklahoma, who, when arguing that Diamond could easily have gotten the gun away from Trudi Doyle without harm, said: "Folks, he'd have been on her like a duck on a bug. He'd 'uv mashed her to the ground in nothing flat, spun her around, disarmed her before she could say 'Howdy.'"

I mention these dialects of populist expression to highlight a broad pattern: both within a place and between one area and another, variety is the rule in local styles. People sharing a cultural tradition (say, rural western or African American) draw on common symbolic resources, yet the particular place where they live also affects their identity. Lawyers like Tony Serra who practice in their home territory benefit, of course, from long intimacy with local ways of speaking and thinking. Transplants like Jo Ann Harris, who grew up in a midwestern farming family, absorb local sensibility and patois, and so pass for native with juries.

The importance of locality surfaces in lawyers' conjectures about how well styles travel. The fabled "Philadelphia lawyer" was greeted as a suspicious type in other jurisdictions. The aggressiveness of Roger King or Bobby Mozenter would probably play well enough in Chicago. But in rural Pennsylvania? Patrick Williams would find a receptive jury if he tried a case in Montana, but perhaps not one that would be as comfortable with his flamboyance as they'd be with a plain speaker like James Goetz.

To be bested by the other side *because* you are the visiting lawyer is to be "hometowned." Recently I heard speculation about whether a New York City attorney had been hometowned when he lost a major case in Boston. He himself wondered if he had, and so did a close colleague. Another lawyer disagreed. The difference in styles between New York and Boston, she thought, wasn't nearly big enough to account for the jury's verdict.

Gendered Plotlines

A case file: Laura Hobson, twenty-two, is the government's key witness in the cocaine trial of her ex-boyfriend, Fred Peters. She had been arrested along with him as they sat in a car parked outside a house while a friend of theirs, William Howell, sold drugs to an undercover agent inside. Hobson is testifying against Peters in return for immunity from prosecution.[21]

Jo Ann Harris, representing the government, conducts the direct exam:

Now did there come a time, Miss Hobson, when you moved in with Fred Peters and had an intimate relationship with him?
Yes.
And when was that?
When I was seventeen.
When you were a teenager, did you use drugs?
Yes.
When did you start using drugs?
After I moved in with Fred Peters.
And did you sell drugs?
Yes.
And when did you start selling drugs?
After I moved in with Fred Peters!

Did you know a man by the name of William Howell?

Yes.

And when did you first meet Mr. Howell?

About three years ago.

And when you sold drugs, who did you sell drugs for?

Fred Peters and William Howell. . . .

Were William Howell and Fred Peters arrested that early morning in Lyle, after you got out there?

Yes.

And were you arrested?

Yes.

Did the arresting officer ask you about what you knew about a drug deal that night?

Yes.

And what did you tell them at that time?

I denied knowing anything about it.

All right. Why didn't you tell him the truth, Laura?

Um, lots of reasons. I was scared. I was a drug user. I didn't know how to get out of a bad situation. I was worried about my friends.

All right. Did you change your mind later?

Yes.

What happened to cause you to change your mind?

Again, a lot of things. Um, I wanted to get these thugs out of my life. And I was also ordered to testify.

All right. Did you basically decide to change your lifestyle at that point?

Yes. Absolutely.

Have you taken any drugs since that night, Laura?

No. Nothing.

Do you know what would have happened to you after the judge ordered you to testify if you hadn't testified here today?

Yes.

What would have happened?

I would have been found in contempt of court and thrown in jail.

All right. What does the judge's order say about your testimony here today?

That what I say here cannot be used against me unless I lie, and if I lie, then what I say can be used against me, and perjury charges can also be brought against me.

Are ya tellin' the truth here today, Miss Hobson?
Yes, I am.
No further questions.

Jo Ann Harris discerns wholesomeness in Laura Hobson. "I was try-ing," Harris says, "to get very close to her." She gets close by the manner in which she cues Hobson's testimony. Study Harris's ways of putting her questions, and you can hear how she uses her voice to enact a relationship of trust. *When you were a teenager, did you use drugs? When did you start us-ing drugs? And did you sell drugs? When did you start selling drugs?* The rhyth-mic tempo, word repetition, and logical sequencing give a firm, reassuring scaffold for Hobson's answers.

Harris's switches between formal and informal address are signals. Her statement *All right. Why didn't you tell him the truth*—and then, after a de-liberate pause, *Laura?*—telegraphs itself as a crucial moment: the move to us-ing Laura Hobson's first name conveys support for the witness at the instant when she has to explain why she lied. The implicit message is that Harris un-derstands why, believes her, stands by her. Harris's next use of the first name—*Have you taken any drugs since that night, Laura?*—is again support-ive: it conveys trust that Hobson is going to answer truthfully and that after the trauma of rearrest she'd not take drugs again. With the final question— *Are ya tellin' the truth here today, Miss Hobson?*—the shift back to formal ad-dress is adroitly balanced by a shift into slang: Harris combines proper dis-tance with a glint of satisfaction at how credible her witness has been.

What is the gist of Jo Ann Harris's story? Laura was young when she moved in with Peters. He hooked her on drugs. She sold them for him, then for Howell. Busted and on probation, headed for hard time if con-victed again, she kept selling. Why? Regard her judgmentally and she's just as bad as they are. But Harris is working from different mythic coordinates. In her telling, Laura Hobson was vulnerable to being exploited because she lacked a sense of self-worth. She found a false security with Peters and Howell. Submerging herself in them and their world, she self-destructively did what they wanted. The arrest precipitated personal crisis. Forced to choose between protecting Peters and having a chance for her future, she finally acted for herself.

The fresh start: a great American dream. We saw Roger King argue, through a Christian lens, that a prosecution witness with a drug habit had found redemption. Here Laura Hobson's life is renewed through a lens of gender. From this perspective her plight has parallels with the situation of many women in this male-dominated society. It's a central insight of contemporary feminism (based on research by psychologist Carol Gilligan) that, as a result of deep-seated differences in social roles and psychological expectations for the two sexes, women go through a different trajectory of moral development than men. Jo Ann Harris invokes this gendered trajectory, this woman-centered plotline, by portraying Laura Hobson as a person at the threshhold of moral maturity. She was unformed before, not evil. Now she has broken through to personal autonomy, redeeming her potential to lead a good life.[22]

For this story to be convincing, Hobson has to cut a sympathetic figure. Harris explains the dynamic:

> Next to the witness's credibility in this courtroom, I think *my* credibility is the single most important thing going on. And if I have established a relationship with this jury that makes them believe that *I* am a credible person, then if I can get close to my witness and not distance myself, I think that my credibility—hopefully—will *wash* over the witness.

Jo Ann Harris trusts the witness. Yet not one among the seven other prosecutors who did direct examinations of Laura Hobson at the Festival—all of them men—got close to her. None of them even tried. One "decided to treat her like dirt," Harris observes, "and then to argue that Peters had chosen her because she *was* dirt, and that they all stuck together." Harris empathizes with the witness woman-to-woman. The male attorneys, skilled as they are, didn't reach out. They lacked feminist insight into her situation.

The most supportive attitude towards Hobson by a male prosecutor—courtliness—was shown by Patrick Williams. Williams, fifty-five, a lean six-foot-six, speaks strongly, with easy confidence:

> *Sometime after you had met Mr. Peters, did your relationship become a little more* dedicated, *as it were?*
> Yes, it did.
> *And would you describe for the court and jury what relationship developed between you and the defendant?*

Well, we were boyfriend and girlfriend, we'd lived together.
Did you have an intimate relationship with him over a period of time?
Yes, sir.
And how long did that obtain?
Two, three years.
Miss Hobson, I'll ask you, please, ma'am, have you ever used drugs?
Yes.
When did you first start usin' drugs?
When I was sixteen.
And how old were you when you met Fred Peters?
Sixteen.
Now having commenced to use drugs, tell the jury, please, what type of drugs you have used over the years.
Cocaine, amphetamines, hallucinogens, marijuana.
I'll ask you, please, ma'am, have you ever been convicted of any crimes against the laws of this state, the United States of America, or any other state?
Yes.
Tell the jury about that, please. When and where did that occur and for what offense?
It was in 1982 for possession of marijuana.

Williams is following standard trial practice: bring out on direct what damages your case, so "the sting won't come out with the defense lawyer." His solicitude may lessen the sting. *I'll ask you, please, ma'am,* bespeaks gentlemanly fastidiousness about her involvement in drug use; *a little more dedicated* and *how long did that obtain* are delicate, if tongue-in-cheek ways of broaching intimate matters. Where Jo Ann Harris wants to make the witness's life poignantly real, Williams prefers discretion. He implies that the defendant introduced her to drugs, but he doesn't push further, to portray her as a victim, or further yet, as a victim turning the tables on her victimizer. If jurors relate to Hobson as Williams relates to her, they will regard her in the traditional gendered role of a woman who, weak and deserving of protection, is less responsible for her crimes than the men who got her in trouble.

Williams's opponent, defending Fred Peters, is Penelope Cooper, who is as scathing with Hobson as Williams is circumspect. Cooper, from

Berkeley, California, is forty-seven years old, five-foot-seven, with a studious presence. Her voice has a slightly nasal quality, but it packs force:

> *Miss Hobson, is that your name?*
> Yes, that's right.
> *I noticed before when Mr. Williams was examining you, and he asked you to identify Mr. Peters, you weren't even hardly able to look him in the eye, were you?*
> I didn't want to.
> *You don't want to even look him in the eye, right?*
> Right.
> *Now I understand that your idea of this immunity agreement, ma'am, is that if you tell the truth, that you won't be prosecuted for the various charges, correct?*
> Yes, that's right.
> *And who will decide whether or not you're telling the truth?*
> I guess the prosecution.
> *And you're going to assist him in that?*
> No. I'm not assisting anybody.
> *Well, you already have a deal, do you not, that you're not going to be prosecuted on these charges, correct?*
> Yes, that's right.
> *Did you feel that you were guilty of these charges?*
> No.
> *You didn't feel that you were guilty of assisting in the conspiracy to distribute cocaine?*
> [*long pause*] I had something to with it, I guess.
> *Did you feel that you were guilty of a conspiracy to distribute cocaine?*
> > WILLIAMS: If the court please, I would object on the form of the
> > question, in that she's calling for a legal conclusion.
> > JUDGE: Overruled.
> *Could you answer the question, please?*
> Well at the time, no, I didn't feel guilty—
> *—You didn't feel guilty.*
> *You didn't think that the fact*
> *that you might have been holding somebody's cocaine,*
> *whether it was Howell's or Peters' or your own,*

didn't make you guilty *of this conspiracy,*
when in fact you drove it across town to distribute it to somebody.
Ya had it in your brassiere, is that correct?
Yes, that's right.
Close to your breasts?
Yes.
I see.
And it was just snuggled there waiting to make the final delivery?
Yes.
You had absolutely no *feeling*
at that time and place,
that you were guilty of assisting any kind of distribution, correct?
I had no feelings of guilt, no.
I didn't ask you if you had feelings of guilt. I asked you if you had any feel-
ings that you were guilty. *No.*
No.

> WILLIAMS: If the court please, I'm gonna object now. She's arguing
> with the witness. That's a distinction without a *difference* where I
> come from!

Pat Williams here tries an I'm-just-a-country-boy routine to deflect attention from Penny Cooper's point: that if Laura Hobson claims she didn't know
her behavior was illegal, she's a liar. Cooper's strategy "is to show that there is-
n't any kind of pattern in this woman's life, nothing that changed her pattern,
to show in any way that she would be telling the truth." The discrediting begins with the first question: *Miss Hobson, is that your name?* The words are dismissive: *you weren't even hardly able to look him in the eye, were you?* Implication:
your betrayal makes you ashamed. Cooper pursues Hobson with steel-trap
logic, gendered barbs, and wry humor. The comic image of the snuggled cocaine, taunting in its intimacy, is deliverable only by a woman. What Harris el-
evates to a young woman's crisis of character Cooper scorns as a young woman's
evasions. You held the drugs at your breast: you were a drug dealer body-and-
soul. Living the life gave you pleasure. I see through you. I expose you.

Like Jo Ann Harris, Penny Cooper has advantages as a woman questioning a woman. She can imaginatively enter the witness's psyche and, if
the witness is an adversary, undermine her without appearing unfair.
Cooper and Harris also benefit from another potential advantage for

women in this heavily male-dominated profession: the appearance of self-lessness. Cooper touched on this in an interview with her law partner Cristina Arguedas. Arguedas asked if she thinks "it is more difficult for a woman to project power in a courtroom than a man." Cooper said:

> I think that depends on one's definition of power. I think what one needs to display in a courtroom is preparation and assertive-ness, oftentimes just to get the judge's attention; but that can be done in a myriad of ways, and it can certainly be done with a quiet voice as well as with a loud voice.

Arguedas wondered how Cooper can "forcefully corner a cop during cross-examination without appearing shrill or bitchy or any of the female stereo-types?" Cooper replied:

> Again, you would be prepared and you should have a goal. During my very first trial, Judge Pulich told me, "Penny, always have a goal when you are examining," and I believe that that has really been one of the most important lessons that I have ever had because I think that if you always keep your mind on the goal, that it focuses you and the trier of the facts on the issues rather than the style of the examiner.[23]

Focusing on substance, Cooper believes, protects her from lethal gender prejudices. Substance is her strength: she is renowned among colleagues as an exacting reader of evidence and determined champion of principle.

But Cooper's preference for issues over style doesn't mean she's free of style. It means that her approach to performance isn't personality-centered. To stress issues and deflect attention from oneself is itself a matter of style, a style that seems particularly congenial to many women attorneys. The association in American society of egoistic traits with men and selfless traits with women can aid women in seizing the high ground of objectivity. The less a lawyer is saddled by ego, the more convincingly she can display dis-interestedness. Penny Cooper doesn't need height or loudness, flash or femininity to work identity to her advantage. She conveys authority through her purity of dedication to her client's cause.

R. Eugene Pincham, sixty years old, an Illinois appellate court judge, used to be a noted defense attorney in Chicago. He describes his style as "extremely intense": emotional, but masked by "levity." With resonant voice, abrasive and ironic tone, he subjects Laura Hobson to bullying cross-examination:

Now. Miss Hobson, you told this jury that you got immunity, right?
That's right.
And,
I take it that you are here
to testify
pursuant to your duties and obligations
of a law-abiding, God-fearing citizen,
that right?
That's correct.
You want to be here,
right?
No, that's not correct—
In fact—well!
[sudden double take at her last response]
Now which one is the jury supposed to believe?
I'm here as a law-abiding citizen, but I don't want to be.
All right. You're here pursuant to your duties *as a citizen.*
I was subpoenaed.
But you're here pursuant to your duties as a citizen.
[no response]
I didn't hear ya.
Yes, sir.
You're here because you want to clean up the community of that despicable
trade of narcotics, right?
I'm here because—
[cutting her off] *Did you hear what I asked you?*
I heard you.
You understand English?
[*faintly*] Very well.
Pardon me?
Very well.

I'm speaking the same language the prosecutor spoke, aren't I?
Uh-huh.
You didn't have any difficulty understanding him, did'ja?
No.
You don't have any difficulty understanding me, do ya?
No, sir.
I'll ask ya again:
You're here because you want to clean up the community because of the despicable trafficking in narcotics, right?
No, sir.

The question about *speaking the same language* has a racial subtext. Eugene Pincham is calling attention to pronounced African American inflections in his own voice, in contrast to the speech of the prosecutor he's been paired with, whom he teasingly refers to as "the all-American boy." He puts jurors on notice that Hobson, who is white, may be prejudiced—and is at the very least snotty. He signals that she's recalcitrant, that he's justified in handling her roughly. In the same vein Pincham makes sure the jury knows William Howell's background:

Black eyes, black hair?
That's right.
Black skin?
Right.
And a natural? Wore his hair straight up? Right?
Yes.

Pincham flaunts the authority of his cultural identity. How can Hobson answer his taunt that she's *law-abiding, God-fearing* and wants *to clean up the community of that despicable trade of narcotics?* What is moral about testifying to save your skin? Morality resides with him—in his imposing bearing and in his sardonic tone that makes the word *despicable* convey that, while the narcotics trade may mean making money and slumming and getting high to her, he has intimate knowledge of its terrible causes and consequences.

His technique, like Cecil Moore's, is to set up resistances in the witness and then break them down, leaving the impression that she is evasive and has to be forced to admit the obvious. He courts her dislike, makes it a mirror to her defective character. He knows jurors may feel he's browbeating her, but says, "It's just a risk you have to take." Race here neutralizes sympathy that could accrue to the witness on account of gender.

The Hobson "case" feeds into our hoary mythology of Beauty and the Beast.[24] Penny Cooper and Eugene Pincham can be seen as attacking the witness for failing to live up to the ideal of womanly innocence, while Pat Williams can be seen as affirming her in it. Even Jo Ann Harris, telling a woman's story about women's autonomy, doesn't mount a headlong challenge to the myth's gendered nature. Her Laura Hobson can be seen as a beauty—possessing beauty of an inner kind, achieved through hard effort.

This deference toward customary beliefs is entirely in keeping with lawyers' respectful personas. They can chide, even goad jurors, but they cannot openly confront jurors' fundamental values. Rarely can they be multicultural in a way that endorses separatist impulses. The emphasis must be on rootedness and cohesion, on a moral perspective that affirms that we-are-all-in-this-together and experience more or less the same world.

A Mix of Class, Gender, and Race

A civil case file: When Scott Freeman was a toddler he swallowed a marble that rolled out of the tray of Marble Mouth, a game his older brother was playing. Now age seven, he has learning and behavioral disorders resulting, his doctors say, from brain damage suffered when the marble lodged in his windpipe. His mother is suing Amerifun, the manufacturer of the game, on the grounds that the game is dangerous for the very young and should have contained a warning label. The corporation's position is that there's nothing wrong with the game and that the fault lies with the mother, who had left her children unattended to go on a job interview just before the mishap.[25]

John Shepherd, sixty years old, from St. Louis, a former president of the American Bar Association, is the civil defense attorney representing the game manufacturer. He calls his style "sophisticated folksy." Jurors, he says, feel if *he* understands the case, "it can't be so very complicated." Shepherd's manner, cross-examining the mother, is at once avuncular and probing:

> *Mrs. Freeman, I have just a few questions to ask you. Other than the time you were in court for a divorce, I guess, this is a new experience for you.*
> Yes.
> *Yes. And I think you said that your husband at the time, when Scotty was*

just, what, six months old, or about a year, did you say, your husband went off to California.

No, he went off to California somewhat after this incident.

Oh, he was here *at the time of the incident.*

Yes.

Yes. So that at that time, the decision to go to work, on your part, was to supplement the income that he *earned.*

No, he was not living with me. The income that he gave me, it wasn't enough.

Did you live at the same place where you live now, at the time?

Yes.

Yes. So the money he gave you at least didn't change that *part of your lifestyle. You stayed in the same home.*

Yes.

And he sends sufficient money, does he—we don't want to burden this on you—but he sends sufficient money for the children?

[*after a long pause*] We can *just* get by.

Just get by.

John Shepherd commiserates, hiding his intent: *Other than the time you were in court for a divorce, . . . this is a new experience for you.* Is he not considerate, putting an inexperienced witness at ease? The innocent question commences his probe into whether Carol Freeman needed money so badly that she was justified in putting her child's safety at risk. His uncertainty about her financial and marital status sows little doubts about her character. A waver in his repetition of her words *just get by* conveys that he's straining to understand her, but doesn't quite get it:

You decided that you would go to work, and this interview was an important thing to you.

Yes.

And you expected the babysitter to be there in five minutes, I think you said.

Right.

And the interview was important enough for you *that you didn't want to wait that five minutes.*

Well. I felt that this was just the kind of job that I had a good chance at. It was the first interview I'd been given. And I had been a math teacher

and this was with a computer company, and I thought that it would
have the kind of flexibility I wanted, to do part-time. And— [*pauses*]
Yeah. So you knew something about the company, evidently.
Well, they were willing to interview me. That was important.
*But you felt they weren't willing to wait five minutes while the babysitter
got there.*
[*agitated*] I had had difficulty getting an interview. I had no job history
for seven years.
I see.
And I had tried to get interviews and I hadn't been able to.
All right. At any rate, [brings both hands down decisively] *you felt that
this company—*
[*interrupting*] I felt if I was gonna call and say, "Can I be ten minutes
late?" that they would just be disposed to say, "This person's going to
present a problem. Don't bother even showing up."
Yeah. And those were the kind of people you wanted to work for.
Well, I felt that they would have a number of people that they could select
from and that they would be discouraged from hiring a single mother—
All right. I see. So—
[*breaking in to finish*]—that presented such problems, that couldn't
even get her act together to have a babysitter to come to an interview.

Shepherd has the posture of attentive listening—he often prefaces
questions by restating what the witness has just said. Yet her actions continue to baffle him. He makes disturbing inferences about them. This fuels her need to explain. Speaking haltingly, he leaves her an inviting wedge
of time to interrupt him, and then he indicates imperceptibly that she's being aggressive, cutting him off, but he, courteous and fair-minded, will let
her. As she tries to justify herself, she raises the specter of panic she might
have felt when faced with the prospect of being late for the job interview.
If she loses composure under his cool contemplation, what does that im-
ply about her judgment at home that day?

So you left the boys there with this game that uses marbles.
Yes.
*And had'ja ever in the eighteen months in any way told Billy, "Now, don't
let Scotty put things in his mouth?*
Yes.

Yeah. How recent to the day of this event?

Well, Billy was pretty good about trying to keep an eye on Scotty. I can't say.

You don't recall when you told him, but you know you'd told him on more than one occasion that he should watch his little brother because babies have a tendency to put things in their mouths.

Well, I felt that actually Scotty was outgrowing that, a little bit . . .

And did you need some company to put a piece of paper in the box to tell you,

now as an experienced mother,

"Remember that children put things in their mouth."

If they had put some warning like that on that game, I think I would have looked at the game differently. I just did not see the game as—

[*slight pause*]

Well, you know—

—a hazard.

—*I don't want to* quarrel *with you, but I think we have to get* this *straight: Is it your feeling* [picking up a marble from the Marble Mouth game] *that the company should put a piece of paper in there to tell an experienced mother that a marble might be put in the child's mouth?*

[pauses]

Is that your feeling?

Yes. I think it would have helped! I think it would have helped. Yes, because the game encourages it.

When did you get the game?

At Christmas.

And when did the accident happen?

In August.

And do you think that between Christmas and August you would have had that piece of paper there every time they got the box out to say, "Now wait, here, I want to read—"

[*interrupting*] No, if that had been on the box, then the game would not have been in my house. . .

So, you say when the game came at Christmastime, and you saw it was a marble game, you never told the children to be careful, and not let Scotty put that marble in his mouth.

No.

Never did!
And you looked at the marble, and you saw the children playing with it,
the thought never occurred to you, *did it, to say, "Don't put these marbles*
in your mouth, you may swallow one!"
Well, it was a game that Billy played with his friends—
Yes.
—and even though Scotty would be around when they were playing, it
was Billy's game.
But knowing that circumstance—
this is what I think *I'm trying to ask you—*
knowing that circumstance,
that an older boy and his friend playing with Scotty *sitting*
right there,
did it ever occur to you
to say, "Now be careful, don't let Scotty get these marbles
in his hand, he may put it in his mouth?"
[long pause]
We just need to know the answer, that's all.
Whether it hurts or helps. I'd just like to know.
No, it did not occur to me.
Never occurred to you.

Shepherd has here secured, he explains, a vital admission: Carol Freeman
worried about Scotty putting objects in his mouth, yet she never connected
the hazard to this particular game. Is that common sense? He brings out the
contradiction repeatedly, the last time (*But knowing that circumstance . . .*)
with rhythmic force. Then he patiently nudges her from silence toward confession—*We just need to know, whether it hurts or helps*—with fatherly objectivity. It was news to him, Shepherd says, that she'd never instructed her children about these marbles. The discovery is "like gold," and he got it "by
waiting, and pacing myself." He would make it "permeate the whole trial":

> If *she* had instructed the children and told them about how
> they have to be careful about it, then that relieves the corporation
> of responsibility, because certainly they couldn't do more than
> have a college-educated person talking to children of *her own* and
> giving them the *very warning* that the lawyers claim the corpora-
> tion should have furnished.

Her failure to warn will enable him to use her professional identity against her: "This is not your average mother who comes into court who had difficulty taking care of the child," he explains. "This is a college graduate, a math teacher. If *she* doesn't take the time to talk to her children—." And what if she *had* foreseen danger in the game? He would have logic ready-to-hand to play it that way, too. If she had warned Billy to make sure Scotty didn't touch the marbles, he would argue that "warning has nothing to do with this lawsuit because the children *were* warned as much as they could be by a company. That changes the case, because it forces the plaintiff then to say that the game should never have been built in the first place."

John Shepherd embraces the identity of an incipient elder, offering a lifetime of experience. Age for him is a camouflage. The affable gentleman who seems a bit slow, baffled by changing mores, conceals a dazzlingly nimble mind and an upper-class sensibility. The persona is a perfect foil for the role of inquisitor. It softens up witnesses and jurors, easing the way for him to appeal to the conservative voice of authority regarding social class and gender that we have internalized within us.[26] Shouldn't a mother put her child's welfare first? Shouldn't she be able to make do with limited means? Shouldn't she have waited to pursue her career until the child was old enough? However committed jurors might be to equality for women in the workplace, Shepherd asks them to be prudent, affirming of maternal responsibility. Because he outwardly sympathizes with the mother, his actual gaze can be pitiless.

Shepherd attacks the mother's moral character with an ethos rooted in class privilege. The strategy is effective because class (unlike race and gender) is seldom overtly acknowledged as a consequential mark of identity in American society. Class is attended to subliminally and for that very reason has special force. Our democratic ideals efface class differences. In our mythology, to be American is to be—or to be striving to become—middle class. But we are nonetheless anxious about our class position. Most of us tend at least sometimes to gaze uncomfortably upward, with a mixture of longing, envy, and self-doubt, at those above us in wealth and social rank. We may scoff at the pretensions of the rich, but they provoke our fantasies of freedom as well as our angst.[27]

Because of Shepherd's folksy personality, his judgmentalness comes across not as condescension but as middle-class common sense. Jurors, without consciously realizing it, respond to him deferentially, by identifying *up*.

Diana Marshall, thirty-seven, a civil defense attorney from Houston, makes no nod at sympathy when cross-examining Carol Freeman. Where Shepherd insinuates doubt gradually, she jumps out swinging. Her voice is vibrant, her speech a rich Texas vernacular, her tone harshly skeptical:

Ms. Freeman, you are askin' that this jury hold Amerifun accountable because, I believe you said, they failed to anticipate *that maybe Scotty would swallow a marble from a game, is that correct?*

I believe that the game was dangerous and it should have had a warning on it.

Okay. Let me ask ya if ya believe that Amerifun should have anticipated that Scotty would swallow a marble.

Not Scotty particularly—

Okay.

—but small children—

All right.

—might be led to imitate the game.

Okay, to swallow a marble. You think Amerifun should have thought that a small child might do that.

Yes.

Now, you were observing your own small child
                    play with that game
from approximately December of '79 until August of 1980, weren't you? Your child Billy. You did observe that, didn't you?

Yes, I did.

And certainly, if you had ever seen him do anything at all
                    that looked dangerous
                    with that game,
you would have taken that game and thrown it RIGHT OUT OF THE HOUSE, wouldn't you?

Yes, I would.

And you NEVER saw that then, did you?

No, I did not.

All right. And you know from the testimony that you've heard here that Amerifun observed dozens of children playing with this game before they put it on the market, didn't you hear that?

Yes, I did.

Okay. Now Ms. Freeman, you didn't believe that Scotty might swallow a marble, did you?

It did not occur to me.

If it had occurred to YOU,
    as a caring mother,
    and an observant mother,
    and an experienced mother—
        if it had occurred to you
        with all of that experience and caring
            you wouldn't have left the game out, would you?

No, I wouldn't.

And if you hadn't left the game out, this incident wouldn't have happened, would it?

Not that time.

Now Ms. Freeman, you ask that Amerifun be held accountable for not anticipating that Scotty would swallow a marble, but not you.

If I had known the game was dangerous, I would not have had it in the house.

You didn't know.

No, I didn't know.

Well, isn't it true that just a couple of months before this incident, where Scotty picked up a marble that rolled away from a game while you were out of the house, it's true that he picked up a DIME and swallowed it, didn't he?

Yes, he did.

Where did he find that dime?

It was—

In the house.

In the house, yes. I think it was in one of the chairs.

Now you don't have some toy that has a
        dime-
        eating
        aspect to it, do ya?

Diana Marshall doesn't try to be understanding, and adopts none of Shepherd's I-hate-to-subject-you-to-this pose. Incredulity shines through. To parody Carol Freeman as *caring, observant, experienced* is to ridicule her mothering. To imagine a toy with *a dime-eating aspect* is to make the lawsuit ludicrous.

Why can Marshall dispense with delicacy? "I think that I would be less offensive questioning the mother's conduct than perhaps a male would," she says. "I would have a substantial advantage because I wouldn't be bullying in the eyes of the jury, even if I were bullying." The cover Shepherd gets by being an old duffer Diana Marshall gets by playing on her youthful womanliness.

Marshall is unusual among women attorneys in the degree to which she infuses gender in her style. She wears colorful dresses in court. (Penny Cooper favors pants and jackets; Jo Ann Harris, skirts and blouses.) She has wavy red hair and the charm, a colleague says, of "a southern belle." Marshall alludes to the regional working-class roots of her persona when she describes Texas-style voir dire:

> With Ms. Meyers [*a prospective juror*], I would have said [*cooing*]: "And what are the names of your little children? Did you name them after your uncle or your husband? And I LOVE your dress! Yellow is your color!"
>
> It really gets terribly, terribly personal and down home. They come to the courthouse *to visit*. In the country areas, especially in Texas. They come there, they bring their lunch. They are comin' there for the *day* to have a good time, and you are supposed to visit with *them* or they'll *do you in* later.
>
> And if you're the out-of-town lawyer, representing the big *company*, and you're *unfriendly*, and you're *not* wearing a dress that looks like you bought it there locally, you're gonna lose! They'll put it on the radio that night! GUESS WHO'S GONNA PAY TOMORROW, BROTHERS?

Diana Marshall grew up in Odessa, Texas. Her father was an oil-field worker who became disabled. "We wound down to poor, and I got ambitious," she recalls. As a teenager she was a typist at local law firms. After working her way through law school, she was hired by Baker & Botts, a large, prestigious Houston firm, where she became one of two women partners.

When a *Time* reporter asked her about the prospects for women in law, she said, "The men are starting to worry about being run over by hordes of ambitious young women, and the woman who tells me she is not afraid of discrimination is too stupid for me to hire." The reporter then asked if male lawyers underestimated her. She replied: "It happens constantly. And I'll admit, I've won a few cases by planting the notion that little old me wouldn't really take a case all the way to trial, without settling first. I'd spend all weekend preparing for trial while my opponent goes to the golf course."[28]

Marshall seems the antithesis of the out-of-town lawyer representing a big corporation. What many jurors see is a smart, beautiful, sassy country girl who's made it in the big city. Her old-fashioned femininity endears her to them. Look how she brandishes it, nonverbally, when she queries a panel of prospective jurors during voir dire in the Freeman case:

> Now I'm gonna be a little bit embarrassed, frankly, to be questioning Mrs. Freeman about her being a bad mother [*shaking her head no as if she doesn't really mean "bad mother," while smiling as if maybe she does*]—I'm not trying to suggest that [*nodding her head in understanding*]: Anybody can make a mistake. And we're going to be havin' to prove that Mrs. Freeman did, and it is not a pleasant task.
>
> And I'm gonna ask you: will you hold it against me, or my client, 'cause I'm having to [*smiles*] accuse this person or question this person's conduct, over something that [*frowns*] I'm sure is a sad and regretful moment in her life. And one which *I* do not choose for her to relive, but I didn't bring this suit.
>
> Now I'm not gonna be able to walk on eggshells about that, and I need to know about it, if it's gonna make you [*a quiver in her voice*] mad at me, for—kinda reminding this lady of what we say she did wrong that day.

Just after her voice catches, in the brief pause between *for* and *kinda*, Marshall purses her lips together tightly and protrudes them in a pout, as if she were at the edge of tears. This conventionalized feminine gesture caps a stretch of talk in which she's oscillated with dizzying speed between condemnation and compassion for the mother. The pout, I think, invites jurors to resolve ambivalent feelings about the mother by identifying with *her*. Marshall offers herself as the heroine, compelled to confront the mother with her failure of care. She asks the jurors' blessing for doing this, in language that takes them into her confidence, welcomes them as friends.

She works the same magic late in the "trial," in her closing argument. William Wilson, the plaintiff's attorney representing the Freemans in this match-up, has claimed that Marshall is saying, "Don't give them anything because of sympathy." He has argued that the Freemans don't want sympathy, they want justice. Marshall replies:

> Yes, indeed, we have been harpin' a little bit on sympathy. I plead guilty to that and that alone.
>
> But'cha know why?
>
> Representin' a big company is kinda scary.
>
> And I'm scared to death about what you'll do about it. I'm sorry. I don't know you well enough to say that I trust ya completely. To leave sympathy right out here where it belongs. If I knew ya better I probably wouldn't be so scared.
>
> But representin' a big company—well, it's not that big, we're not IBM—but, y'know, we're not an individual, either. And we can't come in here and have anything on our side that might automatically be some sort of an emotional appeal to you.
>
> [*warmly*] But we *know* ya have feelings. We know ya that well.
>
> And ladies and gentlemen, sympathy is the only thing I'm afraid of. Because that's the only thought that you can have that might push you toward turning this misfortune into the fortune that Mr. Wilson has asked you for here today.

It's not about sympathy for the family, Marshall tells jurors as she plays on their empathy for her. At the very moment when the logic of her argument would seem to dictate that she warn them to keep feelings out of their deliberations, she lauds them for *having* feelings, implying that they will feel as she feels if they've gotten to know her well enough. Substituting her womanly vulnerability and folksy background for the corporation's policies, her spirited presence for its impersonality, she deflects suspicions that management is unfeeling about children's safety. She imbues the company with her charm.

Diana Marshall's use of identity enables her to establish an unusually personal relationship with the jurors and also to act unusually boldly in her clients' defense. For instance, there was evidence in the Freeman case file that gave a basis for arguing that the marble had *not* caused permanent brain damage and that Scotty's learning problems were independent of the accident. All the male attorneys were reluctant to make much of this angle. But Marshall trumpeted it. "Boy, there are a lot of kids here today who would like to have twenty thousand dollars for saying, 'I don't like to go to school!'" she says in her summation. When Scotty returned from the hospital after the accident, she went on, he was "a happy, healthy, wonderful little child":

> She [*Carol Freeman*] says she did nothing but leave
>   and hope for the best.
> Well, ladies and gentlemen, I want to conclude with suggesting to you that the best *did* happen.
> Very, very fortunately, on August third, 1980,
> when Mrs. Freeman had a lapse in her motherly duties,
> and when her instincts didn't prompt her to do everything she should have done, that day,
>   on that day, when Scott Freeman had that close call,
>   there's a happy, happy ending.
> Mrs. Freeman's conduct didn't turn out to be all that bad after all.
> And I think we should leave it right there.
> Mrs. Freeman's conduct resulted in a lesson to her—not a lesson Amerifun needed to learn, as Mr. Wilson suggests to you—but a lesson to her.

By *leaving it right there* Marshall signals she has the tact not to openly call Carol Freeman a liar. It's kinder to let her save face. By claiming that Scotty got through the accident with faculties unimpaired, Marshall dares debunk the tragic definition of the situation. The lawsuit's a sham. She can be this vitriolic because she comes across savvy and sweet.

While civil defense attorneys in the *Freeman v. Amerifun* "case" cross-examined Carol Freeman, plaintiff's lawyers crossed Martin Nelson, the corporation's head of toy production. All but one of the plaintiff's lawyers vented moral indignation in the course of their questioning. The exception, the one who showed no personal animosity, was James Ferguson, a forty-three-year-old African American from Charlotte, North Carolina.

Facing Martin Nelson, Ferguson speaks fluidly, spontaneously, without a single glitch:

> *Mr. Nelson, did I understand you to say that* you *are the one principally responsible for the* design *of this game called Marble Mouth?*
> Yes, sir, that's correct.
> *You got that idea, didn't you, from* another *game which was similar, which had animals eating the marbles, isn't that right?*
> We did have a competitor that had a game similar to that, correct.
> *Yes. And what you wanted to do was to design and develop a game for* your *company that would sell at a greater rate than the game using the animals, isn't that correct?*
> I would have hoped that would happen, that's right.
> *You wanted a game that would be* attractive *to children, didn't you?*
> Yes, sir, for certain age groups.
> *For certain age groups. And you wanted it to be attractive for whatever children were going to play with that game, didn't you?*
> That's correct.
> *And from that idea with the animals consuming objects from a game, you decided that* children *might be* more *attracted to a game that used*
>   people
>   *eating marbles,*
>   *isn't that correct?*
> I would have to say I disagree with that.
> *Well, you designed the game, I believe you told us, didn't you?*
> Yes, sir.
> *Is this the game that you designed here, that's resting on counsel table?*
> Yes, sir.
> *And you have marbles in the middle here, do ya not?*
> Yes, sir.
> *Now, is this object shown here at this end of the game, would you call that a person?*
> I would call that a caricature of a person.
> *A caricature of a person. But it represents a person, doesn't it?*
> Yes, sir.
> *Now what is that person to* do *in this game, Mr. Nelson?*
> The object is to eat the marbles.
> *That person is to*

eat
          a marble, isn't that correct?

Yes, sir.

NOW we have something here at the opposite end of the game,
          do we not?

That looks to me like a person.

What does it look like to you, Mr. Nelson?

A caricature of a person.

A caricature of a person. That represents a person, does it not?

Yes, sir.

And that person is to
          eat a marble in this game, isn't that right?

That's the intention of the game. That's how you win.

Yes. You win by eating marbles, is that correct?

Yes, sir.

And the more you eat,
          the more you win,
                    is that correct?

That's the objective.

Now the caricature *of the person that you have on this end is not* just *a* person,
          it's a little *person, isn't it?*

I would say it's a small person.

Could we agree that it's a child?

A caricature of a child, yes, sir.

A caricature of a child, representing
                    a child?

Yes, sir.

And what is that child
          doing, *Mr. Nelson,*
                    without the marbles in its mouth?

I would say that the child has the mouth open, the tongue out.

Well, let's talk about the expression on that child's face.

It looks like they're having a good time.

It looks like the child is
                    smiling,
                              isn't that correct?

Yes, sir.

The child is smiling, ready to receive a marble, isn't that correct?

Yes, sir.

Now let's put a marble in the child's mouth and see what reaction we get from the child.

          [Ferguson pops one in.]

Is the child still smiling?

Yes, sir.

So your game
       demonstrates to children that
              putting marbles in the mouth of a child
                    can be a happy event,
                           isn't that correct, Mr. Nelson?

Do I have to answer that?

You don't have to answer that, Mr. Nelson.

What a clobbering! James Ferguson carves two juicy openings out of the witness's answers. First, when Nelson disagrees with his assertion that *you decided that children might be more attracted to a game that used people eating marbles,* the denial gives Ferguson a reason to drag out the most elementary facts: *You designed the game? Is this the game? You have marbles in the middle? This object at the end, would you call that a person?* All this focuses the audience's visual attention on the game. Then Nelson commits his second—his fatal—mistake, calling the object *a caricature of a person.* It was plain then, Ferguson says, "that this was a witness that was going to weasel around and not give it to you straight. Rather than argue with him about whether it was a caricature or not, I simply picked up his term, 'a caricature,' and showed that even in his own terms he had to know what this game was: a smiling child taking marbles, and he can't get away from that."

Ferguson proceeds to lead Nelson on an inspection tour of his own toy. The faces of persons become faces of children. The children are smiling. The smiling faces swallow marbles. The swallowing is a happy event. Each step in this funnel-like progression exposes more of the game's audacious logic. We feel its hypnotic appeal for children, feel what it looks like through toddlers' eyes. The recognition electrifies.

Ferguson brings off the attack without being irate or indignant. There's no trace of scorn in his voice as he inverts the word *caricature,* no smugness or reproach when he says, *You don't have to answer that, Mr. Nelson.* The tone is almost sweet. Emotional triggers would derail his intention. What James Ferguson displays is enjoyment, pure inquisitiveness about the nature of this toy and the character of this witness. Both for him are objects of ironic wonderment.

We will consider sources of Ferguson's authority shortly. First, let's turn to closing arguments in *Freeman v. Amerifun* pitting Lorna Propes, from Chicago, for the plaintiff, against Ralph Lancaster, Jr., of Portland, Maine, for the defense.

Propes, forty-one, sees her manner as "very straightforward, very businesslike." Wearing a stylish dress, she speaks with persistent intensity, her voice high and strong:

> Mrs. Freeman, Mr. Lancaster, ladies and gentlemen of the jury:
> The case you've heard is about a boy who was injured and damaged for life by the recklessness of a corporation. There are mainly *two* questions that you will have to answer in your deliberations.
> The first one is: did Amerifun design the game Marble Mouth in a way so that it is an unreasonably dangerous game?
> The second question is: was the corporation Amerifun *negligent* when they failed to warn the consumer, Mrs. Freeman, among others, that the game was dangerous or could be dangerous for small children?

Lorna Propes has begun by delineating her story in clear, logical terms. She turns folksy for a second—"Now, I'm going to visit with you folks for a while about the evidence that I believe shows that those issues should be decided in our way"—and then plunges into the matter of the mother's conduct, thinking to herself, "I want to get past that as fast as I can":

> But first I want to talk with you for *one* moment about what you will not have to decide.
> You will *not* have to decide if Carol Freeman was a bad mom.
> You will *not* have to decide if SHE was negligent in anything she did.
> You will NEVER hear Judge MacNamara tell you that part

of your duty is to evaluate her conduct or the quality of her behavior or what she did on that day at all.

Because it's not an issue in this case.

And the reason it's not an issue in this case you don't need the
law to tell you, ladies and gentlemen. You have your common
sense. You know that she is not a party here. This is between Scott
Freeman and the Amerifun Company. It is Scott Freeman that was
injured, not his mother.

And it is the question of what Amerifun did when they designed this toy that comes before you.

Invoking *your common sense,* she is sidestepping the fact that the law doesn't
specify how to weigh Carol Freeman's behavior. The phrase *comes before you*
legitimizes Propes's version of events, giving it a legal veneer. Quickly, she
moves to change weakness into strength:

> Now, ladies and gentlemen, you may say, "Well, then, why is
> it that we've *heard so much* throughout this trial about what Mrs.
> Freeman did?"
>
> And I submit to you that the reason why you've heard so much
> about what Mrs. Freeman did is because
>
> this game
> is so very
> very
> hard to defend.

This breaking into rhythm marks the beginning of her offensive against
Amerifun. With rhythmic emphasis she reviews the evil behavior of The
Greedy Corporation:

> Let's take a look for a moment at what the corporation did.
>
> What did the corporation do?
>
> First, they designed the game. They made up the idea. You
> heard Mr. Nelson testify. It was *his* idea and the corporation's idea
> to design a game that had as its principal goal
>
> the *stuffing*
> of marbles
> in the mouth
> of a *child.*

Amerifun didn't decide to make these faces animal faces or just some sort of design or a cube with different shapes or any of the other things they could have done.

Amerifun

　　　　decided to make them the face
　　　　of a little boy
　　　　and a little girl.

And Amerifun decided that the nature of what you'd do in this game is to stuff the marbles repeatedly in the little mouths.

And so, when Amerifun made that decision, and marketed that game, they introduced that game into the *households* of America. Where there were children—not just children ages four to eight but children of all ages.

It is as if

　　　　when you listen to the defense
　　　　in the *Amerifun* American family
　　　　there are only children ages four to eight.

And then in some other homes are the children two and one and eighteen months like little Scotty Freeman. . . .

Taking as her refrain *that's not all the corporation did,* Propes ticks off a string of negligent actions: they failed to incorporate safety features that would prevent the marbles from falling out of the well; they failed to test the toy with children under the age of four; they failed to put a warning label on the box. Propes puts the most damaging evidence last:

> But, that's not all the corporation did. Because the corporation did find out this game was dangerous, didn't they? They did find out.
>
> How did they find out?
>
> Well, first there was that mom from Athens, Georgia, remember, who wrote to the corporation and said, "My little two-year-old child choked on a marble from that game!"
>
> And that mom, that mom who took the time to write that letter, because she thought it was important, that mom said to the corporation, "Why don't you advise *all* the parents that the little kids can imitate this game and they might choke or hurt themselves?"

What did they do?

What did they do?

They wrote back a letter to that woman from a fictitious person, some person that doesn't exist, and they just blew it off. They told her [*Propes's voice turns cynical*]: "Keep enjoying the game, lady, it's intended for children four to eight."

Consider the terms she chooses. *Mom:* as a woman, Propes has rights to use this informality to create a bond with mothers she doesn't know. *Lady:* she delivers the word as an epithet, with a male sneer. Lorna Propes is building to a climax where the subject of the lawsuit is no longer Scotty Freeman but mothers' protective love:

And did they do anything? Did they take action on her suggestion? Of course not.

And then they found out

—here her tone conveys amazement and outrage—

that a child *died,*
that a child had
died
after swallowing one of these marbles,
a little two-year-old child.

And what did they do?

What did they do?

They said, "Don't worry about it."

[*softly*] "It's no problem."

Well, of course it's no problem to *them.* Because, I guess, the game was successful, and it was making millions of dollars.

Ladies and gentlemen, then they found out another little child had died. And still they didn't do any of the things they could have done: recall the game, make a public announcement of a warning, put a warning on the box. They did none of that.

And it was after that time that the Marble Mouth game found its way into the Freeman home.

And it was nine months later

> that little Scotty Freeman
> put the marble in his mouth
> and choked on it
> and was injured.

Amerifun's love of money culminates in Scotty's tragedy. Propes challenges her adversary to address *this* story, and warns the jury that he'll try to evade it:

> Now, ladies and gentlemen, Mr. Lancaster will have a chance to talk to you now, and he's going to talk to you, I think, about what Mrs. Freeman did.
> And I want you to ask *one* question when he's talking to you:
> What did the corporation do?
> What did the corporation do?
> Because that's the issue in this case, ladies and gentlemen.

Ralph Lancaster comments on Propes's strategy: "A good, effective plaintiff's trial lawyer wants to leave it on a high note. You don't want to pick that up, because if you're sustaining that level you're going to be right *with her.* You want a transition period." He is fifty-five, tall and thin, with a speaking manner that's measured, comforting, low-key:

> May it please the court, ladies and gentlemen of the jury:
> You have been very patient throughout the week that we've been here in this hot courtroom, and I want to ask you to bear with me for just a few minutes longer as I try to respond to Ms. Propes's excellent argument, and try to get us back on the track as to what the facts here really are.

Like Boyce Holleman with Tony Serra, Ralph Lancaster is starting by lauding his adversary's ability while dismissing her story. But he does it in a contemplative mood, as if wishing to engage her in collegial dialogue:

> She began by suggesting to you what the case was not about. And I would like to follow that example. Because I think it's awfully important that you realize what the case is not about.

The case is not about sympathy, and the case is not about giving money away.

She's going to have an opportunity to speak to you when I'm finished, and I'm going to ask her to tell you that she agrees with me, that this is not a case in which you should make your decision based upon sympathy, but upon the facts in the case. And if she doesn't tell you that—or whether she does or doesn't—the judge is going to tell you that when he charges.

Because if sympathy controlled
we wouldn't be here.
And if sympathy controlled
we wouldn't have justice in this country.
Justice, as you've seen her, is blind. She has scales.

The reason she's blind is because every single person in this country comes to court *equal*. And I don't care what his color is or his religion is or whether he's a corporation or an individual, whether he's a single mother or a child—you come sworn, sworn before God and your fellow jurors, to find the truth. . . .

The mix of pronouns has subliminal value. Justice is *she:* Lancaster allies himself with women. The single mother is downgraded to *he.* The corporation is humanized as *he.* Lancaster is signaling his support for American ideals of equality—and then stretching the democratic credo to treat Amerifun as though it were a person.

Now I disagree with Ms. Propes on one issue alone, maybe more, but certainly on one; and the judge will give you the law, as to whether what Mrs. Freeman herself did is relevant here.

And the principal reason I disagree with her is that your job is to find out what caused this accident.

No one wanted this to happen. No one set out to have Scotty swallow a marble and choke. What caused the accident?

And what Ms. Propes would have you do is forget Mrs. Freeman played any role in this at all.

What she would have you do is say, "Don't pay any attention to all of the unfortunate facts that surrounded this accident."

Well, that's not what the case is all about. That's not what your job is, and frankly, that's not what her job is.

Our job, as officers of the court, is to tell you, in way of summation, what these facts are, and to ask you to draw certain conclusions from them. And now I'm going to try to refresh your recollection as to what those facts were.

The subtle implication: Propes is exploiting the fact that she and the mother are women. She is manipulative, he's saying, while he is dispassionate. In impartial tones he recounts the story of The Irresponsible Mother:

The morning of August three, 1980, Mrs. Freeman, the mother of two children, one seven—Billy—and one eighteen months—Scott—had an appointment for a job interview. She was separated from her husband at that time. She was anxious about the job interview.

The interview was scheduled at twelve o'clock.

She had made an appointment with a babysitter to come at eleven-thirty, even though she knew that under the best conditions it would take her twenty-five minutes to get to where the interview was going to be held.

I asked her, and you heard me ask her, and you heard her answer, "Why did you have a babysitter?" And her answer was very simple and straightforward. Her answer was "because these were small children and they shouldn't be unsupervised."

Point one. That's what she said! I mean I didn't put those words in her mouth.

He's discrediting the witness with her words, her rationality.

Let me digress for a moment. There's an undercurrent here, that you have to pick up, that's awfully important to this case. And the undercurrent is called common sense.

When you walked into this courtroom, and when you took your oath, you didn't leave your common sense upstairs in the jury room with your hats and your coats. You brought it with you.

Did I have to ask her the question? I mean, is there anyone in this courtroom or in this United States or in the world who doesn't understand that two seven-year-olds playing a game, and an eighteen-month-old particularly, need some supervision? You *just don't walk away* and leave them. I don't care what your needs are, unless the house is burning down or something—you just don't do that. . . .

Common sense is what *he* exudes. He is transfering it from himself to his story, denying it to the mother and Propes.

Ms. Propes says to you [*sternly*]: *This case is not about whether Mrs. Freeman is a BAD mother!*
I agree.
I'm not trying to say Mrs. Freeman is a bad mother.
The question is not evil intent on either side.
The question is negligence, pure and simple.
Negligence is simply the failure to do something that you *should* do. And God help us, we're all human. And God help us, we're all negligent, and we make mistakes. Some are more serious than others, and unfortunately, Mrs. Freeman has to live with hers.
And I want to say to you, please, please, when you go out there, don't say, "How can we
            find
            against that little baby,
            and how can we find
            against that woman,
            because if we do,
            we're going to be hurting her."
That's not the test!
I think she's hurt enough. I really do. And I'm not trying to hurt her any more. But we all live with what we did, and in this case what she did was walk off and leave her children. . . .

Here Lancaster, close to the emotional peak of his speech, is showing himself to be a caring man. He is modeling for jurors how to reject Carol Freeman's case without denying her suffering. They need only affirm the truth of human frailty in God's world.

Suppose we had put, as Ms. Propes suggests, a warning that said, "This game may be dangerous for little children." What would [Mrs. Freeman] have said? "Dangerous? What is there dangerous about that?"

Now by a lot of thinking she might have come to the conclusion, "Oh, I know what's dangerous—if a marble goes in the baby's mouth, he may swallow it." Did we *really* have to tell her that?

I mean, the law *really* doesn't say ya have to do things that are kinda strange.

You're going to ask yourselves, "Yes, but wait a minute now. You got a letter that told you that a small child had swallowed a marble and choked."

The record, as you know, is that we had sold two million of these games,

  two million of these games,

          out across the country.

This is a very litigious society. In case you don't know it, people sue at the drop of a hat.

Are you naive enough to believe that if this game was as bad as people say it is, and people were choking all over the country out there, that we wouldn't have heard from them?

He is appealing to common sense to negate the fact that a *few* children choked.

In fact, let me ask you this question: Is there a mother on the face of the earth who cares about her child who hasn't at one point or another said to that child, "Don't put things in your mouth"?

Is there one mother anywhere who hasn't at one time or another had to pull a child away from something and pull something out of that child's mouth?

If your answer is no, then you haven't raised a child.

I have six, I know.

I've been through this process. And I think Ms. Propes knows.

And I think, in her heart of hearts, Mrs. Freeman knows.

This is a tricky move, for who could deny that children put things in their mouths? Lancaster is making it sound as if Propes and Freeman might well

deny it—that's how irrational their lawsuit is. Having invoked *his* authority as a parent, he concludes by probing Carol Freeman's motivation as a
parent:

> And I think that one of the reasons that we're here is because
> this is one way that she is attempting to assuage her guilt.
> I'm *sorry* to have to say that. But I have to say it because the
> facts are the facts. In plain, simple language, this thing happened
> because children *will* put things in their mouths, and because, in
> fact, she wasn't there, and there was no one there to take care of
> that child, except two little kids who were busily engaged in play-
> ing a game.

To claim *the facts are the facts* is a slippery note to end on, since there's no
proof that guilt is what's driving the mother. But Lancaster can get away
with it because he comes across as such an eminently reasonable man.
    Lorna Propes begins her rebuttal by displaying indignation about this
last tactic:

> Now ladies and gentlemen, I don't know what to say about
> Mr. Lancaster's allegations that Mrs. Freeman has brought this case
> to you to assuage her guilt. I can't answer that, because I couldn't
> answer it from the evidence. Since that allegation isn't in the evi-
> dence, and since that charge [*angrily*] was never even *put* to her on
> cross-examination . . .

Then, for the first time, she speaks openly from the authority of her own
experience as a mother:

> But I'll say this to ya, ladies and gentlemen: I *am* a mother.
> And I know from jury selection that many of you are mothers.
> *Find* me the mother
>   who hasn't turned her back on her children for three minutes,
>   find her for me.
> *Find* me the mother that hasn't gone to the *bathroom*,
>   that hasn't gone out to the yard to do some weeding,
>   that hasn't been making the beds,

that hasn't just even maybe looked at the soap operas
for a few minutes
> long enough
> for a little baby to pick up a marble and put
it in its mouth.

So that's not the issue.

It wouldn't have changed a *thing* if Mrs. Freeman had been
there.

She is speaking passionately on behalf of mothers across America. And that
prepares the way to climax her rebuttal with a shocking analogy:

> And I'd like to talk to you . . . about this notion that a child
> will put a marble in his mouth. Everyone knows that. Ladies and
> gentlemen, this isn't about a marble! It's about a game that *instructs*
> a child to put marbles in their mouths. And I've said that before,
> but it's so very important that you recall it.
>
> And Mr. Lancaster says, "Well, warnings, everybody knows
> marbles are dangerous." True. And everybody knows medicine is
> dangerous for children. But still those medicine bottles have a
> childproof cap. And they bear a warning that says, "Keep this and
> all medicine out of the reach of children."
>
> And we all know rat poison is dangerous. But what if the rat
> poison company, instead of putting the skull-and-crossbones on
> the bottle, put a picture of a little freckle-faced kid drinking the
> bottle of rat poison?
>
> *What about* that?

Gender stereotypes shape both lawyers' calculations as they frame their
stories. Lorna Propes sums up Ralph Lancaster's strategy by saying he

> wants the jury to think, "My God, this woman's hysterical!
> Don't listen to her, she's out of her mind!" If he can do that and
> come off as the *reasonable* type, the fatherly, logical, sensible type,
> that can be devastating to me. It's a big problem to think that the
> other side might appear more studied and thoughtful just because
> they weren't so excited.

Propes has a dilemma. The plaintiff's side in civil suits typically appeals viscerally to feeling, the defense side viscerally to rationality. Lancaster, with his imperturbable calm, is jockeying to turn her expression of emotion against her, to reframe it as emotionalism, to trigger gender in his favor. He wants her intensity to appear shrill. If he succeeds, she and Freeman will look frantic and scheming, a pair of gold diggers.

Propes's position is thus the opposite of Diana Marshall's, whose lavishness with emotion uplifts her corporate client. It is also riskier than the position of the male plaintiff's attorneys who did this demonstration. They felt free to show their emotions. Propes had to be sparing with hers. This need to negotiate one's identity in light of social expectations about gender—to appear strong but not overly aggressive, compassionate but not soft or unstable—is a special burden for women lawyers in trials, where toughness in combat, a male stereotype, reigns.[29]

Lorna Propes finds *her* balance by embedding flashes of moral indignation and assertions of womanly knowledge in a firm, rational stance. Before becoming a lawyer she was a high school history teacher and guidance counselor. The roles of educator and advisor have carried into her courtroom style. She's been cited in a poll by judges as Chicago's best criminal defense lawyer in cases "involving the particularly delicate handling of witnesses, such as an incest, child abuse, or rape." The poll singled out a trial in which she won acquittal for two African American men charged with the gang rape of a pregnant woman who was white. "The defense was that the woman consented, but asserting it required great sensitivity because at the time of the trial the alleged victim was again pregnant."[30] The words "great sensitivity" are, I think, a coded reference to a way of relating much more identified with women than men in American society: one that responds to others as whole persons, regarding them for their own sake rather than instrumentally. Propes doesn't have to stretch far for this effect. She engages, she says, in no "conscious manipulation" of her identity. "It simply never occurs to me, 'Shall I do things differently because I'm a woman?'" Lawyers "who are really good *are* themselves," she believes. Strength as a performer, for her, lies in faithfulness to expressive habits of her everyday life.

Ralph Lancaster is praised by colleagues for his emotional capabilities as well as his technical mastery. He varies his style, he says, "depend[ing] on the case and the circumstances and the lawyer on the other side." This range in repertoire is connected to class position. Raised in Bangor, Maine and a graduate of Harvard Law School, he possesses cultural advantages of both places. He exudes moderation and good judgment, locally prized virtues that make his cosmopolitanism seem homegrown. At the same time he has the mystique of membership in the elite.

As we saw with John Shepherd, social status, when signaled without calling attention to itself, provokes deference. Civil attorneys who defend corporations must be skilled at manipulating this class anxiety. They may, like Ralph Lancaster, offer the jury imaginative identification with the upper-class background into which they were born, or, like Diana Marshall, with the class position they have achieved. In this potent strain of American mythology, people get exactly what they are entitled to in the wealth and status sweepstakes. Class *is* character.

Lancaster's refinement and deportment signify worthiness of character. His elite persona naturalizes the behavior of his clients. Trusting him, jurors accept by extension that things are what they are for valid reasons. An emissary of order, he makes the world look just.

Now let's return to James Ferguson and his summation in the Freeman "case." If attorneys defending corporate America ennoble the mystery of class relations, plaintiff's lawyers expose them. Propes does it by a frontal attack against the corporation's pretense of being a moral actor. But Ferguson, just as he did in cross-examining Martin Nelson, stakes his ground on broader principle and takes the high road to jurors' emotions:

> We have to think about what Scotty Freeman is going through, and we have to think about it beyond just Scotty Freeman.
>
> What we're talking about is how do we as a society protect and take care for our children.
>
> Every civilized society that there has ever been that has survived has had a very healthy and determined and sincere concern for children.
>
> Back in ancient Greece, Socrates spent all of his time going around teaching the youth of the city because he knew that the future of Greece depended upon the mental and physical and intellectual health of the youth. And Jesus said, "Suffer the little children to come unto me." Kahlil Gibran said that the Prophet told us that "your children are not your children. They are the sons and daughters of life's longing for itself."

Did we see any such attitude on the part of Amerifun in taking care of the children?

Amerifun's attitude, which they want you to adopt in this courtroom today, was an attitude of callousness, and coldness and heartlessness when it came to injuries to children.

You'll remember when Mr. Nelson, their manager of product development, took the stand, and we asked him about Amerifun's attempts to avoid injury, and he talked about how important safety was to them, but then he had to come back to the reality of a memo that he had written, and to which he had gotten a response from the vice-president of Amerifun. In that memo that Mr. Nelson wrote to Tom Johnson, the vice-president, he said, "I recently learned that a two-year-old child in Florida choked on a marble from Marble Mouth and died. Do we have a problem here?" And the vice-president of that company wrote him back in his own handwriting, saying, "Marty, Marble Mouth is for ages four and over. A two-year-old child can choke on anything! Don't worry about it."

And they're here telling you today, ladies and gentlemen, that this was not an injury that came from our game. This was something that was going to happen anyhow. His father had problems in school. We can't say that this child was gonna develop as he should have developed. So don't worry about it, ladies and gentlemen. That's the attitude that Amerifun has come into this courtroom with and that's the attitude that they're gonna try to give you, is "Don't worry about it!"

Don't worry about Scotty Freeman.

Don't worry about that little child down in Florida who died!

Don't worry about the other children who have been injured because they constructed a game which invited children to take marbles and put them in their mouths and smile as they put them in and smile as the marble went down because there would be no damage done by this marble.

They want you to take the attitude of "Don't worry about it."

And if you take that attitude, ladies and gentlemen, you're taking that attitude towards little Scotty Freeman, whom you saw take the witness stand just so that you would be able to see with

your own eyes and to feel with your own hearts what that child has
to go through. And it wasn't easy to have that little child come here
in public and sit in this witness chair and to show the world, to
unveil for the world the embarrassment that he'll have to carry
with him for the remainder of his life.

Here is a philosophy of the human condition: that the protection and
care of children is a universal test of the good, applicable to societies
throughout history. The saga of humankind becomes the struggle for the
nurturance of each new generation. The call to jurors is for love, with anger
in love's defense, not for the sake of anger.[31]

As the fate of this unfortunate boy is transmuted into Society's Responsibility for All Children, the story turns mythic. The effect—this is the
nature of mythology-in-action—is to flip back and forth between evidence
and symbol. At one moment we see Scotty in his particular circumstances,
at another as an emblem of human vulnerability. Mythology's simplifica-
tion of reality is most potent when, as in this case, evidence supports it, the
performance skillfully enacts it, and it offers a plausible solution to a real
social dilemma.

James Ferguson's performance is imbued with African American stylistic resources. Yet, unlike Roger King or R. Eugene Pincham, he calls no
overt attention to them or to the fact that he is black. Nevertheless, race,
that most oppressive sign of difference in American society, inevitably sig-
nifies. How does Ferguson deal with the tenacity of race prejudice? African
Americans, wrote Ralph Ellison, "are an American people who are geared
to what *is* and who are yet driven by a sense of what it is possible for human life to be in this society."[32] The high-minded pleasure and cool equa-
nimity with which Ferguson exposes the defective morality behind capi-
talism's unbridled pursuit of profit spring in part from this cultural ground.
Ferguson's courtroom stature can symbolize to jurors how myths of inferiority, being false, are dying away, and how voices from until recently
excluded groups are now in a position to forcefully advocate for democratic ideals. By *not* invoking the identity that visibly sets him apart from the
white majority, Ferguson intensifies the authority race potentially gives him
to represent humanity's best strivings.

Compare Ferguson's stance to that of another outstanding lawyer:
Johnnie Cochran, lead defense attorney in O. J. Simpson's criminal case.

Cochran, according to many commentators on that endlessly dissected trial, played "the race card" to the hilt. That the success of Cochran's defense strategy triggered a national tidal wave of dismay suggests how difficult it is at present for a great many Americans to reckon with either the realities of our justice system or the state of our race relations. For it should be clear that when Johnnie Cochran, an expert on the manipulation of cultural identity, sought to unify jurors to acquit his client in repudiation of racism and slipshod conduct within the Los Angeles police department, he was doing his job.

DECEPTION AND TRUTH

For a long time there had been silence between
us.
When Papa broke it, the famous voice which
had made juries believe that black was white
and, sometimes, the guilty were innocent was
almost the same as of old. "The truth cannot
hurt anybody," he said. "In the end, the truth
is light—always. Remember that, Nora."
            —Adela Rogers St. Johns, writing
            about her father, famed defense
            attorney Earl Rogers[1]

W̲e have seen how the best trial
lawyers throw themselves into their characters. So ready are they to don the
mask that they can fight tooth and nail in a circus tent on behalf of a made-
up client as if they were in court with life itself in the balance. So committed are they to win that they give their all to the fray, trading even on the
deepest sources of their own identity.

The reader may find this compulsion in performance admirable or dis-
heartening. It is perhaps the supreme irony for trial lawyers in our system
of justice. They must play their role to the hilt—even at their soul's peril.

Adela Rogers St. Johns alludes to this irony in the exchange above with
her father. Earl Rogers loved the truth. But he deceived juries. His experi-

ence as a trial lawyer gave him insight into the truth and reverence for it, yet he readily used his special knowledge to persuade jurors that black was white, the guilty innocent. In this conversation, three weeks before his death at the age of fifty from alcoholism, Rogers is consumed with the question of the truth. His daughter wants to write his story. He wrests a promise from her: he will agree to let her do it—but only if what she tells will be "the truth, the whole truth, and nothing but the truth."[2]

The craft, which brings you near the truth, also exiles you from it. How do lawyers deal with this paradox? It is not a subject that lawyers I met broached directly. For a long while I thought they shied away from it because of constraints set by their official position in the judicial system. I see more to their reticence now. It stems, I sense, from their uneasiness about their ambiguous role in the search for justice. Could it be that the need to mislead in the service of client or cause—to create appearances along that slippery slope that runs from shading to distortion to lies—disturbs them? Do uncertainties about where, when, how, and why to draw the line—qualms that have to be repressed for effective performance—cause many of them to feel private distress, if not at times shame?

The place I found attorneys most frankly addressing touchy matters of truth and deception was in the "war stories" they circulate among themselves. These tales about memorable trial experiences are amusing diversions, surefire enliveners of conversation. Telling them, lawyers drop defenses, dispense with bravado. They *show* one another things they know to be true about the lived tensions of the work, which is much easier than trying to *talk* about such matters.[3]

This chapter will look at war stories told at the Festival of American Folklife in 1986. Like all folklore, these narratives cluster around a small number of recurrent, compelling themes: archetypal relationships to the truth and deception as the trade habitually defines them. Through these themes we can explore how lawyers regard their agon, the struggles they wage on stage with other protagonists and inside themselves.[4]

The Client

Let's begin with a tale about the unexpected—and to the lawyer, the quite surprising—emergence of truth in a trial:[5]

ROY BARRERA

Benito Celize was a client of mine who was charged with murder. It seems that he had whittled a guy down with a knife who was about six feet tall right down to about *his* size.

Benito got into an argument *with* this fellow over job hours, as to who was supposed to be on next, on a night watchman's deal. And Benito and his wife and his family were about ready to go someplace, and this other fellow wouldn't let Benito off the job. And they got into an argument about that. During the argument, this big fellow pushed Benito's wife over to one side, and she tripped and she fell.

Well, needless to say about that time Benito got ten feet tall. He ran to the guardhouse. Got out a knife that he had there for paring and cutting his apples. And he came back here and cut *this* guy's apples real good. And killed him. They charged him with murder.

Of course, as all lawyers do, I questioned Benito about his problems, how long he had been married, about his family.

Eventually we were ready to go to court. Benito had five kids— one of a relatively short few months and another one on the *way*. Naturally you want to take advantage of anything and everything that you can, psychologically, within limits. And I told Benito: "You stay outside here in the corridor, with all of your family, until *I* tell you to come on in. *No* one is going to get you to come in there until I tell you to. When I do, I want you to come up front with the baby in your arms, your other older child next, and then next, and next, and next, and your wife will bring up the rear with the one that's still in the basket. I want you to troop in."

By that time, of course, I anticipated the jury panel will be seated, and they're going to be told, "This is a murder case." And here comes the murderer, with his family.

So the case began. The panel came in. The defendant was not there in the hubbub of gettin' everybody seated.

And the judge finally looked around, he said, "Counsel, where is your defendant?"

I said, "Judge, he was here a minute ago, let me see if he's outside."

I go outside. Sure enough, there's Benito.

So I tell Benito, "Come on in."

So he came on in. By that time the jury knows this is a murder case. They're waiting to see the defendant. And here he comes. He troops in with his kids and his pregnant wife. Then he sits down.

The prosecutor turned around to me and he said, "You sonofabitch!"

They put on this murder case against Benito. And it was a fairly good murder case. Except that I felt strongly it's a good self-defense. I felt that notwithstanding he had *gone* to get the knife and come on back, I still had some salvation.

I put Benito on the stand, and he told me about his family, and about what happened, and how it happened, and all that.

The prosecutor, he was choking on something—I didn't know what it was.

Finally he asked him, he said, "Now, Benito, you told this jury a while ago that you've been married for seven years."

"Yes, sir."

"Isn't it a fact that you're not married?"

"That's right."

"Isn't it a fact that this lady is *not* your wife?"

"That's right."

"Isn't it a fact that these children are not yours?"

"Well, that's right."

And it was all downhill from there!

But I didn't hear *any* of the rest of it. I was just so anxious to get him back on. I wasn't concerned about the facts. I was concerned about this fraud that apparently we had perpetrated upon that jury. And I knew that that would hurt him more than anything else.

So then *I* was choking. Until the prosecutor got done asking all these fool questions so I could get him back on.

And finally when I got him back on on redirect, I said, "Now Benito, *I'm* confused. And I'm sure the *jury's* confused. Now you told me about your wife, and your kids"—I wanted them to be sure of one thing if nothing else, that *I* had taken no part of it—so I said, "You told this jury that this was your wife and these were your children. And you told the prosecutor they were not. *Now what is it?*"

And this is something
that can only come
from the mind
and from the heart
of a man who's really pure at heart
and humble.
And things that will surprise you.
He said, "Well, she's really not my wife.
    But really,
    we are.
    Because.
    When we got married,
    her husband had been gone for a long time.
    And I wanted to be her husband.
    And we didn't know if the other fellow was divorced,
                                or not.
    And we didn't have the money to have a big wedding.
    So we just went to the altar
    there at the San Fernando Cathedral.
    And we kneeled down at the altar,
    and we told God we wanted to be husband and wife.
    And that's the way we got married."

So. I was born again!
I said, "Well now,
    these children,
    are they your children or not?"
"Well,
    yes, they are
    and no, they're not.
    I'm not their natural father
    but it's just as if I *were* their father,
    and I consider them mine.
    I raised 'em,
    I educated 'em,
    what little education they've got.
    And I been feedin' them,

and I consider they're mine.
And when I married her,
I married her children also.
The last one that she's gonna have,
that one's mine."

Well, by that time I was really feeling good, and I said, "Well now, where is the natural father? You mean you've been supporting *all* of these kids that aren't yours by yourself?"

"Yes, sir."

"Where's the father?"

"I don't know."

"Has your wife ever filed here with this District Attorney's office to get child support for these kids and make *that* fellow support 'em?"

"No, sir."

"Why not?"

"Well,

when I married her
it was *my* obligation,
and I don't need his money."

And you know, it was jam up for Benito.

But those things will surprise you. As much as I talked to him, I never got to the gut question, which I thought was evident: that was his wife, and these were his kids! And a question like that could kill you. If he had not come back as simply and as humbly as he did, we'd have both been dead. But he'd a gone to the penitentiary.

They convicted him, but gave him a suspended sentence, which means he didn't go to the penitentiary.

He trooped out with his kids.

Roy Barrera's strategy is to create an appearance of truth about Benito Celize, by portraying him as a devoted husband and father. The prosecutor's dramatic cross-examination reframes the story: Celize, it turns out, isn't even married; he and his lawyer have seemingly misled the jury. This reversal is then itself dramatically reversed, with the image of his goodness restored with far more weight than it had had before. Benito Celize reveals his inner grace. (The San Fernando Cathedral, where he and his wife exchanged vows, is a much loved church in the Mexican American community, a folk place of grace.)

Of course, Benito doesn't—can't—actually prove the truth of his account of the crime. In showing the jurors his moral character, he communicates a truth that's as close as they will get to the real truth. Ultimately, *he* must convince them. Roy Barrera, skilled as he is, *lacks the power* to do it for him.

Note that Barrera crosses into poetic diction at the point in his tale that marks the moment of breakthrough, when Benito's character becomes manifest: *This is something/that can only come/from the mind/and from the heart/of a man who's really pure at heart/and humble.* Barrera continues to speak with poetic rhythm as he takes Benito's voice. What is striking about this move is that other lawyers make it, too, to register the same point about a client's character.

James Ferguson told a story about a man he represented in a lawsuit against the police. They'd stopped his client, Bob, in his car on trumped-up charges of possessing drugs, Ferguson claimed, and beaten him because they had a grudge against him. Ferguson, wanting "to make *sure* that [my client] did not give the *appearance* of a dope dealer when he came to court," instructs him: "Bob, dress conservative. Don't wear your pink suit and your bright blue shirt and that little skinny tie that I've seen you wear sometimes. Just dress in a dark suit and a white shirt.'" But Bob arrives on the day of trial in his usual attire. Ferguson is dumbfounded:

> So at a recess I said: "Wait a minute. Why did you do the exact opposite of what we told you to *do* in preparing your dress for court?"
> And he said, "Welll,
> > I'm this way, Mr. Ferguson.
> > I have to be honest about everything I do.
> > And it would be dishonest for me
> > to come and try to appear before this jury
> > in a way that I don't usually dress.
> > So I know you're workin' in my behalf,
> > and you're trying to do what's best for me,
> > and your advice is good advice.

But I have to be myself in this courtroom,
and I have to dress myself in the way I do,
and I hope you don't take offense at that."

Sure enough, they win the case, win big. Afterward, the jury foreman tells Ferguson, "The young man's sincerity when he was on the stand came through."

Bob, like Benito, does something that seems destined to sink him. But instead, since wearing his regular clothes helps him be at ease with himself, it supports the aura of honesty he conveys to the jury. When Ferguson breaks into poetic speech as he takes his client's voice, he signals that Bob *is* a person of integrity.

Diana Marshall recounted a parallel story. Her client is getting badgered on the witness stand. The opposing attorney asks him: "How do you know it was *that* stop sign on the occasion in question? How do you know my client ran that *very same* stop sign? Why do you use those words?"

My client said,
"Sir, it was that stop sign,
that very same stop sign,
not just any stop sign."
"You expect this jury to believe you can tell one stop sign from another? *How do you know it was the same stop sign?*"
And my client said,
"Sir,
when my father was alive,
and there were eleven of us children,
before Gretchen died,
my father took my friend Billy Hunt,
who's sitting back there,
hunting,
with our BB guns
for target practice.
And sir,
when we passed by that particular corner,
there was a cat up on that stop sign,
and that cat had been shot,
and it made me cry.

And I was hurting for the cat.

And my father,

who used to give me some very important and mean-
ingful messages,

said,

'Son, don't cry about it,

do something right.'

So I went to take the cat down,

and there was a bullet hole shot through the cat in the
stop sign.

It was the same stop sign, sir."

We won that one and I didn't say another word.

Another salt-of-the-earth, utterly believable client. He, Bob, and Benito Celize strike me as modern-day incarnations of an old character type,
the wise fool of European folktales. Following instinct, constantly underestimated by others, often aided by magical helpers, this is the heroic figure who proves to be pure of heart and worthy of success.

The lawyers, meanwhile, are reduced in these plots to bystanders. They
pave the way for the client's vindication, but the victory belongs to the
client. *Their* relation to truth is, by comparison, tainted. James Ferguson
ended his story by saying that the foreman was impressed that Bob wore a
cross around his neck, although he himself had never considered that the
cross might have such an effect. Ralph Lancaster, who was sitting next to
Ferguson, joked, "Not much! I bet it was your cross!" That comment hints
at the gulf separating attorneys from other trial participants. Their craft, a
Faustian pact, bars them from fully possessing a truth-teller's authority. Inevitably, they're suspected of guile.

For every story at the Festival about a client vindicating her- or himself,
many more showed clients causing their own convictions. It can happen before trial, with the accused inadvertently providing damning evidence:

JAMES GOETZ

One time I was defending a driving-while-intoxicated case. In
Montana they film these people after they apprehend them, and they
administer these field sobriety tests, having them walk the straight line
and doing the test to touch the nose and so on. And the whole issue

here was whether this guy had been drinking while driving and was intoxicated.

And this was on the videotape that I reviewed before the trial: the officer said, "Well, would you reach out with your arm, with your right hand, close your eye, and then pull your finger over and touch your nose?"

And the witness turned to him and said, "Hell, I can't even do that when I'm sober."

Once at trial, chances for self-betrayal multiply. To wit: when the defense attorney asks prospective jurors during voir dire how many believe cocaine should be legalized, the defendant raises his hand. When the opening statements are being made, the defendant, who has been charged with causing an accident by falling asleep behind the wheel, falls asleep. When a government witness provides an unexpected piece of evidence, the defendant gasps, "Oh my God, how did they find out about that?" When a police officer wavers in his identification of the defendant, the defendant pipes up, "You know it's me, don't lie!" When the judge finds the defendant not guilty of selling drugs but warns him to stop it if he has been, the defendant blurts out: "Yes, Judge, I'm gonna quit. I ain't never gonna sell no more dope as long as I live!"

There are also stories about the most celebrated revelations at trial, confessions under cross-examination:

BOYCE HOLLEMAN

Down in Mississippi we have what we call a Justice Court. It's a misnomer.

It's a lower court where the judge is not a lawyer, and he tries people, and then if they don't like that they appeal the case up to the Circuit Court.

A few years ago, when I was District Attorney down there, I had a Mrs. Ladner. And I tried her down in the Justice Court, and the judge promptly convicted her. And she *appealed* it up to the Circuit Court. Got up in front of the jury and the big court and the judge. Had her lawyer put her on, and she testified.

I got up in absolute amazement when I got up to cross-examine her.

I said, "Mrs. Ladner. Do you remember when we were down in the Justice Court about three months ago?"

"Yes, sir, I remember that."

"Do you remember that you testified down there?"

"Yes, sir, I remember that."

"Didn't you testify to just the opposite down there of what you just told the jury up here today?"

She said, "Why certainly! I lost it down there. I hope you don't think I'm going to say the same thing here!"

R. EUGENE PINCHAM

In Chicago, in the sixties, we had street gangs known as the Blackstone Rangers. By the early seventies they were no longer teenagers, they were grown men. And *this* defendant, whose name was Evans, gigantic six-foot-four fella, handsome, huge guy, was charged with being the hit man for the Blackstone Rangers. And quite frankly, they *were* killing two or three people every week.

This fella was charged with a double homicide. The only evidence they had against him was: some witnesses saw him go into a multiple high-rise apartment building. They saw him come out of the building about twenty minutes later. And shortly thereafter they found these two people in the building hog-tied and shot and killed.

Jim Montgomery, who has just resigned as the corporation counsel of the city of Chicago, was his lawyer. And Jim told Evans, "Now, I cannot anticipate every question that the prosecutor is going to *ask* you. So therefore, you will have to be on your Ps and Qs. And should the state's attorney ask you something on cross-examination that we haven't gone over, you just say, 'Well, not that I remember. I don't recall!' "

And of course, Jim put on his client. And the direct examination went beautifully. Obviously it did, because all the defendant had to say was, "I didn't *kill* the people, I wasn't there."

Prosecutor cross-examined him for about thirty-five, forty minutes. Couldn't shake him, couldn't do anything with him. And finally, in utter frustration, the prosecutor asked him, "DID YOU ON SUCH-AND-SUCH A DATE ENTER THIS APARTMENT BUILDING AND HOG-TIE THESE TWO VICTIMS AND SHOOT THEM IN THE HEAD AND KILL THEM?"

[*Long pause*]

"Welll. Not that I remember."

He's walking off a hundred ninety-nine years now.

This story turns on the traditional folktale plot in which a fool follows instructions literally, with disastrous results.

Unlike pure-of-heart clients, who win over the jury by the gradual revelation of their character, clients in these confession stories signal their guilt with an instantaneous lapse. They blow it because of their naiveté, stupidity, or an eruption from their unconscious, rather than because of the opposing attorney's great skill. Again, the lawyers are on the sidelines. The client reframes the story, becoming the inadvertent agent of the truth.

Clients' breakthroughs to the truth, whether the character they display is good or bad, are memorable because they are unusual exceptions to the normally muddy state of affairs. "This isn't Perry Mason" is a common shorthand used in summations to remind jurors that in real trials they can't expect the witness to be broken, the truth to come tumbling forth. But lawyers can't be sure it won't. These stories tap the element of unpredictability in every trial, the ever-present possibility that the truth will escape the control of one or the other lawyer's craft.

In one such confession story, the lawyer is embarrassed by his own skill:

R. EUGENE PINCHAM

I represented a defendant charged with killing his wife. A very, very horrible murder. The prosecutor had three eyewitnesses, a reenactment of the homicide, three signed confessions.

I tried the case, and argued to the jury. Argued for the morning session of court, afternoon session, walking back and forth, raising my voice, doing all that I could.

And finally when I said to the jury, "When you retire, I'm going to ask you to come back and find this defendant not guilty," and walked back to the counsel table, the defendant jumped up, reached into his pocket, and started giving me some money.

I said, "Don't do that in here, man!" I said, "After all, you have paid me already."

He said, "Yes, I paid you *that* for convincing the *jury* I didn't do it. I'm giving you this for convincing *me* I didn't."

Roy Barrera tells the same tale. He's defending a Mexican American man who's a "marijuana-peddlar," and after his summation the client says, "Mr. Barrera, I have to tell you that I ad*mire* the American system of justice." Barrera, thinking his client has "finally gotten religion," asks, "Why do you say that?" "In your closing argument there," the man replies, "for a while even *I* was beginning to think I was innocent."

For the client to reveal guilt to counsel in this way is deliciously ironic. To convince the guilty party that he or she is innocent is an ultimate tribute to the lawyer's skill—or to the guilty one's gullibility. If the former, your skill has thwarted justice. If the latter, you are in the service of a fool. Either way, the awestruck appreciation of your performance takes away your fig leaf of ignorance about your client's guilt.

The Jury

In public, lawyers praise the collective wisdom of juries. But of course they, like the judicial system and the society, are deeply invested in the premise that juries reliably achieve justice. This faith is hardly subject to scrutiny. There is no objective way to judge jury verdicts, to determine whether they are "correct." Yet we know the lawyers' craft pits them against jurors' efforts to make disinterested judgments. What do lawyers really think about the jury's ability to discover truth?

R. EUGENE PINCHAM

I tried another homicide. I don't know why it is that these men who couldn't get along with their wives would kill them and ask me to represent them.

This case was, again, circumstantial. They found the remains of a female human being in a buried grave. And of course the identification of the remains was by dentist, who testified to the teeth structure and what-have-you. And along with that they put in evidence that my client took out a million dollar insurance policy on his wife three or four days before she mysteriously disappeared, with double indemnity upon her disappearance.

And that's about all they had on him.

And in closing argument, I argued to the jury that "you can't deny a man the precious, God-given right of freedom based upon this kind of meager evidence. The prosecutor really doesn't have a case. He doesn't *think* he has a case. It's circumstantial, and the fact of the matter is he hasn't even proven beyond a reasonable doubt that it was the defendant's wife that they found in the grave!"

And I said, "I don't think even you are convinced. As a matter of fact, there's the wife walking in the door now!"

And all the jurors looked at the door.

I said, "You see, the fact that you looked at the door clearly demonstrates that you didn't believe that it was the defendant's wife they found."

I thereupon sat down, in victory, knowing that I had won this case.

Jury went out and deliberated five minutes and came back and found my client guilty of murder.

Well, after they had retired back to get their clothing, I went and asked them: "How could you find my client guilty? You couldn't possibly have been convinced that the defendant killed the deceased. You weren't even convinced it was his wife! Because when I said, 'Look, she's walking in the door,' all twelve of you looked at the door."

And the foreman of the jury said, "That's right, but your client didn't look at the door."

I think that this demonstrates the astuteness and sophistication of the jury.

The surprise arrival is an old vaudeville gag. I once saw Gregory Hines trick a whole concert hall into craning their heads for the entrance of Muhammad Ali, and then say that the joke had been a staple at the Apollo Theater, with the celebrity usually being Joe Louis. Here the lawyer, mock-heroically fighting insurmountable odds, gets too crafty. His scheme to create the appearance of truth instead yields visible proof of guilt. I recently heard this wife-walks-in-the-courtroom tale from another lawyer. *He'd* heard it from famed Texas attorney Racehorse Haynes, who recounted it as the experience of another famous Texan, Percy Foreman.

Justice Pincham draws a pointed conclusion from the story: juries are smart. Lawyers blow it by selling them short. Many tales about juries locate this intelligence in folk wisdom:

JIM CARRIGAN (*federal judge and former plaintiff's attorney from Denver*)
Juries often bring a little justice in through the back door.

There is the famous trial out in our western part of the country where a man is accused of stealing a neighbor's mule. The evidence was pretty clear that he had stolen the mule, all right. But the jury knew both parties, and they knew the circumstances, and they knew that basically he was an upright and honest man who had a great need for a short time.

And so the jury came back with a very wise, typical jury verdict. The verdict was: not guilty, but he has to return the mule.

Well, the judge took a look at that jury form, and he knew that you can't have an inconsistent verdict. So he instructed the jury, "You're going to have to go back and deliberate again and come up with a consistent verdict."

So the jury went back, and about ten minutes later they come back and reported a new verdict:

"Not guilty and he can keep the mule."[6]

James Jeans, a plaintiff's lawyer from Kansas City, Missouri, had another version: a poverty-stricken defendant accused of poaching confesses on the stand, "I did indeed shoot the deer. I knew it was out of season. We didn't have any meat at home. And I'm married and got five kids." When the jury finds him not guilty, the incredulous judge demands an explanation. The foreman says, "You told us that we were the sole judges of the credibility of the witness. And when Jed said he shot that deer, we didn't believe him."

Since they're not in thrall to the legal system, juries are quite capable of framing the story in a way they know is factually false so they can uphold what they see as a larger moral truth. Judges instruct them on the law and how to apply it, but back in the jury room they may revert to folk standards of justice. Jury nullification—a verdict inconsistent with the facts—is nicely illustrated by the saying I heard attributed to Georgia lawyers that juries in homicide trials ask two questions: did the person deserve to die? And did the right person do the killing?

Lawyers thus may hope to win by covertly appealing to jurors to make their own collective judgment of what's right even when it goes against seemingly damning evidence or formal dictates of law. They encourage jurors to trust the authority of their own experience. In one popular vein of

stories jurors assert themselves by inadvertently uttering "truths" that break
the frame of the trial itself:

MICHAEL TIGAR

I was sitting in [Judge] Charles Bryant's court, and while I had a
jury out he ran another case in. Two young men charged with running
guns from California through false names into the hands of criminals
in New York. A very complicated scam, with a lot of paperwork that
had supposedly been falsified.

And defense counsel thought to make this point that *I* just made.

And so in the middle of his summation in full cry, he walked over
to the prosecution's table, and he grabbed up these papers.

And he said, "Look, members of the jury, LOOK AT THIS PAPER.
WHAT DOES THAT PROVE? WHAT DOES THAT PROVE?"

Juror Number Five said, "Illegal dealing in guns!"

More frame-breakings: a lawyer announces in his opening statement
that he's seeking a $2 million verdict, and a juror whistles in amazement.
A lawyer states he's seeking $250, and a juror offers to pay it out of his own
pocket to avoid sitting through the case. A judge asks prospective jurors,
"Could you, under the appropriate facts, return the death penalty against
a criminal defendant?" and one answers, "Sure, Judge, but it would be a
great help to me if we could do it on Saturday." A young prosecutor reaches
the point of tears during her summation in a rape case, and a woman juror
pats her hand, reassuring her, "Don't worry, we're gonna hang the sonofabitch."

R. EUGENE PINCHAM

I sat as a judge in a criminal court in Cook County for eight years.
I was presiding over a jury trial in which the defendant was charged
with rape.

And the prosecutor put the victim on the stand. A very, very
charming, attractive young lady. And as he brought her to the incident of the rape, he asked her, "Now, would you tell the ladies and
gentlemen of the jury what it is the defendant said to you as he approached you?"

And with that, the young lady broke down and started crying.

And out of deference to her feelings and her past hostile experience, I said to her, "Madam, was what he said to you too vulgar and profane and offensive for you to repeat in this courtroom?"

And she said, "Yes, yes, it was."

I said, "Well, why don't you write it down on a piece of paper."

And she wrote it down and handed it to me. I in turn handed it to the prosecuting and defense attorney. The prosecutor stood and held it.

He then said to the young lady, "Now would you tell the ladies and gentlemen of the jury what it is this defendant *did* to you after he *said* this to you."

And she again broke down and started crying.

Trying to be the dignified, fair judge, I said to her again, "Madam, was what he did too vicious and horrible for you to repeat in open court to the ladies and gentlemen of the jury?"

She said, "Yes, your Honor, it was."

I said, "Well, write it down, what he did."

She wrote it down, handed to me, I read it. I handed it to the defense attorney and he read it and handed it to the prosecutor.

The prosecutor then said, "Well, your Honor, may I have leave to present to the jury what the witness has written down?"

I said, "Leave granted."

He went to the end of the jury box, handed the two pieces of paper to the jurors. They passed it down the aisle.

The eleventh juror was a very attractive woman, and she read it. The twelfth juror was a man. He was asleep.

So when she punched him with her elbow, he starts and awakens suddenly. He read the note, smiled, and put it in his pocket.

Leaning over, he looked at her gleefully and said, "Okay, we'll get to that this evening."

The sleeping juror tale is another classic that Justice Pincham tells in the first person, thus making it vividly his own.

Jurors fall asleep during trial. They fantasize. Ordinary preoccupations of their lives cling to them as they go about the business of judging. There is a gap between their natural response and the behavior officially expected of them that makes them ready targets for lawyers' wiles.

The Judge

With his exaggerated deference toward the distraught rape victim, Justice Pincham humorously depicts proper decorum for a judge. But the dominant tone in lawyers' war stories about judges is not flattering. Instead it shows them exercising power, often in distorted ways:

DIANA MARSHALL

I'm gonna tell one [that] has to do with being a woman trial lawyer. And if I'd planned and worked and fussed and fretted I never could possibly have figured out how to take advantage of that, because at the time that I started being a trial lawyer everybody thought it was a *dis*advantage.

One of my first trials was [before] one of the crustiest [judges]— and some of these judges are just *ill-tempered* people you don't want to be around *ever*, especially in the courtroom when you're scared to death.

And unfortunately I went to trial in one of those courts, and I found out that the judge doesn't like lawyers, he didn't like young lawyers,

> and he *hated*
> *women*
> *young*
> *lawyers.*

And I found that out when he started referring to *me* as "*lady*"— and I don't mean in a fond way—and the other lawyer as "counsel."

So it was, "Overruled, lady," and "Sustained, *counsel.*"

And it was just awful. And I was really upset and hurt about it until I looked over at the jury and I saw these people looking at me like [*sugary*]: "*Poor little Bo-Peep!*"

I thought, "This isn't all that bad, is it?" Representin' AT&T, you really don't get very much sympathy, very often. So I loved it. Although I had not planned on how to handle it, because I didn't really expect it. I let the sympathy for me grow. And the jury was really getting sick of this treatment that I was getting. I couldn't get a fair shot at *any*thing—and it was "Sit down," and "Eeechh," and he was just horrible to me.

So I decided to gradually fight back for myself, and the jury was pulling for me, and it was just great.

And finally I said, "Your Honor, I have to object! Now you have been referring to him as 'counsel' for this whole trial and you've been callin' me 'lady'!"

And he said, "Well. Would you like to be called 'counsel'?"

And I said, "No, I was thinking maybe you would call him 'lady.'"

I thought it was funny, the *jury* thought it was funny, and the judge FINED me fifty dollars!

Penny Cooper told a story that she described as "the last time I wore a dress." She is hoping for leniency for her client in a cocaine smuggling case in Puerto Rico, before a notoriously tough judge:

> So I pled him guilty, only to have to calendar the case to return within a few weeks.
>
> I was wearing a pantsuit. And Judge Pascera had never seen anything like that, and had continually ragged me about it, and said that he didn't appreciate it, and didn't like it, and when I were to come back for sentencing I was to wear a dress.
>
> So the day before I left on the flight to Puerto Rico, my then-partner wheeled me around in a car and took me to one of the flighty stores in Oakland, California, where I bought myself a twenty-five-dollar dress that fit.
>
> I stood in front of that judge, and I *begged* for probation or a shorter sentence than a year, and he looked at me, and he said, "One year."
>
> And I said, "Well, your Honor, I just wanted to tell you that I did come in a dress."
>
> And he looked down at me, and he was furious. And he smacked his hand as hard as he could on the podium. He said, "All right! Six months! Get out of here!"
>
> I threw the dress in the hotel wastebasket when I finished my appearance.

With bravura, Diana Marshall and Penny Cooper triumph over benighted judges. Sexist treatment goes with the territory. They know it's a real problem for aspiring women attorneys. They know it can be overcome. Their expertise at disarming genderphobic stereotypes is part of what makes them formidable.

The judges in these stories, as in many others, treat their courtrooms as fiefdoms. But they don't gaze impartially on the fray from empyrean heights. They're as embroiled as everyone else in American obsessions with gender, race, and class. They have biases and predilections. They react volatilely to certain lawyers and witnesses. They abuse their institutionalized power:

JAMES FERGUSON

It was a murder case. The facts are not that important. But there was one witness for the prosecution who was on the stand, and we were doing what we had hoped was a fairly *vigorous* cross-examination of this witness. We had done fairly well with that, and the prosecutor came back to do a redirect. And the manner in which the prosecutor was asking the questions, I felt, was objectionable.

You've seen lawyers object: so I would object. And in this particular case we had a judge who was very friendly with the prosecution. And instead of *ruling* on my objections—because he knew he had to overrule those objections in order to prevent the case from getting reversed on appeal—he *called* the prosecutor up to the bench. And when he said, "Mr. Prosecutor, come up," I went up to the bench as well. Because I felt like I ought to *be* there, that was my place.

And I got there, and he suggested to the prosecutor how he ought to ask the questions the next time.

And I said at that time, "I object to your Honor coaching the prosecution in this case."

And the judge said, "Go back and sit down."

So this time we went back, and the prosecutor, being the bright star that he was, started asking the questions the same way—again.

And I, of course, objected in the same manner. And the judge, to be sure, sent the jury out, and this time called the prosecutor up and said, "Come up here."

And I got up to go up to the bench, just as I had the time before.

And at that time the judge motioned to me: "No, you sit down, Mr. Ferguson."

At that moment the prosecutor had already reached the bench. I turned to the court reporter to say, "I would like to have the record reflect that the judge is allowing the prosecutor to come to the bench and not allowing defense counsel an opportunity to do the same."

As I said that to the court reporter, the judge was already talking to the prosecutor. And there was a trial lawyer who had been privately brought into the case to assist the family in the case. And as I was talking to the court reporter, this lawyer stands up and says: "Your Honor!! Mr. Ferguson's telling the court reporter to put something in the record that your Honor can't hear!!"

And the judge then bristles up and leans over the bench, points his finger at me:

"Mr. Ferguson,

> in this courtroom,
> NOTHING goes into the record
> that the court can't hear."

And I very calmly said, "Your Honor, what I said to the court reporter I said loud enough for everyone in the courtroom to hear. And perhaps if your Honor didn't hear me, it was because you were engaging in the very activity I was complaining about: conferring with the prosecutor in my absence."

"Don't you get smart with this court, Mr. Ferguson! Do you want to apologize for that remark?"

And I thought about it, and tried to see if I had any reason to apologize. And couldn't think of one!

So I said, "No, your Honor, I don't care to apologize."

And at that moment he said, "LOCK HIM UP, sheriff."

And the sheriff carted me away.

James Ferguson's contempt story, like Diana Marshall's, follows a common pattern. The teller, pushed to the edge, acts out of principle. The judge is ill-tempered, capricious, pompous, partisan, maybe dumb. These judges are extreme, but a larger craft critique, an indirect defense of the jury system, is implied: judges are not superior to juries as arbiters of truth. In fact many, hardened by their position of authority, are worse.

In the stories I heard, far more loathing was expressed toward judges than toward opposing attorneys. Stephen Delinsky, a criminal lawyer from Boston, described how an adversary of his dealt with a judge's abusiveness:

Out of the corner of my eye I could hear the jurors going all hushed and appearing to be in shock. I turned around and there was this defense attorney apparently going through the throes of a heart attack brought on by this judge. He was gasping for breath, one of the jurors was coming over the rail to help him, and the courtroom was cleared. Needless to say, after a continuance of about three hours he regained his composure, the court came back into session, and the judge was solicitous of him.

Delinsky's sympathies went to his opponent, not the judge. With judges, lawyers must be at once deferential and cagey. They hide anger with humor:

JAMES JEANS

There was a lawyer in Kansas City who was arguing a motion before a judge. And he made an impassioned plea, and the judge says, "That's overruled."

And as he turned to leave the bench, he muttered under his breath, "That sonofabitch."

And the bailiff heard him.

So as soon as he had started to leave the courtroom, the bailiff came up to the judge. He said, "Your Honor, that fella just cursed you. He said, 'That sonofabitch,' after you ruled."

[The judge] said, "Bring that lawyer back in here!"

So he brought the lawyer back in there, and he said, "Bailiff said that you cursed after my ruling. You said, 'That sonofabitch.' Is that true?"

He said, "Well, yes it is, your Honor. But he didn't hear *all* of what I said. I said, 'That sonofabitch sure knows the law.'"

A lawyer's well-known retort when a judge puts a bad question to a witness is, "Judge, if you asked that question for my opponent, I object; if you asked it for me, I withdraw it." A retort when a judge takes over the lawyer's questioning is, "Judge, I don't mind you trying my case, but for God's sakes don't lose it!"

There is a vein of stories about lawyers' subordination to judges that feature the delight they take in discomfiting attorneys. A Tennessee judge greets a visiting Illinois lawyer in front of the jury with, "We're glad to have you here, and we're going to treat you the same way that we get treated when we go to Chicago." A judge known to fall asleep on the bench makes a practice of feigning sleep, so lawyers never know whether he's dozing or

listening. A judge denies a lawyer's request for a break to stop the pound-
ing his client is getting on cross-examination by saying, in the jury's presence, "You never call off the dogs when you got the coon treed!"

The Expert

Judges must be shown deference. The other side's witnesses have to be
handled gingerly, lest the jury think the lawyer unfair. With opposing experts, however, the gloves can come off. They are supposed to clarify facts
for the jury. But in war stories they seldom deserve respect:

JAMES GOETZ

I had a case one time: it was on a motion to suppress, and it involved
hashish that was boxed and sent in Hawaii. The agricultural inspectors
inspected it, found it was hashish, boxed it up again, and shipped it to
the Bozeman, Montana, police department. And the police had it delivered in a controlled stakeout, and then went in for their arrest.

They brought for the suppression motion a witness from the police department in Honolulu. And he was testifying in response to the
county attorney's questions. And the question was, "Where does
hashish come from?"

And the witness said, "Well, you're not gonna believe this, but," he
said, "in the Middle East they have these fields of growing marijuana.
And what they do is they turn a bunch of camels loose and they eat this
marijuana and then what they defecate turns out to be hashish."

At that point I said, "Your Honor, may I approach the bench?"

And I walked up, and we had a sidebar up there, and the county
attorney walked up.

I said, "I have a motion to make."

And the judge looked at me, and said, "Yes, counsel, what is your
motion?"

And I said, "Your Honor, I have to move to dismiss this case."

And the judge said, "On what grounds?"

And I said, "On the grounds that this is not hashish. This is camel
shit."

Lawyers relish this moment of discrediting the opponent's expert. Experts' authority as truth-tellers derives from their control of the esoteric

knowledge of their fields. But what do they actually know about the subject in question in the courtroom? Is their authority legitimate or bogus? The lawyer tests them, matches wits, and pounces if they stumble:

WILLIAM DWYER (*plaintiff's attorney and later a federal judge in Seattle*)

I remember one case in which I was defending the will of a sweet old lady who had died and left a fortune to charity.

And her relatives were very surprised. She had no children, but she had some distant relatives, and they were surprised and distressed, and they filed a will contest case. And I defended the will.

They were claiming the old lady had lost all her wits and had not had the capacity to make a will; that she had been suffering from arterial sclerosis of the head, or senility, and couldn't have made a valid will. And of course we claimed she was sound as a dollar and the will was perfectly good.

Well, the relatives put on the witness stand a doctor. The doctor had seen the old lady a few times shortly before she died. And he testified that yes, in his opinion, she *had* been suffering from senility, and because of that she had not had the capacity to make a will.

So on cross-examination I asked just the kind of questions you'd expect.

"Doctor, what is this thing we call senility?"

He said, "Well, it's a hardening of the arteries in the brain."

And I said, "Now, at what age does this ordinarily come upon a person?"

And he says, "Well, it usually starts somewhere in middle age, to some degree."

I said, "For example, several of us here in the courtroom would be suffering from some degree, wouldn't we?"

He said, "Well, maybe."

I said, "For example, I myself, my opposing counsel, perhaps even his Honor, we may all have a touch of this?"

He said, "Yes, that's true."

And I said, "Now doctor, what is the main sympton of this thing you call senility?"

And he said, "Well. The main symptom is, um—um—um—uh—"

I said, "Is it forgetting what you're talking about?"

And he said, "Yes, yes, that's it!"

The mistakes both these experts make are unpredictable. The lawyers score because they've got the poise to seize the chance. Like guilt, error and fatuousness are revealed spontaneously. They're not ferreted out by calculated questioning:

JIM CARRIGAN

These courtroom demonstrations with demonstrative exhibits can be dangerous sometimes. One example that comes to mind is right out of the case that formed the basis for the Johnny Diamond case, in which [an FBI] ballistics expert was flown out from Washington, D.C. to this small town in Colorado, to testify about his opinion that this gun could not have fired accidentally.

And in doing so, he got on the stand, and explained in minute detail all the different safety mechanisms the gun had—it was a Browning automatic, a very fine weapon—and in fact began to disassemble the gun right on the witness stand in front of the jury, and took it all apart.

And pretty soon he had springs flying all over the courtroom, and little parts dropped on the floor, screws here and parts over there.

And then he began to put it back together again right in front of the jury's eyes, and he couldn't get the damn thing back together.

So we sat and watched him. We had our own ballistics expert, and we sat and watched him while he writhed and suffered.

And then I stood. "Your Honor, our expert, who *knows* about this gun, would be willing to help the FBI agent put it back together."

And he let us do it, in order to get the trial moving again. So our expert went ahead and put the gun back together.

When the opponent's experts take the stand, lawyers get to step out of their usual role. They become skeptical laypersons, drawing nearer to the position of the jury. The onus is less on the lawyers and more on the experts to prove they know what they're talking about. The stakes, at least in the stories I heard, are limited. When experts fail, the wound isn't fatal. They provide comic relief. They're sideshows.

The following story is different. It features the expert as truth-bearer, a lawyer's perfect accompanist:

ARTHUR RAYNES (*plaintiff's attorney from Philadelphia*)

Up in Philadelphia we have a lot of ethnic groups, and we always try to make some ethnic identification with the plaintiff and the people on the jury.

Well, I had a case where I represented Eric Rosenblith, who was the concertmeister of the Indianapolis Symphony Orchestra. He was injured in Allentown when this finger on his left hand was injured when a Hertz Rental man slammed the door shut when he was getting his violin case out.

Eric Rosenblith wanted to be a virtuoso—that is, somebody who would be an artist on his own. But because he was the kind of person that he was and had the kind of ego that he had, he couldn't admit that he played the violin any less well *after* the accident than before the accident.

So I had to figure somebody who would come in to testify who had seen Eric Rosenblith play before, who knew that he had the technical artistry to be a virtuoso, and who had seen him play afterwards and knew what his problems were, and somebody who was an expert qualified to give that opinion.

And I was lucky enough to get the famous Isaac Stern, who was appearing in Philadelphia at the Academy of Music. And I had the trial set down for that day.

On the Saturday before the Monday that Isaac Stern was to appear . . . when I went over the case with him, he said to me, "Well, now, how's your *jury?*"

I said, "Well, Mr. Stern, I'm kind of worried about the jury."

[He] says, "What do ya mean?"

I said, "Well, you know, I'm Jewish. And you're Jewish. And Eric Rosenblith is Jewish. And I have Isler Solomon, the conductor of the Indianapolis Symphony Orchestra, on. He's Jewish. And there's nobody that's Jewish on the jury."

He says, "Don't worry. *I'll* handle it."

I said, "What are you gonna do?"

He says, "Don't worry."

We showed up in the courtroom. I called all my friends up, had standing room only. And [Stern] wanted to demonstrate to the jury why this finger is the most important finger. And he turned to the judge. Could he use his Stradivarius, which he *just* happened to have in the courtroom, to demonstrate to the jury why this finger is so important and what this injury meant to Eric Rosenblith?

Of course there was an objection from the defense lawyer, but Judge Sheridan said, "There's no way that you're going to prevent Isaac Stern from playing his violin in my courtroom."

And he handled the problem for me. You know what he played for the jury?

Ave Maria.

Isaac Stern has a master performer's consummate flair for cultural symbolism. Arthur Raynes is right to expect that his appearance will lend dazzle to the whole case.

The Lawyer

Lawyers' war stories, being expressions of craft outlook, are often cautionary, if not downright self-deprecating, about the trade itself:

JAMES FERGUSON

This was up in a rural area [in North Carolina], where on Friday afternoon court would usually adjourn around twelve or one o'clock because everybody wanted to go home. But on this particular day, there was a case remaining that the judge wanted to finish up before the week was out. And they thought that they could get it done very quickly, because the facts were very clear.

And I'll tell you what they were, very briefly, and then tell you what happened.

The facts were that the defendant was charged with murder, and he had stabbed the decedent eight times. And his defense was that he was sitting on the corner with his knife, peeling an apple, and the decedent came around the corner, slipped on a banana peel, and fell back on his knife eight times.

So the judge naturally felt that it wouldn't take long to resolve this case. But he needed a jury. And everybody had gone home except some lawyers who were hanging around the courthouse telling tales like we're doing now.

The judge said, "We'll just get a jury of these twelve lawyers, and they'll understand this case, hear it very quickly and get it over with."

So the case was presented in about thirty, forty-five minutes. No defense put up except what I told you. And this jury of twelve lawyers went out to deliberate in the case.

The judge expected that they would be back in about ten or fifteen minutes because the facts were so clear.

So after they had been out about an hour and a half, the judge called them back in, wondering what in the world was taking so long.

And he said, "Do you have a verdict yet?"

And nobody would say anything. Nobody said a word. They just all looked at the judge.

So he said, "Well, all right, obviously you don't, go back and deliberate some *more*."

So he sent these twelve lawyers back into the jury room, and they deliberated a while longer.

And the judge waited, and they were still in the jury room, and he called them out about *four* hours later. Now that's getting to be after six o'clock on Friday.

So the judge called them out and said, "Have you *reached* a VERDICT yet?"

One of them stood up and said, "Your Honor, we haven't reached a verdict yet, but we have had the nominating speeches for foreman. If you could give us about another hour, I think we could conclude that part of the case without too much difficulty."

With their workweek over, these lawyers regress into a timeless state where language becomes its own end, and they are finally free to strut verbal, legal, and interpersonal talents before peers, who, unlike jurors, can appreciate the finer points of their forensic abilities. Ferguson spoofs the trade's tendency toward fetishizing of voice and persona that, if not checked, debases practice.

This is the lawyer's deadly sin of self-importance. It is an occupational pathology. Intoxicated by the sound of your voice, you lose proportion. You become trapped in a puffed-up, static sense of self, out of touch with ordinary human concerns. One symptom is rigor mortis of the repertoire:

BOYCE HOLLEMAN

There's a lawyer down in Houston, Texas, named Racehorse Haynes that some of you may have heard of. . . .

He always says that you must go scalp your opposition. So if he has a case in a certain section of Texas, he goes ahead of time and looks over the District Attorney, and kind of sees how he does. Because most of us, when we prosecute, we fall into a pattern of final arguments, and we have certain things we like to say.

This particular District Attorney was little, beady-eyed, bald-headed, short-cut hair, and he just looked like the chairman of the board of deacons of the local church. He looked like a fellow that would prosecute his own mother. He was just a typical prosecutor type.

Racehorse scouted him. And he found out that this District Attorney, at some point in his final argument, would always come to a certain spot. And [Racehorse] didn't know exactly how he'd fit it in, but he'd always say, "IN THE PITS OF DEGREDATION!" He'd always say it.

So [Racehorse] said he made a note of that. When he was making his argument—the District Attorney was waiting to argue—he got up and told the jury, he said, "Now, ladies and gentlemen," he said, "Mr. Johnson, at some point in his argument, is gonna come right here"— and he took a piece of chalk out—"right here, and he's gonna say, 'IN THE PITS OF DEGREDATION!'" And he said, "I don't want you all to be persuaded by that in any way!"

Then he finished his argument and sat down.

So the District Attorney got up and he *wound* up and he took off and after about thirty minutes he looked and he was standing right on the chalk mark and he was saying, "IN THE PITS OF DEGREDATION!"

And Racehorse won that case.

Haynes grasps the exact nature of his adversary's compulsion. Overestimating one's authority as a performer—the egocentric craving to hold forth, to argue, to be heard, to control the floor, to dominate—is a constant danger.

One well-known spot where these tendencies bite lawyers is the urge to ask one question too many in cross-examination:

BOYCE HOLLEMAN

Clarence Darrow liked to tell a story about lawyers asking too many questions.

This young lawyer was defending a fella. The charge was biting another fella's ear off in a fight. There was only one witness, and he had this witness on the stand. And after a number of questions he got to the big question.

He said, "Did you see my client bite this man's ear off?"

[The witness] said, "No, sir, I didn't see that."

He oughta set down. But he didn't. He said, "Well, then, how is it you come here and tell this jury that he bit his ear off? How'd you know that?"

He said, "I saw him spit it out."

RALPH LANCASTER

I come from Maine, and Maine is a fairly rural state, as you know.

There was an accident case some years ago in which a man was driving a wagon. He had a dog up on the wagon seat with him, and a horse was pulling him. He came up over a curve, a car came around the curve going too fast, bang—the horse ended up in one gully, the dog ended up in another, the man ended up underneath the wagon.

He sued the driver of the car. He's on the stand.

Cross-examination by defense counsel: "And isn't it *true*, that just after the accident, a man came up to you and said to you, 'How do you feel?' And you said, 'I feel *great*, I never felt better in my life'?"

Answer: "Yes."

Redirect examination: "Now would you tell us what happened just *before* that?"

"My horse was lying over in the gutter with two broken legs. Man walked over, he looked at the horse, pulled out his revolver, and shot the horse in the head. He walked over to the other gutter where my dog was lying with a broken back, and he shot my poor dog right through the head. And then he walked over to me and he said, 'And how do YOU feel?'"

Both tales are classics in oral tradition. The cross-examiner presses on. Just one more jab will clinch the point, will defeat the witness and prove the apparent truth of your story. But just as you close in on the effect you want, you open yourself to a surfacing of actual truth that blows the frame you are trying to create. The scent of the kill throws off your judgment, and you forget that the truth may lie in waiting and that the witness isn't on a string. Many lawyers have personal accounts of such embarrassments:

TOM ALEXANDER (*civil defense attorney from Houston*)
I started practice with a great man. He was charming, entertaining, a great lawyer. His name was Newton Crane. He's with the Lord now.

He took me over to try my first case. And we were trying the issue of whether or not the Washington National Insurance Company owed nine hundred dollars on a claim for a man that had been operated on for a hernia. Washington National claimed that he had the hernia before he had the insurance policy, and he claimed he had the insurance policy before he had the hernia. And that was the issue in the case.

I was voir diring the jury panel to see who ought to serve on this jury, and I thought it important to ask if anybody'd ever had a claim that was disputed by an insurance company.

A hand goes up. Big fella.

He said yes, he had.

I said, "What was the nature of that claim, sir?"

"Well," he said, "it involved surgery."

I was hot on the trail then. I figured I had a disqualified juror. So I said, "What kind of surgery did it involve?"

He says, "Personal surgery."

Well, that wasn't satisfactory for me. Finally I pressed him, and he allowed, in a very gruff [voice], kind of looking down, "Well, it was hemorrhoids."

Oh, now I'm mortified! I've embarrassed a man. I've embarrassed him in front of the panel. I've embarrassed myself. And I don't know what the hell to do!

Now then, up comes a note to me, from the great Newton Crane. I figured that's my salvation, now I'm gonna get out of this.

So I opened the note. Newton says, "You forgot to ask him to show you the scar."

The stakes in Tom Alexander's first trial are paltry, yet he inflates his role and is hung up before he even gets out of the gate. His mentor's note epitomizes the craft's sink-or-swim approach to novices. Alexander is on his own. He has to face his insecurities and learn humility fast.

The consuming passion of trial practice is winning. Some war stories directly pose the thorny paradox of this commitment. Win at what cost? Win just for the client—or for principle, or glory, or money, or sport? Is winning a fetish? Is there a point where the lawyer, in framing appearances of truth that deceive about what is really true, is degraded by the work?

Percy Foreman, like Racehorse Haynes the subject of many tales recounted among Texas attorneys, was scathingly candid about motivation:

TOM ALEXANDER

Percy represented a fella that was involved in a three-way business partnership, and two of his partners conspired against him—*truly* did. Rather than solving it in civil court, he solved it himself: he killed one of them. So now there were only two partners.

He was a little bitty fella, and in addition to that had lost a leg.

In Percy's closing argument, defending this fella, he carried him in his arms before the jury, while he made his speech.

And, predictably, got him off on self-defense.

Someone asked him after a bit, said, "Percy, what did you charge that fella?"

Percy said "Two hundred and fifty thousand dollars." Now, this was when two hundred and fifty thousand dollars, as Everett Dirksen would say, was real money.

He said, "*Percy*, how can you charge a man that much just for one case?"

He says, "*Some*body's got to punish the sonofabitch."

The questioner in Alexander's story isn't a bit concerned about the ethics of getting a guilty man off—it's the cost. Percy Foreman's reply zeroes in on the incongruity of his own talent. Master that he is, he can thwart the truth. Is that a sin? What else *can* he do? The exorbitant fee, Foreman slyly suggests, balances the scales, cleanses in an ersatz sort of way. It inflicts the only pain the client will suffer with Foreman as his protector. And it assuages the lawyer for doing venal work.

Should we take Percy Foreman at his word? His biography confirms the points Alexander makes. "My clients don't want justice," Foreman declared. "They want their freedom." The onus is on them. He does their bidding. But, he said, "I don't represent wealthy clients. If they aren't poor when they come to me, they are when they leave. If a case is so nefarious that a man is going to the electric chair except for my efforts, I have no compunction about charging all that the traffic will bear. My fee is my clients' punishment." Notice Foreman's indirect admission that he is motivated by more than money. He'd take poor clients if he liked the case.[7]

For socially committed lawyers, the ultimate motivation can be loyalty to human life:

PENNY COOPER

This is not a funny story.

During the penalty phase [in a death penalty case], the prosecutor is allowed to introduce any kind of evidence—some of which has nothing to do with the case—that might [shed light on] whether or not the person should either live or die. . . .

There were four people involved in an armed robbery. After the police were chasing the car, there was a shoot-out. One defendant faced off against a police officer, and the two of them killed each other. So there were two dead bodies—although my client hadn't done the killing. Another one of the defendants had gone to his home, having escaped from the robbery, and committed suicide.

So that left only two people to be prosecuted. One person was able to avoid arrest for several days, and they could never prove he was at the scene of the shooting. It was only my client at the scene of the shooting, so he was charged, vicariously, with the deaths of one of the people that committed the robbery plus the police officer.

He was convicted of first-degree murder on the theory that he was involved in the robbery, and therefore, by the felony murder rule, involved in first-degree murder.

During the trial, I received some information indicating that my client, who had spent most of his life in prison, was a member of a white racist organization called the Aryan Brotherhood.

And it turned out that there was a gentleman who was being prosecuted in various states; he was in a high security prison where my client was being kept—on the tenth floor of the jail at Oakland, California. And this was a man who demonstrated that he was Jewish by always wearing a yarmulke, a skullcap, on his head.

My client apparently did not like Jews. During a fight in the jail—during the time that his [case] was being tried—he put this man's eye out.

So I found myself during the penalty phase of the trial facing the evidence that my client had actually maimed a person entirely because of the fact that he was Jewish.

So here I had come months through this huge, long trial, and I found myself *now* in front of a jury—myself being Jewish—arguing to the jury that my client really wasn't a Nazi, he really hadn't any kind of preferences in that respect.

There I was, arguing to the jury that they should *not* kill my client, he wasn't a Nazi, I was a Jew—and why would I be representing him?

It just shows you the circumstances that one can find oneself in in the business of being a trial lawyer.

Here is a stomach-turning test of commitment. The client abhors your very identity, stands with those who exterminated your people and might relish the slaughter if the chance came again. What will you do to help such a man? Strange as it may make her feel, Penny Cooper goes as far as she must. She shades what she knows, sets aside her personal history, indeed calculatedly invokes her Jewishness, which isn't an explicit part of her courtroom persona, on her client's behalf. What Percy Foreman claims to have done for money, Penny Cooper does out of devotion to principle. It's the cost of being true to her vision of her craft.

Our last story broaches the enigma of the sources that impel performance.

JAMES FERGUSON

Let me tell you something about what *may* have changed a trial for me. Now, nobody's going to believe this. I still don't believe this story myself.

Except that it happened to me.

This was a criminal trial some years ago. And I was representing a young man who was charged with murder. As a matter of fact, he had already been convicted of murder before I got the case. We took it on appeal. Got it reversed on some grounds, and then tried the case again.

It was one of strongest circumstantial cases I have ever seen.

The man was murdered at a store, and he was robbed, and there was marked money taken from the robbery. And when my client was arrested at home, some of this money was found there, in his pocket.

There were two witnesses who testified that he had come by their house immediately *before* the murder took place and said that he was going to this place to rob it. There were three other people at a house that said he came by there within fifteen minutes [after] the time that the murder took place. And all of his alibi witnesses ultimately said that he was not with them, as he said he was.

And there was a tire print found at the scene which matched the tire print of his car.

There was a cigarette there that had some saliva on it that came out in a test that matched his saliva.

We presented no defense at all. We didn't put on any witnesses. Didn't call any witnesses. We thought that this was an open-and-shut case. And this was the time when the death penalty and the issue of guilt [were] decided at the same time.

And this case took place in Wilmington, North Carolina, at a time when there was a lot of racial strife there, and it was a black defendant and a white victim.

So we felt that we had *no* real chance at all.

So on the day of closing argument—we all like to feel that closing argument can make the difference in the case, but we don't really *believe* that—I got ready to go in the court to make my closing argument. And my client's brother came up to me, and said—they call me Fergie—said, "Fergie, I have something I want you to do for me. I know you don't believe in this. But I wish you would take *this,* and put it in your pocket while you're arguing your case." And he said, "This old lady, who's a friend of ours, went out last night, down through a creek and across the swamp, and found this up under a tree stump. And she wanted you to just put this in your pocket to argue."

I said, "Well, Vince, I don't believe in this kind of stuff, but if it makes you and the lady happy, I'll do it."

So when I walked in the courtroom, I was really still wondering what I was going to say in closing argument. But I got up to argue the case, and for some reason the words just came, they just flowed. And for two-and-a-half or three hours, I talked with this jury. And it was an all-white jury.

And after the argument was over—I had the last argument—and the judge had given his instructions, the jury went out. And we felt that we'd have at least forty-five minutes or an hour before the jury came back.

And this is the quickest verdict I've ever gotten in *any* kind of a case. The jury came back in *ten* minutes. I hadn't even had time to smoke a cigarette, because I smoked at that time. And the jury came back in ten minutes and knocked on the door.

Well, I thought that they were knocking on the door to ask for a question, because I never thought a jury could decide a case, *any* case, that quickly, particularly one that involves both guilt-innocence and life or death.

And the judge said, "Do you have a question?"

The foreman said, "No."

Said, "Well, do you have a verdict?"

And the foreman said, "Yes, we have a verdict."

So the judge said, "What's the verdict?"

And at that time, the foreman would just stand up in court and announce the verdict.

And he said, "Not guilty."

And my client, not hearing the "not" part of it, put his head down on the desk, thinking that the jury had said, "Guilty."

And I said, "Chris, congratulations, you just won your case!"

And he said, "What? Oh hell, I can't believe it!"

So when the jury filed out of the courtroom, we wanted to talk to them and find out why they had ruled that way.

And they wouldn't talk to us. The jury was angry at us. And my client's mother went up to thank the jury for saving her son's life.

And *each* juror, down to the twelfth juror, looked at her and said, "Don't thank us."

And they walked away from the courtroom, angry.

And I've never understood to this day why the jury ruled the way it did. But I reached back in my pocket, and I found this little doll that this lady had given to me.

I found my client's brother. I said, "Vince, about this little doll that this lady gave me. You think she'll let me hold on to it?"

With this amulet, this object of folk conjuration, in his pocket, James Ferguson finds an eloquence far beyond his conscious control. Is persuasive authority yoked to powers that can't be grasped by reason? To origins buried deep in one's cultural background? To forces outside ordinary human experience? Ferguson doesn't know. But he submits to the mystery. Defeating great odds, he attains his craft's boundless dream.

CONCLUSION

IN THE SERVICE OF . . .

> In one sense every developed craft has its own
> morality, which consists of the virtues that
> must be cultivated if standards of
> craftsmanship are to be met. The master virtue
> is commitment to excellence, and subsidiary
> virtues include self-discipline, respect for tools
> and materials, and concern for the user or
> consumer. But a craft morality is at best
> rudimentary if it is not connected to and
> governed by a more general ethic.
> —Philip Selznick[1]

Jury trials are storytelling contests.
Lawyers reach for drama, metaphor, voice, gesture, persona, myth, and
other expressive resources of the storyteller's art to give authority to their
accounts. The need to perform arises from the American commitment—
highly unusual among the world's societies—to trial by jury. Professional
judges would not be receptive to the craft's method of telling stories. Lay
jurors are.

But isn't all this compelling reason (as if any more were needed) for the
public to distrust lawyers? Their own war stories attest to the uneasiness
they as performers feel about their official role in the search for justice.

In public, certainly, attorneys play down this conflict. When asked, for instance, if they believe what they say in court, they typically reply that they have to be convinced within themselves of the case they're going to make when they go before a jury. No doubt for many that's true. But this is no more than saying that sincerity is the base paint for the mask of performance. Sincerity can be coaxed through suspension of disbelief in a client's account as well as from genuine belief, and it can be detrimental to earnest performance to distinguish between the two. (A similar dynamic seems to occur in clients: if they convince themselves of their sincerity they can fortify their attorneys to act with sincerity on their behalf. O. J. Simpson may have been such a client.) "I am not interested in the truth outside me," Konstantin Stanislavsky said. "What is important to me is the truth in me."[2] Intense focus on inward truth makes the actor believable.

Another lawyerly defense against criticism is to assert that despite the attorneys' efforts at persuasion, juries still decide the great majority of cases on the basis of the evidence. Many in the justice system believe this to be a strongly established finding of social science research. It isn't. One vein of research indeed concludes that evidence is usually the crucial factor in verdicts. But many other studies are resolutely agnostic on the matter, focusing instead on the influence of "extra-evidentiary" factors: the composition of the jury; the attractiveness, race, social class, and speech styles of defendants and plaintiffs; and so forth. The research literature has made little headway in determining the relative weight actual juries give to evidence compared to other factors. And it has paid scant attention to the effect of lawyers' skills—perhaps because, since they infuse the trial, they can't be measured. Obstacles to assessing the validity of jury verdicts are formidable, especially given the fact that observers are barred from viewing actual jury deliberations. Except in unusual circumstances—for example, where there has been flagrant error by lawyer or judge—it is dicey to second-guess what a jury decides.[3]

Trial lawyers, in short, must live with the consequences of their craft. This leaves a nagging question at the end of my study: what *are* these lawyers' moral responsibilities? We should consider the situation of lawyers not in isolation, as though they bear a unique burden for the shortcomings of the justice system, but rather in connection to dilemmas faced by every profession at a time in our national life when the very idea of moral purpose is seriously in doubt.

*   *   *

Let us grant that lawyers rightly prize excellence in their craft as a high virtue. But as sociologist Philip Selznick reminds us, mastery by itself is only a rudimentary morality. Skill in the trial craft obviously serves the purpose of winning. Unless governed by a more general ethic, does it also serve justice?

Plato took up this question in the *Gorgias,* a Socratic dialogue about the morality of crafts of persuasion. Socrates, in conversation with Gorgias, a rhetorician, asks him to explain what rhetoricians do. Gorgias replies that he can convince juries and political gatherings to adopt his opinions. He can even convince sick people to submit to treatments when their own doctors can't. But under Socrates' prodding, Gorgias admits that, unlike crafts such as medicine, mathematics, and shipbuilding, which are based on actual knowledge, his craft is not. So, Socrates presses, the rhetorician "doesn't know the things themselves, what is good or bad, what is fine or shameful or just or unjust, but has devised persuasion about them so that though he doesn't know, among those who don't know he appears to know, rather than the man who knows."[4] Socrates asks: if a student came to you without knowledge of what is just and unjust, would you have to teach him about justice before you could teach him rhetoric? Gorgias says yes. Now Socrates has him. Gorgias is forced to admit that what is just matters and that rhetoricians *should* serve justice.

Plato, through the skepticism of Socrates, is raising the most basic questions about the purposes of persuasion. If the aim is solely to win for your client—or to exercise power—then you tell the audience whatever you think they need to hear to get them to side with you. Socrates counters, as he often does, by proposing a harder path: to seek the good. What kind of a life, he asks, is best for a person? And for a society?

Can lawyers defend themselves against Socrates' criticism? James Boyd White imagines a modern lawyer explaining to Socrates how he can justify his need for scruples to a client:

> If I were habitually sleazy and manipulative, signs of that would appear and make me less effective as a speaker for you; if I were habitually ethical but occasionally sleazy, I am sure that my discomfort would be less than completely hidden. I can hardly exaggerate the importance of what I am saying: what the Greeks called the "ethos" or character of the speaker is among the most

powerful sources of persuasion. In any case in which I act, my own sense that I am speaking properly, asking for what I am entitled to ask for, functioning out of a sense of fairness, is essential to my ethos and therefore to my success. And for success in two ways: not only in the material sense of gaining so many dollars by settlement or trial, but in the much larger sense of helping you to give this difficulty a meaning that is most valuable and appropriate to you.[5]

Strategy and ethics, White is saying, must be joined. The interests of clients and of justice are *both* best served when attorneys act with integrity. Is this pie-in-the-sky idealism? White makes no claims about present norms of the profession. He describes what he thinks lawyers *should* strive for, what is better and worse for society—and for their own souls. He does not think the path is well flagged. "Every day the lawyer faces questions of right and wrong that have no ready answer," White's modern lawyer tells Socrates.[6] The work is full of challenges that can build—or diminish—character.

Ways of dealing with ethical decisions are shaped partly by professional socialization, but many such choices a lawyer makes are, finally, matters of personal conscience. In the midst of a death penalty hearing, Penny Cooper found herself denying that her client was a Nazi. She was trying to save his life. Did she cross a moral line? Cooper could put the same question to the DA's office. They sought her client's death. He hadn't actually killed anyone. Would it have been more ethical for them, using prosecutorial discretion, to seek life imprisonment?

The issue of conduct in court is: how far will you go in your advocacy to get the results you want? As we've seen in this book, moral conviction easily works *against* restraint. Maybe you pull out the stops because the other side does, or because the odds are stacked against you, or because even though you've got the edge, you leave nothing to chance. You're driven to do it. If you get squeamish, if ethical doubts cause you to hesitate, you are liable to weaken your performance in the heat of battle.

So, while reflection on the moral choices faced in advocacy is surely desirable—and is often called for by those concerned about lawyers' ethics—it's unrealistic to hope that by itself it can improve the moral tenor of the profession. Personal integrity is largely a private matter. And self-examination is constrained by the demands of practice.

But what about the *structural* change of the trial system? Can lawyers act *publicly* to improve the chances for justice?

The most visible calls for reform in recent years involve the selection and treatment of juries. As things stand now, many good potential jurors are removed by lawyers' peremptory challenges or by exemptions, resulting in juries that are often unrepresentative of their communities and that lack the breadth of judgment a diverse makeup makes possible. And as things stand, jurors are often confused during trials about parts of witness testimonies and about the laws they are supposed to apply.

Innovative judges, experimenting in their courtrooms, have shown that these obstacles to reasoned deliberation can be reduced. Courts could rein in peremptory challenges and exemptions. Jurors could be urged to take notes and allowed to put their questions about testimony to the judge, who could seek clarification from witnesses. The judge could give legal instructions at the start of the trial instead of just at the end, and could make them clearer. These procedural reforms can aid juries in their efforts to reach just verdicts. "None of the suggested approaches to helping them do this job better is particularly difficult to pursue," legal journalist Stephen Adler writes. "Many, though, are politically chancy because they siphon power from lawyers or require judges to work harder or, at least, differently."[7] To date bar groups have tended to be lukewarm if not hostile to most of these proposals. But in the interests of justice they should actively support them. If reforms pushed many lawyers to hew more closely to evidence and law, that would be all to the good!

As helpful as these changes could be in empowering juries, however, there are higher moral stakes for trial lawyers at the present moment in American history. These are times of the sharp upward distribution of wealth, resources, and power. For a great many people on the wrong side of hardening class lines, access to such basic goods as education, medical care, and legal protection is, at best, tenuous. What is in jeopardy is the American commitment to moral equality—"the postulate," as Selznick puts it, "that all persons have the same intrinsic worth." Selznick points to the historical role American courts have played in the advancement of moral equality:

> Baseline equality [*the minimum basic goods to which all persons are entitled*] is contingent, not absolute. Its level is sensitive to changing expectations. This is perhaps best seen when we consider

"equal justice under the law" and "equal protection of the laws."
In these phrases "equality," though rhetorical, is more than empty
rhetoric. It is a mandate for *extending* legal protection to all persons, and especially to those hitherto disadvantaged or excluded.
The legal effect is to enlarge the category of who is to be treated as
a full citizen or, in the case of non-citizens, as one whose person-
hood is recognized and protected.[8]

Trial lawyers, I think, have a special responsibility to defend equal justice under the law in the face of assaults on moral equality. For they pos-
sess, at the heart of their craft tradition, an elemental insight into the nature of justice. Their craft axiom, "The more skilled the lawyer, the better
the chance of winning," has a corollary that, while seldom articulated, has
profound ethical implications: "*The more evenly matched the lawyers, the
better the chances of justice.*"

The logic is straightforward: when opposing attorneys are of similar
caliber and when each has adequate resources to devote to trial preparation,
the chance that jurors will be able to judge a case on its merits is optimized.
The lawyers in effect neutralize each other. The evidence each can adduce
then comes to the fore. Jurors will be less likely to conflate an imbalance in
skill or resources with the quality of the evidence.

The criteria for adequate representation are, of course, complex and
debatable. But the undesirability of unequal matchups is clear. A rough
parity between sides is the key to a fair shot at a just verdict.

This craft-based awareness, it seems to me, places a trust on trial
lawyers as an occupational group: to strengthen the institutional infra-
structure that promotes parity in court for those who otherwise would lack
a decent chance at justice. This protective structure includes the public defender system, legal aid services, death-penalty defense organizations, and
public-interest law groups—agencies often underfunded, understaffed,
and dependent on idealistic young lawyers; the court appointment system
that assigns attorneys to indigent defendants, and the pro bono work that
attorneys volunteer for clients and causes; and policies of recruitment that
diversify membership of the profession. The scope of these forms of representation and the fairness they foster are largely the result of judicial and
legislative responses to social movements, in the past century mainly those
seeking civil rights, labor rights, equality for women, and consumer and

environmental protection. Supports for parity of treatment under the law, in other words, are the fruit of historical struggles. They are vulnerable to being weakened, even eviscerated. Instead they need to be defended, expanded. Trial lawyers, with their intimate knowledge of the court system in their communities, are especially well positioned to try to extend the means of access to equal justice.[9]

Certain lawyers, including some who have appeared in these pages, make this fight a personal mission through their choice of clients. Consider one example from my fieldwork: I saw Tony Serra represent, at his own expense, a young man accused of a brutal assault. Serra had taken the case at the urging of the man's parents, who had seen the lawyer portrayed on *Sixty Minutes* as a brilliant, conscience-driven throwback to the sixties who, living under a vow of poverty, ploughs money from paying clients back into cases he believes in. Serra was convinced the man was innocent. The attack had occurred in the dark, and the victim's identification of the defendant was highly suspect: her brother had shown her the high school yearbook, which had two African American males in it, and she'd picked one. Still, Serra feared he might lose. The trial was in conservative San Jose, California. His client, too poor to post bail, had been raped in prison and seemed to be losing his mind. Serra worked tenaciously. He went so far as to enlist the aid of Elizabeth Loftus, a nationally recognized authority on eyewitness identification. Loftus, who agreed that the identification was egregiously weak and who admired Serra, testified for a fee of two thousand dollars (a five hundred dollar discount), which Serra paid out of his own pocket.

Tony Serra won. But such commitment is rare. And for that reason, attitudes like his raise prickly issues about justice in the justice system. What constitutes adequate representation by a counsel? What special barriers are likely to be encountered by a person who is poor, or uneducated, or not white, or not fluent in English, or facing death row, or bringing suit against a large corporation—barriers to *effective* representation? It would be disingenuous for lawyers to reply that any qualified trial lawyer could have pulled off Serra's victory. They know that the threshold of competence and resources required by the justice system is nominal compared to craft standards. They know there's a great discrepency between the economics of the legal profession and the rigorous efforts often needed to insure equal treatment under the law.[10]

Some of these economic inequities can be addressed only on a national scale. For example, plaintiffs' lawyers for cancer victims and their families failed for many years in the lawsuits they brought against tobacco companies; it took a change in presidential policy and concerted, coordinated efforts by many states' attorneys general to pierce these corporations' hitherto invincible legal armor. Many barriers to equal treatment involve local jurisdictions, however. The ineptitude of John Guilfoy's performance against Roger King in the Blaylock trial was no freak event in Philadelphia; it is an all-too-frequent sort of occurrence dictated by the very structure of a justice system that devalues the defense of poor people—usually young, male, and black—who are accused of homicide.

The problem in Philadelphia is instructive regarding moral challenges facing legal communities. For two decades, concerned criminal lawyers have pressed the Philadelphia Bar Association and the Court of Common Pleas to reform procedures in these homicide cases. Crucial pressure for change was generated by a 1992 *Philadelphia Inquirer* exposé. Wrote reporter Fredric N. Tulsky:

> In repeated cases, an Inquirer review shows, defendants have been convicted of murder after their attorneys failed to take basic steps that legal experts say should be routine.
>
> Attorneys have gone into court without having interviewed their clients; without having tracked down potential witnesses; and without having fully researched legal issues, the review shows.
>
> "The issue is not whether these are people who deserve to be punished severely," said Gerald Dugan, a former homicide prosecutor. "The issue is whether they had a fair trial. And too often, that is a legitimate question."[11]

The *Inquirer* series documented the failure of a system that barred public defenders from handling homicides. Some of the private attorneys who were awarded these cases weren't well qualified; judges appointed them anyway, at times because of personal or political ties. All received much less money to mount a defense than did their counterparts in other jurisdictions. Investigators were hired to assist in fewer than half of the cases, and paid a pittance. In the wake of the series, the money-strapped City Council appropriated funds to allow the public defenders' office to shoulder a portion—20 percent—of the city's indigent homicide defense work.

What kind of record have public defenders amassed under the new policy? Paul Conway, chief of the Defender Association's homicide unit, told me that during the first five years of the program, none of the hundreds of clients represented by his lawyers received a death sentence. During this same period, however, more than fifty clients defended by private, mostly court-appointed attorneys have been condemned to death. Furthermore, in the cases that public defenders have tried before juries (rather than handled through plea-bargains or degree-of-guilt hearings before a judge), they have won outright acquittals for their clients 40 percent of the time. Conway credits this extraordinary success rate to the skill of his lawyers, all of whom, he says, have at least ten years hard-core trial experience, and to having the resources to do a thorough job. A team of four is assigned to each case: two lawyers, an investigator, and a "mitigation specialist" who prepares for the eventuality of a death penalty hearing. Experts—a neurologist, a psychologist, an authority on DNA or ballistics—are brought into the case as needed. With this level of support, Conway says, lawyers no longer "have to fight with their hands tied behind their backs." The odds that an indigent homicide defendant in Philadelphia will get a public defender, however, are one in five. It's strictly the luck of the draw.

Socrates asks the question of what one is in the service of. In the service of the client one does what one can to win. But if justice is be served, society needs fairness in the terms on which trials—and appeals—are waged. This effort can't be fobbed off on beleaguered sectors of the profession, on lawyers who represent despised clients or underdog causes. It is a collective stewardship. Greater parity of representation is hard to pursue, hard for many lawyers even to admit the need for. It is in conflict with the vast powers of business and government, whose interests in litigation most attorneys serve. The prospects for more justice in American criminal and civil courts, dim as they may seem in this era of unleashed economic self-interest, rest on the chance that lawyers, despite their employment by well-heeled clients, will nurture a robustly critical guild mentality about how the trial system can make good on the moral promise of democracy.[12]

Parity in representation would in time affect lawyers' conduct, tempering excessive zeal more effectively than pleas for ethical self-restraint ever will. In a climate where, for example, prosecutors routinely anticipated that their opponents would mount a strong defense, they would find it riskier to press for questionably harsh verdicts. Defense lawyers who didn't feel the odds were unfairly stacked against them would have less incentive to resort to desperate measures on their clients' behalf. In a fair system, space widens for moral action. It becomes possible to gain a more honorable win, to accept a more honorable loss.

In the court of popular opinion trial lawyers often stand convicted of blatant disregard for justice. The best of them may be masters of persuasion, but they are tainted by suspicions of lying, money-grubbing, and debasing American ideals—by the scent of doing the devil's handiwork. Is this condemnation justified?

O. J. Simpson's criminal trial is a recent case in point. The verdict stoked fires of public indignation, in part because televised coverage of the proceedings turned many Americans into armchair jurors who were convinced that Simpson was guilty, however badly prosecutors and police may have bungled the case. This animosity against the defense lawyers was fueled, notably, by the press.

Consider the confessions of Jeffrey Toobin, who covered the trial for the *New Yorker.* After the verdict, Toobin claimed that he and fellow reporters, despite their better judgment, had abetted attorney Johnnie Cochran's race-based strategy. "Cochran never seemed to miss an opportunity to play racial politics in [Judge Lance] Ito's court," Toobin wrote. For instance:

> On September 11th, in the midst of the [Detective Mark] Furman controversy, Cochran arranged for the entire defense team to wear African kente-cloth ties in front of the jury. These antics brought hoots from the reporters watching the trial on the closed-circuit feed into the media compound, on the twelfth floor of the courthouse, but when it came to actual reporting on the trial we all turned into a remarkably timorous crew. The reporters were an overwhelmingly white group, and, as far as I could tell, no one ever worried that their treatment of the defense was unduly favorable.

Toobin is charging that the press corps, although keenly aware that Cochran kept playing the race card, steadily underreported it. Indeed, he says, they went to extremes to make the defense's flimsy case look credible. Reporters were intimidated, Toobin believes, because they were white:

Fear of being called racist transcended everything in that newsroom. This extended, I think, even to discussions of the evidence. The safe course for those of us covering the case was to nit-pick along with the defense attorneys. . . . Our caution and fear, however, simply misled. The case against Simpson was simply overwhelming. When we said otherwise, we lied to the audience that trusted us.[13]

In Toobin's view, Cochran succeeded in manipulating race to control not only the trial but also the national discourse about the trial. While Toobin critiques the journalists, he also justifies their conduct. What else could be expected, he implies, in a nation so riven with racial fears but that the truth would fall victim to skilled exploitation of racial identity?

In shifting blame to Johnnie Cochran, Toobin eases himself and his colleagues off the hook. Yet it was no secret to knowledgeable observers that Cochran, who, as Toobin put it, "has made a handsome living over several decades by representing well-heeled black men accused of crimes and by suing the City of Los Angeles on behalf of black people mistreated by the L.A.P.D.," uses race as a weapon in the stories he tells in court.[14] Shouldn't Toobin, a former prosecutor, have been prepared for this? The journalists' failure, it seems to me, was not that they took the defense attack on prosecution evidence too seriously—their task, after all, was to report, not to judge—but rather that, collectively, they framed the story *they* were telling in an oversimplified way. They offered little to help their mass audience make sense of the cultural dynamics of the trial's unfolding drama. Reporters were hampered in part because, being an "overwhelmingly white group," they were too inhibited, intimidated, or ill-informed to deal openly with the supercharged racial tensions for which the trial became a lightning rod.

But the coverage *could* have been different. Had black reporters and intellectuals been a significant presence in that media compound, *they* likely would not have been so tongue-tied. Some of them possessed the requisite personal authority to take the lead in diagnosing racial stratagems resorted to by both sides. Commentators such as Stanley Crouch, whose pretrial speculations in the *Los Angeles Times* about the power of the race card proved prescient, and Henry Louis Gates, Jr., whose incisive postverdict interviews with African American thinkers appeared in the same issue of the *New Yorker* as Toobin's article, conveyed a much better grasp of the symbolic force of race in present-day America and the Simpson trial than did reporters and pundits who wrung their hands at its intrusion into the courtroom and blamed the defense for putting it there.[15]

In slamming the defense, members of the press led the chorus in a typical American form of scapegoating: they displaced their own uneasiness about evils afflicting society by laying them on the heads of certain usual suspects, thereby absolving themselves. But the Simpson defense was not at fault for outperforming the prosecution. It would be better for journalists to look self-critically at how well *they* and the media corporations that employ them live up to *their* public trust to investigate and report what they find.

Trial lawyers make easy targets. But are they less moral than journalists—or other professionals? In this era of doubts and disillusionments about the ability of American institutions of all kinds to promote human well-being, who in a position of trust has a conscience free of moral conflicts? Every occupation has long-standing troubles its practitioners must face if they are to reach beyond narrow craft standards and self-interest to act for the larger good.

To speak, as seems only fair, of my own trade, scholars involved in cultural studies study how people find meaning in their lives and how they are affected by the workings of power. We want to reveal society's symbolic codes. Folklorists bring a special slant to this work: we explore the place of artful expression in human experience, in the most integrative ways we can.[16] But ironically, the esoteric theory and arcane writing in much cultural studies research, even that of folklorists, render it inaccessible to all but very small audiences. All too often, its potential to contribute to public understanding is diminished or lost.

Our narrowness is part of the general historical weakness of American colleges and universities in meeting the stringent test of education in a democracy: to prepare students for lives of morally informed citizenship. This, John Dewey's vision, is as urgent now as it has ever been.[17] Democratic renewal in a world awash in sophisticated, conglomerated media requires that Americans see beyond images produced for public consumption by our major institutions—business, government, media, education, medicine, law. Young people especially need chances to cultivate their critical awareness of how the crafts of a society are practiced, how interests are served, how decisions of consequence are made. Whatever absolution we may think our scholarship confers on us, academics enjoy no moral advantage over lawyers or reporters. Our teaching and research are shadowed by the specter of bad faith toward students. How well will what they learn with us help prepare them to grasp the circumstances in which they will later find themselves and to recognize for themselves what is right?

Are trial lawyers untrustworthy? As advocates they have an ulterior motive, of course: winning. The conclusions they want juries to reach must be scrutinized with doubt. The trick, for jurors, is not to confuse the moral impulse that inspirits the lawyer's story with the story's actual truth. Skepticism about moral appeals is crucial to reasoned judgment in trials.

But not only in trials. Skepticism is just as indispensable elsewhere. It's our best defense against the salesmanship behind *all* the crafts of persuasion—including public rhetorics of politics, advertising, entertainment, and personal relations—that crowd the contemporary scene.

Do the stories lawyers tell have redeeming value? The news and entertainment industries employ vast personnel and resources to crank out continuous streams of artfully made stories, disseminated via television, newspapers, magazines, movie theaters, theme parks, staged events, and the Internet. The effect of much of this spectacle is to amuse and distract us, not to focus our attention on things that deeply matter. We long for these deeper connections, for "the pleasure," as Saul Bellow puts it, "that comes from recognition or rediscovery of certain essences permanently associated with human life. These essences," he thinks, "are restored to our consciousness by persons who are described as artists."[18]

This book has described trial lawyers as artists, albeit of a necessarily concealed kind. Their art is ungainly, at times grotesque. What it lacks in elegance, though, it makes up for by its unique character as storytelling about events that matter—conflicts of honor and dishonor, family and property, love and sex, life and death—events that are consequential because they are real and because their recounting will change people's lives.

Where else in our distracted society are audiences assembled for days, weeks, even months on end, their attention more or less assured, in intimate proximity to the performers? Where else will they experience such intense, detailed exposure to stories whose fateful outcome they alone judge? Where else might they be even be lucky enough to encounter an advocate so engrossed in the work at hand that he or she approaches it with love?

The jury trial in these respects is unmatched as an American occasion for oral performance. "[T]he performer," Bellow says, "must have the power to impose himself."[19] In court this power turns on the ability to convey to jurors, through the medium of the case, essences of what they live and yearn for. The best lawyers know that, despite the bewilderments of modern existence, people continue to hunger for significance, to shun evil, to desire the good. They know from their craft tradition that hope is at the core of the human condition. And they know how to show their audience that moral ambiguity too is part of human nature.

These lawyers know, as other artists know, how to be a conduit for what moves us by embodying it within themselves.

NOTES

1. Kittredge (1992), 67.

2. For an account of trials from the point of view of "court buffs" in Brooklyn, see Singer (1984).

3. Except for Roger King and Judge Stout, names of the main trial participants have been changed. Dates have been omitted.

4. In transcriptions I will try to suggest certain qualities of speech. When the speaking is rhythmic I treat it poetically, breaking it into lines. I divide paragraphs by taking account of voice intonation, pauses, and the sense of the passage. I use italics when words are uttered with special emphasis and all capitals when they're shouted. This ethnopoetic approach draws on Glassie (1982), 39–40, 44–45.

5. Performance, as Bauman (1977, 11) defines it, "consists in the assumption of responsibility to an audience for a display of communicative competence." Hymes (1974, chs. 1, 2) lays the foundations for this ethnographic approach. He explores the implications of "full" performance in "Breakthrough into Performance" (Hymes, 1981). V. Turner (1988) works with the closely related concept of "cultural performance." For art's "virtual" relation to reality, see Steiner (1995).

6. These features of performance are set out in Bauman (1977).

7. According to current estimates, "In the civil area, jury trials take place in fewer than 1 percent of cases disposed of in state courts and in only 2 percent of cases terminated in federal courts," while on the criminal side, "less than 5 percent of state felony criminal cases are disposed of through jury trial" (Abramson, 1994, 8, 252). Still, the United States accounts for an estimated 80 percent of the world's jury trials (Hans and Vidmar, 1986, 31). Flemming et al. (1992) examine how defense attorneys, prosecutors, and judges work separately and together to expedite criminal cases. Maynard (1984) analyzes the process of plea bargaining. Nader and Sursocks (1986) argue that, despite variations in how justice is pursued, concern for justice is central to every human society.

8. For the idea of craft as tradition, with intrinsic standards of excellence developed through generations of practice, see MacIntyre (1981). For a folklorist's ethnography of an occupational culture, see McCarl (1985). For a fiction-like rendering of lawyer talk, see Joseph (1997).

9. All quotes below are from Spence (1986).

10. The best piece I know on the power of folktales to give counsel is Benjamin's (1969) essay "The Storyteller: Reflections on the Works of Nikolai Leskov," first published in 1936. Warner (1995) shows a keen sense of the mythic underpinnings of stories. Kittredge (1987, 62) defines mythology as "a story that contains a set of implicit instructions from society to

its members, telling them what is valuable and now they are to conduct themselves if they are to preserve the things they value."

11. Timothy Egan, "Rebuking the U.S., Jury Acquits Two in Marshal's Killing in Idaho Siege," *New York Times,* July 9, 1993, A1.

12. Pye (1978) defines craft as work that involves risks from the beginning to the end of a project.

13. All names have been changed, including the lawyers'.

14. Durkheim ([1912] 1995), 429. Durkheim held that societies renew themselves—and that their members reenergize themselves—through sacred ritual activities.

15. On disputes over the framing of experience, see Goffman (1974, esp. 321–38). Saint Augustine (1949) is an early source on authority: his right to speak for God came from his experience as a sinner. White (1994) investigates how authority is challenged and created in conflict-laden experiences of life and law.

16. This summary is drawn from Jo Thomas, "Oklahoma Bombing Trial Goes to the Jury in Denver," *New York Times,* December 17, 1997, A1; Jo Thomas, "Nichols Convicted of Plot and Manslaughter Counts but Not of Actual Bombing; Could Face Death," *New York Times,* December 24, 1997, A1; Jo Thomas, "Bomb Jury Hears Testimony in Sentencing Phase of Case," *New York Times,* December 30, 1997, A8; James Brooke, "Nichols Life Was Saved by a Handful of Holdouts," *New York Times,* January 11, 1998, A10.

17. The program I curated, American Trial Lawyers, took place from June 25 to July 6, 1986.

18. Ted Koppel reported this on *Nightline,* May 14, 1996.

19. Regarding *language use* in court, see, for example, Conley and O'Barr (1990) on the impact of class-linked speech styles; Atkinson and Drew (1979) on the social organization of speech; Danet (1980) on the struggle over the meaning of words; Gumperz (1982) on the miscommunication resulting from linguistic and cultural differences; and Mertz (1994) for references to recent research.

On *stories,* Bennett and Feldman's (1981) cognitive model of how lawyers construct narratives is a landmark study. Amsterdam and Hertz (1992) analyze stories told in closing arguments, with attention to the influence of myth and pop culture. Schuetz and Snedaker (1988) look at the rhetorical efficacy of lawyers' stories in historically notorious trials. Matsuda (1989) and Delgado (1989) point to story as a primary means for outgroups to seek justice. LaRue (1995) discusses Supreme Court decisions as more or less persuasive stories. Jackson (1988) develops a semiotic theory of the place of narrative in law. See also nn. 20 and 21 below.

On *disputing,* see Greenhouse et al. (1994) on the symbolic role of courts and law in American towns; Merry (1990) on working-class dealings with courts in family and neighborhood disagreements; and Brenneis (1988) for references to research on wrangling of many kinds in many societies.

On *law and life,* among the most searching commentators are White, who has mapped connections of law, literature, and community in a series of works (most recently, 1994); Williams (1991), who asserts the authority of personal experience in her critiques of subordination in the law; Minow (1990), who examines dilemmas of difference in legal treatment of different groups; Ball (1981, 1993), who uses theological insights to grasp what is at stake in the practice of law; and Cover (1992), who studies legal conflicts over fundamental values that pit government against particular communities.

20. The idea that lawyers give performances at trial is consistent with much of the scholarship cited above, but its implications have yet to be developed. Ball (1981) is one of a small number who have worked directly with metaphors of theater and performance; he cites others who have, too. White (1994, ix) uses "performance" creatively to mean the conscious art of human conduct in challenging situations. A performance approach considers affective (including nonverbal) dimensions of storytelling alongside the cognitive ones that have occupied most scholars of narrative in trials (e.g., Bennett and Feldman, 1981). This can lead to a fuller, more integrated grasp of what trial stories do.

21. Pennington and Hastie (1991) use a series of studies to show that jurors reach their decisions by following a process of story construction and by matching the story to the available verdict that best fits.

22. Felstiner and Sarat (1992) scrutinize the complex dynamics of lawyer-client relationships. Cunningham (1992) describes, with himself as an example, how difficult it often is for lawyers to hear their client's story rather than forcing it into legal categories. Blanck et al. (1985) find that judges may nonverbally "leak" to jurors their personal views about defendants' guilt or innocence.

23. My ethnographic method is in the tradition of symbolic anthropology described by Geertz (1973, ch. 1).

Chapter 1

1. Sophocles (1954), 31.

2. Todorov (1977) makes this observation about the double character of narratives in detective fiction.

3. The following account is based on official court transcripts, field notes, and taped interviews with Roger King.

4. In a leading manual on trial practice, Mauet (1980, 56) writes: "It is difficult to imagine a situation where a party, either plaintiff or defendant, would find it advantageous to waive making an opening statement." Guilfoy also passed on his opportunity to give an opening later, when he began to present his case.

5. Ferguson (1953), 25–53. He draws his terms "purpose," "passion," and "perception" from Kenneth Burke's ([1945] 1969, 38–41, 264–65) use of the Greek words *poiema*, *pathema*, and *mathema*, respectively. Three-part movements—the first an initial state, the second a journey, and the last a return in a transformed state—are a recurrent pattern in Western folk experience and storytelling. See, for instance, F. Turner (1986), 87–88.

6. Aristotle (1987), 32, 42–43, 44–47 (chs. 2, 11, 13, 14).

7. Esslin (1976) describes these elements of drama.

8. These lines are broken to suggest the speech's poetic rhythm. See Introduction, n. 4.

9. Angelou (1986), "Caged Bird," 183; Dunbar (1907), "Sympathy," 162.

10. Sperber (1974) explains how cultural symbolism guides—but doesn't dictate—the associative pathways of the mind. Fernandez (1986) examines the transformative power of metaphor in performance.

Chapter 2

1. Sontag (1966), "On Style," 32.

2. Names of participants in the series of trials described in this chapter, except for the lawyers and judge, have been changed. I draw from official trial transcripts, tape recordings of closing arguments, witness testimonies, field notes, and taped interviews with Mozenter and King.

3. In the following, a * marks the omission of a segment of the summation. An ellipsis means that I've left out a short amount of speech. An extra space between lines indicates a longer-than-usual pause and, at times, a shift of topic. For ways of reading poetic transcription, see Introduction, n. 4.

4. "Language lives only in the dialogic interaction of those who make use of it," wrote Bakhtin (1984, 183). "The entire life of language, in any area of its use (in everyday life, in business, scholarship, art, and so forth) is permeated with dialogic relationships." For Bakhtin's detailed description of dialogic varieties of speech, see the chapter "Discourse in Dostoevsky." My discussion in this section is much indebted to Bakhtin. American social theorists such as Mead (1934), Birdwhistell (1970), and Bateson (1972) have reached conclusions paralleling Bakhtin's about the centrality of relationship to communication.

5. American Bar Association (1981), EC 2–26, EC 2–30, EC 7–1.

6. Bateson's (1972) "Style, Grace, and Information in Primitive Art" trenchantly explores the relation between conscious and unconscious skill. Performers' repertoires are a subject of long-standing interest in folklore scholarship. See Ives (1978) for an exemplary study of one songmaker's repertoire that delves into his life's preoccupations and the cultural traditions that shaped his art.

7. Pioneering studies by Lord (1960), on Yugoslavian epic singers, and by Propp ([1928] 1968), on Russian folktales, demonstrate how oral composition entails the use of already-known elements to fill structural slots. Kuiper (1996) shows that oral formulae are endemic to speech and that the degree of speakers' reliance on them depends on the nature of the pressures presented by each distinctive type of performance situation. Bauman (1986, 96–98) discusses parallelism in story performance.

8. Davis (1985), 18.

9. Davis (1985) discusses circularity on pp. 27–30, syllogism on pp. 76–78, open-endedness on pp. 80–81.

10. In capitalizing these themes, I follow Barthes (1972), who uses this device to illustrate how myth operates. In myth, Barthes wrote, a concept (like Home or Redemption) attaches itself to a specific experience and leeches the experience of its complexity. The result, he argued, is a story with a ready-made, comforting interpretation that confirms ideology or stereotypes.

11. Harr (1995), 374–76. Italics in the original.

12. Sontag (1966, 24–25) develops this line of argument.

13. Goffman (1959), 249.

14. Bateson (1972), 129.

1. Zora Neale Hurston (1973, 228) defines "handkerchief-head" as a "syncophant type of Negro; also an *Uncle Tom*."

2. This discussion relies on the *Philadelphia Evening Bulletin* clipping files at the Temple University Library Archives. It also draws on articles in these files from the *Philadelphia Inquirer, Philadelphia Daily News, Philadelphia Tribune, Philadelphia Guardian, Jewish Exponent,* and *New York Times.*

3. Moldovsky and DeWolf, (1975, 124–35). Moldovsky, a Philadelphia defense attorney, devotes a chapter of his autobiography to Moore's tactics.

4. On ritualized insults see Abrahams (1970, 39–60) and Labov (1972, 297–353). These are a subset of the broad rhetorical practice of signifying, analyzed in depth by Gates (1988). On black forms of discourse in relation to black culture see Smitherman (1977).

5. On black folk heroes see Roberts (1989) and Levine (1977, 367–440).

6. Lewis (1960), 14.

CHAPTER 3

1. Ellison (1986), 19.

2. Mindfulness, like grace, can be seen as a universal human capacity. Attention to it is highly developed in some Buddhist traditions. For a recent treatment, see Klein (1995, 61–88).

3. Ellison (1986), 164. Ellison's far-reaching grasp of the pluralistic dynamics of American artistic communication has shaped my approach to cultural identity in this chapter.

4. I extended invitations based on recommendations solicited from various attorneys and judges, gathered largely through phone interviews. I tried to get a broad geographical and cultural representation. Participants attended the Festival for two or three days and took part in mock summations, direct exams, and cross-exams, as well as "war story" sessions. For an analysis of the Festival of American Folklife as a site for the display of culture, see Cantwell (1993).

5. Ellison (1986), 279.

6. For example, Toni Morrison (1992, xv) analyzes the racial stereotyping of *both* Thomas and Anita Hill by Thomas's supporters on the Judiciary Committee:

> Thus, the candidate was cloaked in the garments of loyalty, guardianship, and . . . limitless love. Love of God via his Catholic school, of servitude via a patriarchal disciplinarian grandfather, of loyalty to party via his accumulated speeches and the trophies of "America" on his office walls. The interrogator, therefore, the accusing witness Anita Hill, was dressed in the oppositional costume of madness, anarchic sexuality, and explosive verbal violence.

Morrison points out that this is the mythology whites have traditionally held about black people: they "are used to signify the polar opposites of love and repulsion."

7. Rosaldo (1993) explores the "multiplex" nature of American cultural identity.

On divisive uses of identity, see Douglas (1966), who shows how the enforcement of boundaries between groups are tied to taboos about bodily pollution, and Rieder (1985), who documents the resistance of white ethnic groups to the breaching of social boundaries.

The following accounts are based on audiotapes of the sessions, transcripts of these tapes, videotapes of some sessions, my conversations and interviews with participants and their colleagues, and biographical materials (including journalists' sketches of their work) that they supplied. On the devices used in transcribing the material, see Chapter 2, n. 3. On ways of reading poetic transcription, see the Introduction, n.4.

8. This case file was prepared for the Festival by attorney Harold Rosenthal.

9. Ages given are lawyers' ages in 1986, the year of the Festival.

10. See Paredes (1958) for a folklorist's study of traditional Border culture. Fischer (1986) explores how ethnicity continues in contemporary society to shape people's sense of who they are and to give them insight into the broadest human concerns.

11. For studies of the use of emotional discourse in a range of societies and contexts, see Lutz and Abu-Lughod (1990).

12. See, for example, hooks's (1992, ch. 1) critique of the position of African Americans who have "a vision of cultural homogeneity" and deny significance to race.

13. Darrow (1957), 48.

14. Darrow (1957), 36.

15. Darrow (1957), 80.

16. Darrow (1957), 52.

17. Baldus et al. (1990) and Nakell and Hardy (1987) give convincing analyses of race bias and arbitrariness in death sentence decisions.

18. The *State v. Diamond* case file was developed for trial training workshops by the National Institute for Trial Advocacy (Seckinger and Broun, 1983).

19. Finnegan (1998), 56.

20. Harris (1984), 153.

21. The Peters case file comes from the National Institute for Trial Advocacy (Seckinger and Broun, 1983).

22. For instance, Gilligan (1982, 94) describes the development experienced by a woman of twenty-five faced with a painful decision about having an abortion:

> Within the new framework, her conception of herself and what is "right for myself" is changing. She can consider this emergent self "a good person" because her concept of goodness has expanded to encompass the feeling of "self-worth," the feeling that "you are not going to sell yourself short and you are not going to make yourself do things that you know are really stupid and that you don't want to do."

Goldberger et al. (1996) present a range of current thinking in this moral development perspective.

23. Arguedas (1985), 37.

24. Warner (1995), 63–81.

25. The *Freeman v. Amerifun* case file was created by attorney Edward Stein of Ann

Arbor, Michigan, for use in his trial advocacy workshops. It was slightly modified for the Festival.

26. On the internalization of this voice of authority, see "the internal interlocutor" discussed by Willis (1981, 166–69).

27. On class envy, see Lapham (1988); on the politically conservative impact of class fears, see Ehrenreich (1989).

28. Bennett H. Beach, "The New Women in Court," *Time,* May 30, 1983, 60–61.

29. Epstein (1983) examines gender stereotyping in the profession. For an ethnographic study of relations between men and women trial lawyers in law firms that documents how emotions play into the subordination of women, see Pierce (1995). Hagan and Kay (1995) offer a sobering study of how women lawyers have fared in their careers.

30. Keith D. Picher, "Chicago Lawyer Poll: Who Are the Best Criminal Defense Lawyers in Town?" *Chicago Lawyer* 8, no. 4 (April 1985): 9.

31. This concern for "natality" is at the heart of Hannah Arendt's (1958) philosophy.

32. Ellison (1986), 112.

Chapter 4

1. St. Johns (1962), 3.

2. St. Johns (1962), 4.

3. Wittgenstein ([1921] 1961) investigated this distinction between saying and showing.

4. The war stories retold here were tailored to a very public setting: groups of four to six lawyers, most newly acquainted, sitting in a semicircle, taking turns, sharing mikes, with an audience looking on. In the right leisurely circumstances war stories can be far longer than these—many-layered sagas about events.

Bellow and Minow (1996) present first-person narratives written by lawyers as "case studies" of their experiences. Anecdotes that sometimes sound much like ones told at the Festival are submitted by readers to the "War Stories" column in the *American Bar Association Journal.*

5. For the conventions of transcription followed below, consult the Introduction, n. 4, and Chapter 2, n. 3.

6. In a New South Wales version of this tale, the country jury delivers a verdict of "not guilty, if he returns the cows," and, after chastisement by the judge, comes back with "not guilty—and he doesn't have to return the cows" (Gilbert, 1986, 11–12).

7. Dorman (1969), 28, 60.

Conclusion

1. Selznick (1992), 325.

2. Stanislavsky (1950), 22. See also Goffman (1959), 17–21.

3. Kalven and Zeisel's (1966) often-cited report of results from the 1950's University of Chicago Law School's Jury Project is a primary source for confidence in jury verdicts: they found that judges agreed with their juries' verdicts 78 percent of the time. Guinther (1988, xvi–xxviii) discusses some limitations of these findings as well as those based on mock

juries and juror surveys. Ford (1986, 26), reviewing the literature on the role of extra-evidentiary factors in jury verdicts, notes, "While trial manuals advise attorneys about the importance of their behavior in influencing jurors, few studies have manipulated these variables to assess their effect." Visher (1987, 5), although arguing for the importance of evidence, notes how little research has been done measuring its role: "The research emphasis on extralegal influence and juror competence has created a void in the literature, and research on the role of legally relevant factors—witnesses' testimony and exhibits—in jurors' decisions is lacking."

4. Plato (1979), 27.

5. White (1983), 892.

6. White (1983), 893.

7. Adler (1994), 241. He describes judges' reforms and shows, through case studies, why they are needed. Note-taking is the one change that has become fairly widespread. Adler's call to completely eliminate peremptory challenges seems extreme to me. See Abramson (1994) for a lucid argument showing the importance of the jury, as a deliberative body, for American democracy.

8. Selznick (1992), 485.

9. On the law's indebtedness to social action, see, for example, Higginbotham (1992).

10. On unequal treatment under the law because of race, see Kennedy (1997) and Mann (1993). On unequal treatment because of class, see Smith (1991).

11. Fredric N. Tulsky, "Big-Time Trials, Small Time Defenses; Many Lawyers, Even the Well-Connected, Do Top Work, Others Are Not Up to the Task." *Philadelphia Inquirer,* September 14, 1992, A1. The first installment appeared the previous day: Tulsky, "What Price Justice? Poor Defendants Pay the Costs as Courts Save on Murder Trials," September 13, 1992, A1. The controversy over the appointment and funding of counsel for indigent homicide defendants can be traced in these *Inquirer* articles: Tulsky, "Standards Approved for Lawyers—Defenders Face New Guidelines," November 1, 1983, B1; John Woestendick, "ACLU Questions System for Choosing Murder-Trial Lawyers," April 23, 1985, B1; Woestendick, "Philadelphia's Prominence on Death Row Debated," August 22, 1986, B1; Woestendick and Susan Caba, "Attorney Standards Toughened; Judge Sets Appointment Rule," May 20, 1988, B1; Linda Loyd, "Lawyers Sue over Lack of Pay; Represent Poor in Criminal Cases," April 7, 1989, B1; Henry Goldman, "Bar Panel Shifts on Role of Defenders," February 1, 1991, B7; Tulsky, "Bar Chancellor Criticizes City on Defense for Poor," September 21, 1992; Tulsky, "Murder Convict Says Lax Lawyer Did Him In; At Issue: A New Trial, and Attorney's Efforts," December 18, 1992, B1; Tulsky, "Philadelphia's Top Pay to a Lawyer for Poor: $358,000 in 3 Years," January 10, 1993, A1.

12. Gordon and Simon (1992, 257) call for the American Bar Association and other bar associations to "concretely back up their commitments to public service by the bar, and [to] serve as sources of influence to counter the economic pressures of private practice that severely discourage engagement in non-billable ventures of any kind." Carlin (1966) describes how the milieu of practice shapes lawyers' ethics.

13. Toobin (1995), 46.

14. Toobin (1995), 42.

15. Crouch (1995), 77–80; Gates (1995).

16. Bauman (1986, 114), describing his own work on narrative, catches the scholarly impulse behind much folklore research, including my own:

> [T]o seek an "interdisciplinary" solution is to concede the legitimacy of disciplinary differentiation to begin with, whereas I have preferred to align myself with the integrative vision of language, literature, and culture in which folklore was itself first conceived. More particularly, though, with regard to narrative, I believe that "the fullness of the work in all its wholeness and indivisibility" [he is quoting Bakhtin (1981:255) here] demands and is better served by the kind of integrative vision offered by the performance-centered analysis I have pursued in these pages.

17. I am not harkening back to some mythic time, imagined into being by some conservatives in "the culture wars," when the academy supposedly lived up to its ideals. It never has. See Levine (1996) for a strong defense of multicultural education against the ahistoricism of its critics.

18. Bellow (1994), 168.

19. Bellow (1994), 164.

BIBLIOGRAPHY

Abrahams, Roger D. 1970. *Deep Down in the Jungle.* Chicago: Aldine.

Abramson, Jeffrey. 1995. *We, the Jury: The Jury System and the Ideal of Democracy.* New York: Basic Books.

Adler, Stephen J. 1994. *The Jury: Disorder in the Courts.* New York: Doubleday.

American Bar Association. 1981. *Model Code of Professional Responsibility and Code of Judicial Conduct.* Chicago: National Center for Professional Responsibility.

Amsterdam, Anthony G., and Randy Hertz. 1992. "An Analysis of Closing Arguments to a Jury." *New York Law School Law Review* 37:55–122.

Angelou, Maya. 1986. *Poems.* Toronto: Bantam Books.

Arendt, Hannah. 1958. *The Human Condition.* Chicago: University of Chicago Press.

Arguedas, Cristina C. 1985. "Interview: Penny Cooper." *California Attorneys for Criminal Justice Forum,* 12, no. 1 (January–February):36–39.

Aristotle. 1987. *The Poetics of Aristotle.* Trans. Stephen Halliwell. Chapel Hill: University of North Carolina Press.

Atkinson, J. Maxwell, and Paul Drew. 1979. *Order in Court: The Organization of Verbal Interaction in Judicial Settings.* Atlantic Highlands, NJ: Humanities Press.

Augustine. 1949. *The Confessions of Saint Augustine.* Trans. Edward Pusey. New York: The Modern Library.

Bakhtin, Mikhail 1981. *The Dialogic Imagination.* Trans. Caryl Emerson and Michael Holquist. Austin: University of Texas Press.

———. 1984. *Problems of Dostoevsky's Poetics.* Trans. Caryl Emerson. Minneapolis: University of Minnesota Press.

Baldus, David C., George Woodworth, and Charles A. Pulaski, Jr. 1990. *Equal Justice and the Death Penalty: A Legal and Empirical Analysis.* Boston: Northeastern University Press.

Ball, Milner S. 1981. *The Promise of American Law: A Theological, Humanistic View of Legal Process.* Athens: University of Georgia Press.

———. 1993. *The Word and the Law.* Chicago: University of Chicago Press.

Barthes, Roland. 1972. *Mythologies.* Trans. Annette Lavers. New York: Hill and Wang.

Bateson, Gregory. 1972. *Steps to an Ecology of Mind.* New York: Ballantine Books.

Bauman, Richard. 1977. *Verbal Art as Performance.* Rowley, MA: Newbury House.

———. 1986. *Story, Performance, and Event: Contextual Studies of Oral Narrative.* Cambridge: Cambridge University Press.

Bellow, Gary, and Martha Minow, eds. 1996. *Law Stories.* Ann Arbor: University of Michigan Press.

Bellow, Saul. 1994. *It All Adds Up: From the Dim Past to the Uncertain Future.* New York: Penguin Books.

Benjamin, Walter. 1969. *Illuminations.* Trans. Harry Zohn. New York: Schocken Books.

Bennett, W. Lance, and Martha S. Feldman. 1981. *Reconstructing Reality in the Courtroom: Justice and Judgment in American Culture.* New Brunswick, NJ: Rutgers University Press.

Birdwhistell, Ray L. 1970. *Kinesics and Context: Essays on Body Motion Communication.* Philadelphia: University of Pennsylvania Press.

Blanck, Peter David, Robert Rosenthal, and LaDoris Hazzard Cordell. 1985. "The Appearance of Justice: Judges' Verbal and Nonverbal Behavior in Criminal Jury Trials." *Stanford Law Review* 38:89–151.

Brenneis, Donald. 1988. "Language and Disputing." *Annual Review of Anthropology* 17:221–37.

Burke, Kenneth. [1945] 1969. *A Grammar of Motives.* Berkeley: University of California Press.

Cantwell, Robert. 1993. *Ethnomimesis: Folklife and the Representation of Culture.* Chapel Hill: University of North Carolina Press.

Carlin, Jerome. 1966. *Lawyers' Ethics—A Survey of the New York City Bar.* New York: Russell Sage Foundation.

Conley, John M., and William M. O'Barr. 1990. *Rules Versus Relationships: The Ethnography of Legal Discourse.* Chicago: University of Chicago Press.

Cover, Robert. 1992. *Narrative, Violence, and the Law: The Essays of Robert Cover.* Ed. Martha Minow, Michael Ryan, and Austin Sarat. Ann Arbor: University of Michigan Press.

Crouch, Stanley. 1995. *The All-American Skin Game, or, The Decoy of Race.* New York: Vintage Books.

Cunningham, Clark D. 1992. "The Lawyer as Translator, Representation as Text: Towards an Ethnography of Legal Discourse." *Cornell Law Review* 77:1298–1387.

Danet, Brenda. 1980. "'Baby' or 'Fetus'? Language and the Construction of Reality in a Manslaughter Trial." *Semiotica* 32, no. 3/4:187–219.

Darrow, Clarence. 1957. *Attorney for the Damned.* Ed. Arthur Weinberg. New York: Simon and Schuster.

Davis, Gerald L. 1985. *I Got the Word in Me and I Can Sing It, You Know: A Study of the Performed African-American Sermon.* Philadelphia: University of Pennsylvania Press.

Delgado, Richard. 1989. "Storytelling for Oppositionists and Others: A Plea for Narrative." *Michigan Law Review* 87:2411–41.

Dorman, Michael. 1969. *King of the Courtroom: Percy Foreman for the Defense.* New York: Delacorte Press.

Douglas, Mary. 1966. *Purity and Danger: An Analysis of Concepts of Pollution and Taboo.* London: Routledge & Kegan Paul.

Dunbar, Paul Laurence. 1907. *The Complete Poems of Paul Laurence Dunbar.* New York: Dodd, Mead and Company.

Durkheim, Emile. [1912] 1995. *The Elementary Forms of the Religious Life.* Trans. K. Fields. New York: The Free Press.

Ehrenreich, Barbara. 1989. *Fear of Falling: The Inner Life of the Middle Class.* New York: Pantheon Books.

Ellison, Ralph. 1986. *Going to the Territory.* New York: Vintage Books.

Epstein, Cynthia Fuchs. 1983. *Women in Law.* 2nd ed. New York: Anchor Books.

Esslin, Martin. 1976. *The Anatomy of Drama.* New York: Hill and Wang.

Felstiner, William L. F., and Austin Sarat. 1992. "Enactments of Power: Negotiating Reality and Responsibility in Lawyer-Client Interactions." *Cornell Law Review* 77:1447–98.

Ferguson, Francis. 1953. *The Idea of a Theater.* Garden City, NY: Doubleday Anchor Books.

Fernandez, James. 1986. *Persuasions and Performances: The Play of Tropes in Culture.* Bloomington: Indiana University Press.

Finnegan, William. 1998. "Defending the Unabomber." *New Yorker* (March 16):52–63.

Fischer, Michael M. J. 1986. "Ethnicity and the Post-Modern Arts of Memory." In *Writing Culture: The Poetics and Politics of Ethnography* (pp. 194–233). Ed. James Clifford and George E. Marcus. Berkeley: University of California Press.

Flemming, Roy B., Peter F. Nardulli, and James Eisenstein. 1992. *The Craft of Justice: Politics and Work in Criminal Court Communities.* Philadelphia: University of Pennsylvania Press.

Ford, Marilyn Chandler. 1986. "The Role of Extralegal Factors in Jury Verdicts." *The Justice System Journal* 11, no. 1:16–39.

Frank, Jerome. 1949. *Courts on Trial: Myth and Reality in American Justice.* Princeton: Princeton University Press.

Gates, Henry Louis, Jr. 1988. *The Signifying Monkey: A Theory of Afro-American Literary Criticism.* New York: Oxford University Press.

———. 1995. "Thirteen Ways of Looking at a Black Man." *New Yorker* (October 23):56–65.

Geertz, Clifford. 1973. *The Interpretation of Cultures.* New York: Basic Books.

Gilbert, Michael, ed. 1986. *The Oxford Book of Legal Anecdotes.* New York: Oxford University Press.

Gilligan, Carol. 1982. *In a Different Voice: Psychological Theory and Women's Development.* Cambridge, MA: Harvard University Press.

Glassie, Henry. 1982. *Passing the Time in Ballymenone: Culture and History of an Ulster Community.* Philadelphia: University of Pennsylvania Press.

Goffman, Erving. 1959. *The Presentation of Self in Everyday Life.* Garden City, NY: Anchor.

———. 1974. *Frame Analysis: An Essay on the Organization of Experience.* New York: Harper Colophon Books.

Goldberger, Nancy R., Jill M. Tarule, Blythe M. Clinchy, and Mary F. Belenky, eds. 1996. *Knowledge, Difference, and Power: Essays Inspired by Women's Ways of Knowing.* New York: Basic Books.

Gordon, Robert W., and William H. Simon. 1992. "The Redemption of Professionalism?" In *Lawyers' Ideals, Lawyers' Practices: Transformations in the American Legal Profession* (pp. 230–57). Ed. Robert L. Nelson, David M. Trubek, and Raymond L. Solomon. Ithaca, NY: Cornell University Press.

Greenhouse, Carol J., Barbara Yngvesson, and David M. Engel. 1994. *Law and Community in Three American Towns.* Ithaca, NY: Cornell University Press.

Guinther, John. *The Jury in America.* 1988. New York: Facts on File Publications.

Gumperz, John J. 1982. "Fact and Inference in Courtroom Testimony." In *Language and Social Identity* (pp. 163–95). Ed. John J. Gumperz. Cambridge: Cambridge University Press.

Hagan, John, and Fiona Kay. 1995. *Gender in Practice: A Study of Lawyers' Lives.* New York: Oxford University Press.

Hans, Valerie P. and Neil Vidmar. 1986. *Judging the Jury.* New York: Plenum Press.

Harr, Jonathan. 1995. *A Civil Action.* New York: Vintage Books.

Harris, Jo Ann. 1984. "As Federal Prosecutor: Talking Man to Man." In *Women Lawyers: Perspectives on Success* (pp. 153–64). Ed. Emily Couric. New York: Harcourt Brace Jovanovich.

Higginbotham, A. Leon, Jr. 1992. "An Open Letter to Justice Clarence Thomas from a Federal Judicial Colleague." In *Race-ing Justice, En-gendering Power* (pp. 3–39). Ed. Toni Morrison. New York: Pantheon Books.

hooks, bell. 1992. *Black Looks: Race and Representation.* Boston: South End Press.

Hurston, Zora Neale. [1942] 1973. "Story in Harlem Slang." *The American Mercury* 45 (July):84–96. Reprinted in *Mother Wit from the Laughing Barrel* (pp. 222–29). Ed. Alan Dundes. Englewood Cliffs, NJ: Prentice-Hall.

Hymes, Dell. 1974. *Foundations in Sociolinguistics: An Ethnographic Approach.* Philadelphia: University of Pennsylvania Press.

———. 1981. "*In Vain I Tried to Tell You*": *Essays in Native American Ethnopoetics.* Philadelphia: University of Pennsylvania Press.

Ives, Edward D. 1978. *Joe Scott, the Woodsman-Songmaker.* Urbana: University of Illinois Press.

Jackson, Bernard S. 1988. *Law, Fact, and Narrative Coherence.* Roby, UK: Deborah Charles Publications.

Joseph, Lawrence. 1997. *Lawyerland.* New York: Farrar, Straus, and Giroux.

Kalven, Harry, Jr., and Hans Zeisel. 1966. *The American Jury.* Boston: Little, Brown and Company.

Kennedy, Randall. 1997. *Race, Crime, and the Law.* New York: Pantheon Books.

Kittredge, William. 1987. *Owning It All.* St. Paul: Graywolf Press.

———. 1992. *Hole in the Sky: A Memoir.* New York: Vintage Books.

Klein, Anne Carolyn. 1995. *Meeting the Great Bliss Queen: Buddhists, Feminists, and the Art of the Self.* Boston: Beacon Press.

Kuiper, Koenraad. 1996. *Smooth Talkers: The Linguistic Performance of Auctioneers and Sportscasters.* Mahwah, NJ: Lawrence Erlbaum Associates.

Labov, William. 1972. *Language in the Inner City.* Philadelphia: University of Pennsylvania Press.

Lapham, Lewis H. 1988. *Money and Class in America: Notes and Observations on the Civil Religion.* New York: Ballantine Books.

LaRue, L. H. 1995. *Constitutional Law as Fiction: Narrative in the Rhetoric of Authority.* University Park: The Pennsylvania State University Press.

Levine, Lawrence W. 1977. *Black Culture and Black Consciousness: Afro-American Folk Thought from Slavery to Freedom.* New York: Oxford University Press.

———. 1996. *The Opening of the American Mind: Canons, Culture, and History.* Boston: Beacon Press.

Lewis, Arthur H. 1960. *The Worlds of Chippy Patterson.* New York: Harcourt, Brace and Company.

Lord, Albert B. 1960. *The Singer of Tales.* Cambridge, MA: Harvard University Press.

Lutz, Catherine A., and Lila Abu-Lughod, eds. 1990. *Language and the Politics of Emotion.* Cambridge: Cambridge University Press.

MacIntyre, Alasdair. 1981. *After Virtue.* South Bend, IN: Notre Dame University Press.

Mann, Coramae Richey. 1993. *Unequal Justice: A Question of Color.* Bloomington: Indiana University Press.

Matsuda, Mari. 1989. "Public Response to Racist Speech: Considering the Victim's Story." *Michigan Law Review* 87:2320–81.

Mauet, Thomas A. 1980. *Fundamentals of Trial Techniques.* Boston: Little, Brown and Company.

Maynard, Douglas W. 1984. *Inside Plea Bargaining: The Language of Negotiation.* New York: Plenum Press.

McCarl, Robert. 1985. *The District of Columbia Fire Fighters' Project: A Case Study in Occupational Folklife.* Washington, DC: Smithsonian Institution Press.

Mead, George Herbert. 1934. *Mind, Self, and Society.* Chicago: University of Chicago Press.

Merry, Sally Engle. 1990. *Getting Justice and Getting Even: Legal Consciousness among Working-Class Americans.* Chicago: University of Chicago Press.

Mertz, Elizabeth. 1994. "Legal Language: Pragmatics, Poetics, and Social Power." *Annual Review of Anthropology* 23:435–55.

Minow, Martha. 1990. *Making All the Difference: Inclusion, Exclusion, and American Law.* Ithaca, NY: Cornell University Press.

Moldovsky, Joel, and Rose DeWolf. 1975. *The Best Defense.* New York: Macmillan.

Morrison, Toni, ed. 1992. *Race-ing Justice, En-gendering Power.* New York: Pantheon Books.

Nader, Laura, and Andree Sursocks. 1986. "Anthropology and Justice." In *Justice: Views from the Social Sciences* (pp. 205–33). Ed. Ronald L. Cohen. New York: Plenum Press.

Nakell, Barry, and Kenneth A. Hardy. 1987. *The Arbitrariness of the Death Penalty.* Philadelphia: Temple University Press,

Paredes, Américo. 1958. *"With His Pistol in His Hand": A Border Ballad and Its Hero.* Austin: University of Texas Press.

Pennington, Nancy, and Reid Hastie. 1991. "A Cognitive Theory of Juror Decision Making: The Story Model." *Cardozo Law Review* 13:519–57.

Pierce, Jennifer L. 1995. *Gender Trials: Emotional Lives in Contemporary Law Firms.* Berkeley: University of California Press.

Plato. 1979. *Gorgias.* Trans. Terence Irwin. Oxford: Clarendon Press.

Propp, Vladmir. [1928] 1968. *Morphology of the Folktale.* Trans. Laurence Scott. 2nd ed. Austin: University of Texas Press.

Pye, David. 1978. *The Nature and Art of Workmanship.* New York: Cambridge University Press.

Rieder, Jonathan. 1985. *Canarsie: The Jews and Italians of Brooklyn Against Liberalism.* Cambridge, MA: Harvard University Press.

Roberts, John W. 1989. *From Trickster to Badman: The Black Folk Hero in Slavery and Freedom.* Philadelphia: University of Pennsylvania Press.

Rosaldo, Renato. 1987. *Culture and Truth: The Remaking of Social Analysis.* Boston: Beacon Press.

St. Johns, Adela Rogers. 1962. *Final Verdict.* Garden City, NY: Doubleday.

Schuetz, Janice, and Kathryn Holmes Snedaker. 1988. *Communication and Litigation: Case Studies of Famous Trials.* Carbondale: Southern Illinois University Press.

Seckinger, James H., and Kenneth S. Broun. 1983. *Problems and Cases in Trial Advocacy.* Law school ed., vol. 2. South Bend, IN: National Institute for Trial Advocacy.

Selznick, Philip. 1992. *The Moral Commonwealth: Social Theory and the Promise of Community.* Berkeley: University of California Press.

Singer, Mark. 1984. "Court Buff." In *The Literary Journalists* (pp. 238–63). Ed. Norman Sims. New York: Ballantine Books.

Smith, Christopher E. 1991. *Courts and the Poor.* Chicago: Nelson-Hall.

Smitherman, Geneva. 1977. *Talkin and Testifyin: The Language of Black America.* Detroit: Wayne State University Press.

Sontag, Susan. 1966. *Against Interpretation.* New York: Farrar, Straus and Giroux.

Sophocles. *Oedipus the King.* 1954. Trans. David Grene. In *Sophocles I* (pp. 9–76). Chicago: University of Chicago Press.

Spence, Gerry. 1986. "How to Make a Complex Case Come Alive for a Jury." *ABA Journal* 72 (April 1): 62–66.

Sperber, Dan. 1974. *Rethinking Symbolism.* Cambridge: Cambridge University Press.

Stanislavsky, Konstantin. 1950. *Stanislavsky on the Art of the Stage.* Trans. David Magarshack. London: Faber and Faber.

Steiner, Wendy. 1995. *The Scandal of Pleasure: Art in an Age of Fundamentalism.* Chicago: University of Chicago Press.

Todorov, Tzvetan. 1977. *The Poetics of Prose.* Trans. Richard Howard. Ithaca, NY: Cornell University Press.

Toobin, Jeffrey. 1995. "A Horrible Human Event," *New Yorker* (October 23):40–49.

Turner, Frederick. 1986. "Performed Being: Word Art as a Human Inheritance." *Oral Tradition* 1, no. 1:66–109.

Turner, Victor. 1988. *The Anthropology of Performance.* New York: PAJ Publications.

Visher, Christy A. 1987. "Juror Decision Making: The Importance of Evidence." *Law and Human Behavior* 11:1–17.

Warner, Marina. 1995. *Six Myths of Our Time: Little Angels, Little Monsters, Beautiful Beasts, and More.* New York: Vintage Books.

White, James Boyd. 1983. "The Ethics of Argument: Plato's *Gorgias* and the Modern Lawyer." *The University of Chicago Law Review* 50:849–95.

———. 1994. *Acts of Hope: Creating Authority in Literature, Law, and Politics.* Chicago: University of Chicago Press.

Williams, Patricia J. 1991. *The Alchemy of Race and Rights.* Cambridge, MA: Harvard University Press.

Willis, Paul. 1981. *Learning to Labor: How Working Class Kids Get Working Class Jobs.* New York: Columbia University Press.

Wittgenstein, Ludwig. [1921] 1961. *Tractatus Logico-Philosophicus.* Trans. D. F. Pears and B. F. McGuinness. London: Routledge and Kegan Paul.

INDEX